Catholicism in Modern Italy

Catholicism in Modern Italy is the first work in English to explore fully the role that religion has played in Italy since its unification in 1861. John Pollard shows how the religious beliefs, practices and experiences of the Italian people have changed over the last two centuries. He examines the key question of whether the Catholic Church was consistently anti-modernisation, as is often claimed.

Covering not only Catholicism but also the role of religious minorities such as non-Catholic Christians, Jews and Muslims, John Pollard expertly examines the changing impact of religion on Italian society, and the role it has played in Italian politics in the modern period. In particular, the book considers the extent to which Italian society has been 'secularised', but it also analyses the factors that led to the development of religious pluralism in present-day Italy.

Surveying the cultural, social, political, legal and economic dimensions of the Catholic Church, *Catholicism in Modern Italy* explores the Church's relationship to the different experiences across Italy over this dramatic period of change and 'modernisation'. It demonstrates how Italian Catholicism has seen off successive challenges from liberalism, Fascism and Communism, in large part thanks to the presence of the Papacy in the peninsula. John Pollard ends by concluding that, despite the processes of secularisation and the emergence of religious pluralism, the Catholic Church remains a major force in Italian society and politics today.

John Pollard is Fellow in History at Trinity Hall, Cambridge, and researches the modern history of Italy, the papacy, and Fascism and religion. His publications include *Money and the Rise of the Modern Papacy: Financing the Vatican, 1850–1950* (2005).

Christianity and society in the modern world
Series editor: Hugh McLeod

Catholicism in Modern Italy

Religion, Society and
Politics since 1861

John Pollard

Routledge
Taylor & Francis Group

LONDON AND NEW YORK

First published 2008
by Routledge
2 Park Square, Milton Park, Abingdon, Oxon OX14 4RN

Simultaneously published in the USA and Canada
by Routledge
270 Madison Ave, New York, NY 10016

*Routledge is an imprint of the Taylor & Francis Group,
an informa business*

© 2008 John Pollard

Typeset in Bell and Perpetua by
Florence Production Ltd, Stoodleigh, Devon
Printed and bound in Great Britain by
T.J.I. Digital, Padstow, Cornwall

British Library Cataloguing in Publication Data
A catalogue record for this book is available from the British Library

Library of Congress Cataloging in Publication Data
Pollard, John F. (John Francis), 1944–.
    Catholicism in modern Italy: religion, society, and politics since
    1861/John Pollard.
        p. cm. – (Christianity and society in the modern world)
    Includes bibliographical references and index.
    1. Catholic Church – Italy – History – 20th century.
    2. Italy – Church history – 20th century. 3. Catholic
    Church – Italy – History – 21st century. 4. Italy – Church
    history – 21st century. I. Title.
BX1545.2.P65 2008
282'.4509034 – dc22   2008003887

ISBN10: 0–415–23835–8 (hbk)
ISBN10: 0–203–89319–0 (ebk)

ISBN13: 978–0–415–23835–9 (hbk)
ISBN13: 978–0–203–89319–7 (ebk)

For James Walston and Nora Galli De' Paratesi

CONTENTS

ACKNOWLEDGEMENTS

It would be impossible to thank all the people who have helped me in the archives and libraries where I have worked over the years, but one library that has proved to be of unfailing help has been Cambridge University Library. I must thank David Wilson for acting as my research assistant on an early project examining the role of the Church in the crisis of the Italian Republic between 1991 and 1996 whose results have been incorporated into this study. Oliver Logan once again very generously gave me advice on the early chapters, drawing on his exhaustive knowledge of the Church in Italy in the nineteenth century. James Walston did the same for Chapters 7–9 and was remarkably patient and helpful when I badgered him with numerous queries. Jeremy Morris kindly read the Introduction and made suggestions. I am also grateful to Alessandro Iandolo, Camilla MacDonald and Rob Page for sharing their thoughts with me on various aspects of the post-1945 Communist experience. Of course, I alone bear responsibility for any errors of fact or judgement that this book contains.

Much of Chapter 4 was published in my previous work, 'Religion and the Formation of the Italian Working Class', in Rick Halpern and Jonathan Morris (eds), *American Exceptionalism? US Working Class Formation in an International Context*, Basingstoke: Macmillan, 1997, pp. 158–80, reproduced with permission of Palgrave-Macmillan.

I must also record my gratitude to Hugh McLeod, and to successive editors at Routledge, for their extraordinary faith and patience over the years, and especially to Eve Setch and Lizzie Clifford who have seen the book into print. Finally, I owe a huge debt of gratitude to John Ainscough.

Chapter 1

INTRODUCTION

THIS IS A STUDY OF THE COMPLEX SET of relationships between religion in Italy and the forces of change, or 'modernisation', that swept over the peninsula in the nineteenth and twentieth centuries. Its purpose is to provide a synoptic historical account of the changing role of religion, very largely but not exclusively Catholicism, in the life of Italian people, civil society and politics since the unification of the Italian State in 1861. Where appropriate, I shall focus attention on the vicissitudes of the religious minorities in Italy, Jews, non-Catholic Christians and, more recently, non-Christian religions such as the Buddhists and Muslims, as well as tracing the development of secularist and more nakedly anti-clerical opposition to the power of the Church. The principal focus will be on the development of the religious beliefs and practices of the Italian people and of the institutional church in Italy, and their responses to successive waves of 'modernisation'.

By 'modernisation' I mean, first of all, those political ideas and policies emerging from the Enlightenment and French Revolution with which their protagonists, in a rationalising and reforming programme, sought to 'modernise' the functioning of the Church and its economic and legal roles in civil society, and its relations with the state, in the late eighteenth and early nineteenth centuries. The ecclesiastical policies of the 'Liberal Revolution' in the period from 1830 onwards was, of course, derived from that programme, but in one particular respect they went beyond it. Because the moderate liberals were engaged in uniting Italy between 1858 and 1870, the policies were potentially more dangerous to Catholicism throughout the peninsula. In particular, they sought to downplay the Roman character of Italian Catholicism, i.e. its ultimate loyalty and obedience to the papacy in Rome, subordinate the Church to the (liberal) State and destroy the temporal power of the popes, i.e. the territorial sovereignty that they had enjoyed for over a thousand years as rulers of the Papal States of central Italy. The central ideas of the Enlightenment – rationalism, secularism, deism and even atheism – would endure and prove subversive of Catholicism as it was believed and practised.

A further experience of 'modernisation' came with the advent of industrialisation, *la prima industrializzazione,* in Italy from the 1880s until just before the outbreak of the First World War. The economic and social changes – migration and the creation of industrial towns and cities–which that process generated, and their political consequence, the emergence of a revolutionary Socialist working class movement with a materialistic and atheistic ideological base, were to present a major challenge to Italian Catholicism over the next century and, in the short term, to bring a new, though limited, form of secularisation in their wake. By 'secularisation' I mean 'the historical process whereby society and culture is liberated from the control of religion.'[1] The depth and breadth of that process would vary throughout the period with which we are dealing. In this context, the word 'lay' is used here in relation to those members of the Church not belonging to the clergy. It is also used in relation to those individuals, groups or political parties that opposed Church influence on Italian society and the institutional state: the words 'laic' and 'secularist' are used in the same sense.

Another major process of secularisation was set in train by the economic 'miracle' and American cultural 'invasion' of the 1950s and 1960s. The effects of these two phenomena were to prove more far-reaching than the changes of the *prima industrializzazione* of the 1880–1914 period. The 'new secularisation' that they produced signified the turning away of a large part of the Italian population from the traditional, 'official' Catholicism of the institutional church to a more nebulous, 'private' religious belief and (non)practice from the 1960s onwards, or to other, non-Catholic, religions. Coupled with the effects of the Second Council of the Vatican (1962–65), it also seriously shook the internal structures of the institutional church by creating communities of 'dissident' Catholics. Arguably, these tendencies were accentuated by the massive structural changes in the Italian, and global, economy, especially the communications 'revolution' in the last two decades of the twentieth century. They were reinforced by other effects of globalisation on Italy from the 1980s onwards, especially immigration and related new religious and cultural influences.

Two totalitarian political movements emerged in the twentieth century to pose a potentially serious challenge to Italian Catholicism – Fascism and Communism. While Communism may be regarded as an 'outgrowth' of the Enlightenment, albeit one refracted by the dominant influence of the Russian experience of Marxism in practice, Italian Fascism was much more the ideological product of the late nineteenth and early twentieth century anti-rational revolt *against* the Enlightenment. Consequently, Catholicism would more readily adapt to Fascism and, indeed, in the short term seek an accommodation with it. It sought no such accommodation with Communism, and in the decades following the end of the Second World War Catholicism and Communism would be engaged in a fierce struggle for cultural, social and political hegemony in Italy.

Throughout this book, a key focus of analysis will be the tension between the 'official' religiosity of the institutional church as that essentially established by the Council of Trent in the mid-sixteenth century and 'popular religion', the beliefs and practices of the people, which in some places were often in conflict with it. It is clear that, as in other parts of Europe, in certain regions of Italy that tension was acute, especially in the south. This brings me to the phenomenon of regional diversity in Italy. The relationships between the forces of modernisation and Italian Catholicism were bound to be complex given the diversity in economic and social structures, popular culture and religiosity not only between north and south but between regions and even within the narrower bounds of individual provinces in the peninsula. With generations of undergraduate students I have encountered the assumption that Catholicism, the Church, was 'stronger' in the south of Italy because that area was more rural, agrarian, 'backward' and poorer than the north. Until recently, it could be argued that the reverse was true, that the official religiosity of Catholicism, the role of the institutional church in civil society and the capacity of the Church to mobilise Catholics in order to influence politics was much stronger in certain, albeit largely rural, regions of northern and central Italy than in the south. Indeed, many Italian historians have talked about the survival of pre-Christian religions, paganism and superstition, as being distinguishing features of society in southern Italy.[2] Other factors, legal, financial and social, meant that in the post-unification period the Church in the south was institutionally weak, and this persisted even beyond the Fascist era. The wide-ranging diversity of Italy's regions, north and south, both in terms of its historical division into a number of states, but also stark regional variations within the pre-national states, makes it more appropriate, therefore, to talk about 'Italian churches' rather than a single national church, at least until the late nineteenth and early twentieth centuries. To avoid confusion, it should be noted that historians and ecclesiologists also sometimes refer to individual dioceses as 'churches'.

This is not essentially a research monograph, that is, the direct product of substantial fresh research into archival and other primary sources; rather it is the indirect product of research, reading, writing and teaching going back many years. Hence, those familiar with my previously published work will find some strong echoes of it in this book. The book is intended as a general introduction to a subject that has been many, many times touched on in monographs and other studies, but not focused upon in the way in which I do here. It is not primarily intended for an exclusively scholarly readership; it is, in the first instance, aimed at lecturers and teachers of elements of modern Italian history and modern Italian studies, as well as students at sixth-form, undergraduate and graduate levels and at the more general public. I hope that it will also be used as an essential reference work for scholars in the field of religious history, particularly those who do not have a reading knowledge of Italian because there is an almost complete absence of studies of the history of religion in Italy in the English language.

The book is thus intended to fill a gap: much has been written in English on the history of religion in most countries of western Europe in the modern period, most notably the Benelux countries, Britain, France, Germany and Spain.[3] One of the most formative from my point of view is Hugh McLeod's *Religion and the People of Western Europe 1789–1970*,[4] and another is Frances Lannon's *Privilege, Persecution and Prophecy; The Catholic Church in Spain 1875–1975*.[5] What distinguishes my approach from that of McLeod is my emphasis on the role of religion/the Church in politics: this book is, therefore, closer to that of Lannon in scope and spirit as I have tried to keep in balance the personal experience of religion, its role in society and the influence of the Church in politics. But it is also clear that the Italian experience differs in one crucially important respect from that of other European Catholic countries. Italy is, of course, the seat of the papacy: the bishop of Rome is not only the metropolitan of the Roman Province and primate of Italy, he is also supreme pontiff, and as such is the infallible head of the Roman Catholic Church throughout the world. This presence has inevitably rendered Italian Catholicism more, much more, 'political' in its manifestations, and for this reason it has not always been possible to preserve a perfect balance, chapter by chapter, between religion, society and politics. Indeed, religion and politics in Italy have been inextricably intertwined during the period covered by this book, and still are, in a way that is not comparable in other European country.

A work that perhaps comes closest to mine in its purpose is Atkin and Tallett's *Priests, Prelates and People: A History of European Catholicism since 1750*.[6] That said, their book is obviously very much wider in geographical scope than this one. David Kertzer has tried to provide a brief guide to some of the issues discussed here for the nineteenth century in his essay, 'Religion and Society, 1789–1892', and Alice Kelikian has attempted much the same in her 'The Church and Catholicism' for the twentieth century.[7] Jon Dunnage also provides some excellent insights into the role of the Church/religion in Italian society in his book, *Twentieth Century Italy: A Social History*.[8] Otherwise, books dealing with Catholicism in modern Italy tend to focus on relations between church and state, such as Carlo Arturo Jemolo's magisterial treatment of the subject in *Church and State in Italy, 1850–1960* or Daniel Binchy's *Church and State in Fascist Italy*,[9] or my own *The Vatican and Italian Fascism, 1929–1932*.[10] Alternatively, they focus on the Catholic/Christian Democratic movement, such as Richard Webster's *The Cross and the Fasces* or John Molony's *The Emergence of Political Catholicism in Italy*.[11] Needless to say, there is an enormous literature on the post-1945 Christian Democratic Party.[12]

I have tried to keep notes to a minimum. Where they are provided, they are mainly as references for quotations or to give substance to major statements, but sometimes also as suggestions for contextual or further specialist reading. I have endeavoured to provide reading in English, but sometimes that is clearly not possible. I have also sought to place the history of Catholicism in Italy in its necessary economic, political and social contexts. Lest the complexities of the hierarchical organisation and practices of the Roman Catholic Church, which were effectively shaped in Italy under the influence of the late Roman Empire, are unfamiliar, I have provided a glossary of (especially ecclesiastical) terms. Where not otherwise stated, all translations are by the author.

Chapter 2

CATHOLICISM AND THE LIBERAL REVOLUTION (1815–70)

Introduction

ITALIAN CATHOLICISM FACED ITS FIRST SERIOUS challenge from 'modernisation' during the period of the Risorgimento, that is between 1815 and 1870 when the liberal and national movements in Italy developed, matured and eventually achieved Italian independence from Austria and unification under the House of Savoy, the ruling family of Piedmont-Sardinia, with the capital at Rome. The chief casualty of the 'Liberal Revolution' thus carried out in Italy was undoubtedly the Church. Its property, privileges and legal status in civil society were severely curtailed by the secularising legislation of successive moderate (conservative) liberal governments first in Piedmont-Sardinia and then in the new Kingdom of Italy. Perhaps even more significant for the future development of the Catholic Church as a whole was the fact that in the process of unification the 'temporal power' of the popes, their political sovereignty over a swathe of territory in central Italy, was finally abolished. The pope's reaction to that event, along with the proclamation of the doctrine of Papal Infallibility at the First Council of the Vatican (1869–70), helped to accelerate the development of the process whereby the papacy was transformed into a modern, highly centralised institution.

The background: the impact of the Enlightenment and French Revolution on Italian Catholicism

Under the *ancien régime* in Europe, Catholicism as an established church was not only deeply embedded in the institutions of the state; it could be described as a major part of the institutional structure of monarchies. It was also deeply embedded in civil society, since its laws governed so much of the life of the people, marriage, education, and the provision of medical care and poor relief etc., a sort of 'cradle to grave' material and spiritual welfare state.[1] Moreover, possession of such rights of citizenship as existed under the *ancien régime* was restricted to those who conformed to the state religion (which was, of course, also true in Protestant states). Monarchs exercised varying degrees of control over 'national' churches, at the expense of the papacy, utilised their legal structures (canon law) as part of their rule and appointed their servants and friends to the highest ecclesiastical offices as rewards. In broader terms, those offices were a happy hunting ground for careers for large sections of the nobility, the parochial clergy being largely drawn from the urban and rural middle class, and the peasantry.[2]

Much of this changed in the period after 1750. So the structures of the institutional church in Italy, and to a lesser extent the religiosity of the people, after the end of the Napoleonic occupation in 1815 were very much the product of processes of reform and revolution going back 50 or 60 years. The first changes had come in the 1750s, 1760s and 1770s, as a result of the introduction of the ideas of the Enlightenment into Italy. Despite the flourishing of a specifically Italian form of enlightened Catholicism during the pontificate of Benedict XIV (1740–58), the ultimate development of the Enlightenment in Italy, and especially the ideas of men such as Ludovico Antonio Muratori and Carlantonio Pilati, were used in battles against the Church, the consequent development and implementation of the programmes of ecclesiastical reform of the 'enlightened despots' in Lombardy, Tuscany, Parma, Piedmont and the Kingdom of Naples.[3] Anticipating the more radical reforms after the French invasions, the measures introduced by the Habsburg rulers of Tuscany and Lombardy, Grand Duke Leopold II and his elder brother the Emperor Joseph II, aimed at remedying such abuses as pluralism, reducing the economic, landowning weight of the Church through the introduction of laws abolishing or limiting mortmain (the ban on the 'alienation', i.e. sale of Church property), suppressing 'useless' monastic houses, male and female and, above all, restricting papal jurisdiction over the Church in individual states, most especially the power of the Holy Office of the Inquisition.[4] All of these 'Josephenist' reforms had a strong tinge of *Jansenism* to them: Italian Jansenism, like its counterparts elsewhere in Europe, sought a more rigorously internalised religiosity and a strong resistance to the power of the papacy in the affairs of the Church.[5] The conflict between this reforming movement and the 'official' church came to a head in 1786 when Bishop Scipione Ricci called a reforming synod in the diocese of Pistoia, but was thwarted by popular opposition and the unwillingness of Grand Duke Leopold to support him.[6] The reforms also smacked of Febronianism, the anti-papal spirit of church reform in Germany. At the heart of the Enlightenment attacks on the Church in Italy was the doctrine of *jurisdictionalism*, the theory and practice of extending the power of the state by curtailing the legal jurisdiction the Church had exercised for centuries in civil society. In the eighteenth century, as later in the nineteenth, a major target of the reformers was the Jesuits. The expulsion of the Jesuits from the Italian states (and from other European states) demonstrated the weakness of the papacy vis-à-vis the other Italian monarchies. Atkin and Tallett explain that weakness:

> Preoccupied with Italian politics, constantly engaged in backstairs intrigue, undermined by the Curia, economically enfeebled, unable to stand up to the emerging great powers and theologically discredited, the papacy in the eighteenth century acted as little more than a referee rather than a judge in both international and domestic affairs.[7]

But the invasions of the French revolutionary and Napoleonic armies in the 1790s would come close to destroying the papacy altogether. During the first wave of French invasions, between 1796 and 1800, 'sister' republics were set up in various parts of Italy on the French model. During their short-lived existence they enacted wholesale expropriation of church lands that were then sold on the open market, abolished monastic houses and institutions of ecclesiastical charity and the tithe, and emancipated Jews and Protestants. They were short-lived because they had little mass popular base and depended on French bayonets to survive. When the French withdrew in 1799, they perished, in the case of the Parthenopean (Neapolitan) Republic in a veritable bloodbath.[8] Significantly, there was a strong element of outraged popular religious sentiment in the largely peasant class revolts against the French and their Italian Jacobin collaborators; the most outstanding example of this was Cardinal Ruffo's 'Christian Army' to defend the Holy Faith in Calabria.[9]

The French returned after the decisive victory over the Austrians at the battle of Marengo, 14 June 1800, and Napoleon proceeded to reconstruct peninsular Italy (Sardinia and Sicily were never conquered by the French) along French lines, dividing it into three major sections – the Italian Republic (later Kingdom) of eastern, north and central Italy, the Kingdom of Naples and western Italy – Piedmont, Tuscany and present-day Latium – which was directly incorporated into the French Empire. Despite the boundary divisions, in ecclesiastical matters there was a general uniformity based on Napoleon's original concordat with the pope of 1801, which operated in the Imperial territories, another of 1804 very similar to it for the Italian Republic/Kingdom and a third for Murat's Naples.[10] The sale of confiscated church lands was confirmed, state nomination of bishops was continued, and episcopal authority over the parochial clergy was restored.[11] The deaths in exile of two popes, Pius VI and Pius VII, their saintliness and 'martyrdoms', gave back a certain prestige to the papacy. Despite his rough treatment of the occupants of the throne of St Peter, the emperor rather opportunistically decided that there could ultimately be no social and political stability without religious peace, and he adapted his policy towards religion and the church in all of his domains accordingly. As a result, 'In the new state and new society sought by Napoleon the "ecclesiastical world" found itself irrevocably and in every way "regulated", "protected" and "under the orders" of the political *status quo*.'[12]

Religion in Restoration Italy, 1815–48

For the Church, the balance sheet of the experience of the French occupations was not a good one. Atkin and Tallett claim that:

> In 1814, the secular clergy were in a sorry state. Priests might have welcomed state salaries and the re-drawing of parishes, but there was a real crisis of recruitment as elsewhere in Europe and the clergy lost some of its control over the religious beliefs and practices of the people. In 1809, the Bishop of Vercelli bemoaned the fact that a third of the faithful no longer attended Easter communion.[13]

Roger Aubert says that though there was a 'superabundance of clergy', many were employed as private chaplains and private tutors to wealthy and bourgeois families, while others worked in essentially secular pursuits as administrators of estates. And others lived a nomadic life, migrating from place to place in search of a benefice: Rome, naturally, became the goal of the vagrant southern priest in particular.[14] The intellectual, spiritual and moral qualities of some clergy left much to be desired. By mid-century, serious concern was being expressed at all levels of the hierarchy about the quality of the clergy. In the first year of his reign, Pius IX issued an encyclical on the evils that afflicted the clergy, including sexual immorality, their ignorance of spiritual matters and their lack of a sense of ecclesiastical *esprit de corps*.[15] As Rosmini pointed out in *Le Cinque piaghe della Santa Chiesa* ('On the Five Wounds of the Holy Church'), much of this was a result of inadequate priestly education.[16] Many priests came from families with no culture of the liturgy and little of Christian doctrine, and the teaching of scripture in seminaries was abysmal. Many candidates for ordination to the priesthood were *esterni*, that is, they lived outside the seminaries, usually with their families. Indeed, for many students the seminary was simply a cheap form of secondary education.[17]

The question of the adequacy of priestly formation was an important one given the sensitive role that the parochial clergy played in Italian society of the Restoration period. Beyond the walls of church and sacristy, the clergy exercised what can only be described as regulatory 'police' functions. They issued certificates to prove that parishioners had fulfilled their Easter duties, which were essential to qualify for some public offices and go to university. They inspected medical certificates permitting parishioners to buy certain foods on days of abstinence, and kept an eye on the morality and social behaviour of their flocks. In some instances, they even acted as censors of locally produced publications. The performance of these functions, in addition to the exaction of church taxes, chiefly the tithe and *diritti alla stola* (fees for the performance of such ceremonies as baptism), could easily make the clergy objects of popular resentment.[18]

The situation with the regular clergy (members of religious orders and congregations such as monks and friars) was arguably worse: literally thousands of male (and female) religious houses had been dissolved in northern and southern Italy under French rule. As far as the financial condition of the Church is concerned, largely as a result of the dissolutions, the clergy possessed less than 13 per cent of the peninsula's property in 1815, compared to 25 per cent at the beginning of the century.[19] But there were some positive features of the situation: thanks to the various concordats, the relationship between bishop and parochial clergy, in the north at least, was now more stable and regulated and already in the restoration period there were signs that some new religious congregations, with charitable and teaching functions, were beginning to appear.

Consolidation of the parochial system of church organisation (one priest, with perhaps subordinates, ministering to the pastoral needs of souls within distinct fixed boundaries) had been one of the major reforms proposed by the Council of Trent at the end of the sixteenth century.[20] At that time, as well as this parish 'ideal type', there were two other systems of pastoral care under the bishop: in many areas there was the *pieve*, a system whereby a college of priests based on a 'mother church' administered to souls in a city or large town using subordinate churches.[21] The 'mother church', sometimes a cathedral, would be the only one to contain a baptismal font. Despite the objections of those ecclesiastics with vested interests, the *pieve* system was substantially eroded in northern and central Italy by the application of the Tridentine reforms there in the seventeenth and eighteenth centuries.

But whereas the diocese-parish structure had become the key element in the functioning of the institutional church in northern and central Italy by the nineteenth century, the situation was very different in the south, in the mainland

Kingdom of Naples. Here, apart from the fact that there were a large number of small dioceses with limited resources, especially with regard to seminary training, there were also many, many fewer parishes per diocese. The latter was in part the result of the *chiese ricettizie* system, which accounted for between 40 and 75 per cent of all churches in the south at the end of the eighteenth century.[22] It is nigh impossible to translate the term into English; the nearest, but not close, analogy would be the 'minster' or collegiate churches of medieval England served by a group of priests. It is probably best, therefore, simply to explain how it worked in comparison to the conventional parish. Rather than a clearly defined unit of ecclesiastical jurisdiction, and therefore an ecclesial community, with usually a single parish priest who derived his and the rest of the parish's income from an endowment of landed and other property, the southern *chiesa ricettizia* was an agglomeration of clergy, sub-divided by title and function, who drew income from the *massa commune*, that is, a collection of usually landed properties whose income was shared out between them. They did not lead a common life, but lived with their families. They would collectively provide a village or several villages, or even a substantial small southern town, with the necessary religious services.[23]

A typical example of a *chiesa ricettizia* was that of Pisticci, an agricultural/ pastoral town in the Basilicata region, which was composed of a total of 36 priests who served the church, various chapels and the private chapels of leading families.[24] For the local bishop, in this case Acerenza (Basilicata), the *chiesa ricettizia* was a problem. Although he had to ordain its priests and confirm them in office, he had very little control over them and their activities by comparison with the diocesan ordinary in the north. The history of the *chiesa ricettizia* system is a long chronicle of disputes with the bishop, particularly over the payments from them, which he believed were his due. The fundamental characteristic in economic terms of the *chiesa ricettizia* system was the strongly *private* element: it was regulated and controlled by private individuals and families, unlike the parish churches of the north that operated within the legal framework of the institutional church. It should also be said that many of the southern clergy were noted for being more immoral, blasphemous and litigious, and obsessed with business affairs than their northern counterparts. While the very poor provision for seminary training in the south had something to do with this, it clearly derived in large part from the private nature of the *chiesa ricettizia* system.[25]

'Elite' or 'institutional' religion and 'popular religion'

What is apparent from the Restoration period onwards is that there were not only different 'churches' in Italy but, in a sense, different versions of religion, that Catholicism was not lived and experienced in the same way by different individuals, genders and social groups, and by different regions. There was, as there had been for centuries, a tension, sometimes even a conflict, between the 'official' religion of the institutional church and forms of 'popular religion', that is, the way in which it was practised by the mass of the largely rural, agrarian population.[26] Giuseppe De Rosa, Italy's leading ecclesiastical historian, in a seminal work, makes the point that fundamentally there was a difference between the religion of the clergy and that of the laity, regardless of class. He is adamant that 'religious practice, even when it was essentially part of a framework of magic and superstition, was to be found in all classes: day labourers, tenant farmers, landowners, gentry, and even the clergy'. He also argues that some elements of nineteenth and twentieth century popular religion derive from the superstitious, pagan practices of the fourth and fifth centuries and that some 'Christian' practices, such as the cult of the Virgin and the saints, and pilgrimages, have their origins in pagan religious practice, 'baptised' by the Church in the age of mass conversions.[27]

The insistence on Latin as the liturgical language ensured a separation between the roles of the clergy and the laity, priests and people, in the central act of Christian worship, the Eucharist. As the priest celebrated the Mass, the congregation 'prayed' it, using various prayer-forms, litanies to the saints, the rosary etc. The only coming together of celebrant and congregation took place at key 'magical moments' such as the Consecration and the Elevation. As literacy in Italy spread in the late nineteenth and early twentieth centuries, books of specialist prayers, even 'twin-texts' of the missal in Latin and the vernacular appeared, but still the congregation remained largely excluded from the liturgical dialogue, their place being taken by the altar server. Infrequent communion, only obligatory once a year and then around Easter time – compared with the priest, who usually communicated on a daily basis – further emphasised the distance between priest and people. The promotion of Benediction of the Blessed Sacrament, which became a feature of the late nineteenth century Catholic 'revival', still did not bridge the divide, the Host remaining an essentially magical object to be adored by the people at a distance.[28]

In such a situation, the cults of the Virgin and the saints, especially local patron saints, was critically important in a largely rural society based on an agrarian economy. The celebration of patronal festivals, and the festivals of other local saints, accompanied by processions, became key moments in a local community's year.[29] This, and not the Mass, was at the heart of community religion. It could be argued that this was a feature of rural as opposed to urban Catholicism throughout Italy, but it was to be found particularly in the south, where the strength of urban cults of the saints is testified by those of

San Gennaro at Naples and San Nicola at Bari. It is demonstrative of the power of the cult of San Gennaro that eighteenth and nineteenth century conquerors of Naples, the French and Garibaldi included, ensured the successful outcome of the ceremony of the liquefaction of the saint's blood.[30]

Atkin and Tallett make the point that:

> Popular religiosity in the North of Italy was clerically centred and focussed on the parish and sodalities. By contrast, in the South it retained a concern with local saints and was closely linked to family and village networks and sociability patterns.[31]

Religious practice certainly was parish-centred in the north and centre, whereas in the south there was a strong focus on the cult of images (mostly the Madonna), shrines and *romeaggi* (processions of the images of the saints) organised by powerful sodalities (lay people's associations), which tended to be more concerned with charity and other good works in the north. This can largely be explained by geography: the further from northern Italy one goes, the further one is from the kind of Tridentine Catholicism that the Church had sought to impose in the centuries following the great council of the Catholic reform movement. Whereas most of the dioceses of northern and central Italy saw the zealous application of the purifying reforms of the Council of Trent, as exemplified by the work of Saint Charles Borromeo, archbishop of Milan, south of Rome they had patchy, limited impact. The problem of the north–south divide in Italy, the 'Southern Question', has been addressed as an essentially economic and social issue. In fact, the cultural aspect would appear crucial and, of course, the essential component of southern culture, its value and belief system, was religious. That religious component was largely untouched by the reformism of the Council of Trent. As Borzomati, a leading historian of religion in the south, points out: 'The episcopate [then] never succeeded in creating in the churches of the South a "Tridentine" clergy and rarely tried to adapt their pastoral activity, which was very conventional, to the traditions of the same local churches'('churches' here should be understood to mean dioceses).[32]

Religious minorities in Restoration Italy

Non-Catholic religious minorities in Italy were inevitably exiguous. The minuscule Greek rite communities scattered over Apulia, Calabria and Sicily (from whom, in the latter case, the late nineteenth century conservative liberal statesman Francesco Crispi sprang) were in communion with Rome and therefore Catholic. Thanks to the work of the Counter-Reformation in

Italy in the sixteenth and seventeenth centuries, and especially the operations of the Index and the Inquisition, there was little in the way of dissent from Catholicism in Italy. Virtually the only coherent Protestant community in Italy at the beginning of the nineteenth century was constituted by the Waldensians (Valdesi) in a few valleys of western Piedmont. They had survived despite ferocious persecution in the seventeenth century at the hands of the dukes of Savoy, ancestors of the Italian royal house. That persecution was immortalised in Milton's lines:

> Avenge O Lord thy slaughtered saints whose bones
> lie scattered on the Alpine mountains cold.[33]

The 30,000-strong Waldensians faced a renewed threat of persecution after 1815 when the Napoleonic edict of religious toleration was rescinded and the bishop of Pinerolo, whose diocese encompassed the Waldensian valleys, embarked upon an aggressive campaign of conversion.[34]

A not dissimilar fate awaited the Jews of Italy after the Restoration. The 31,000 Jews of 1800, living in 40 ghettos, soon enjoyed a regime of toleration under Napoleonic rule. After Napoleon's fall, there was a return to the previous situation of repression, and the Jews' enthusiasm for Enlightened ideas aroused Catholic suspicion and stimulated anti-Semitism.[35] By 1840, the Jewish population had increased to 37,000 spread throughout Italy, but with the concentration of a third of the total number of Jews in the Papal States: Rome itself had between 3,000 and 4,000 Jews. Conditions for the Jews varied from the most repressive in the Papal States, where Jews were ordered back into the ghettos under the reactionary rule of Leo XII (1823–29), to enlightened toleration in Tuscany.[36] Not surprisingly, many Jews, and to a lesser extent Waldensians, would identify with the religious programme of emerging Italian liberalism during the Restoration period.[37]

Church and state in Restoration Italy

After the upheavals of the previous 25 years, the relationship between the Church and the state authorities in Italy was a complicated, messy and unstable one. To regularise this relationship required the new agreements between the Holy See and the Italian states, covering such matters as appropriated church lands, mortmain, the future of the regulars (monastic orders), especially the Jesuits, the states' roles in the appointment of bishops, free communication between the Holy See and the bishops, diocesan boundaries and, in the Kingdom of Naples, the future of the *chiese ricettizie* system. But 'Josephenism' had not ended with the deaths of Joseph II and his brother Leopold; nor did 'caesaropapism' end with the fall of Napoleon. All Restoration rulers, however personally devout in their religious practice and however desirous of using an established church as a prop to what turned out to be their shaky restored rule, wanted to retain as much control and jurisdiction as possible over the Church in their dominions. Another significant factor in the outcome of negotiations for concordats between the Holy See and the Italian states in this period was the natural unwillingness of those who had acquired former church lands over the previous decades, whether nobles or bourgeoisie, to give them up. In consequence, from the Church's point of view, the outcome of the negotiations as far as its loss of property was concerned was almost invariably disappointing, except in Piedmont where some land was restored to the Church and in Naples where unsold land was handed back.[38]

In the central duchies – Lucca, Modena, Parma and Tuscany – generally speaking rulers retained a fairly tight administrative control over the Church. In Tuscany, for example, the Jesuits were still banned and the laws on mortmain continued.[39] It was essentially the same in the Habsburg territories of Lombard-Venetia.[40] The situation in the Kingdom of Naples after the Concordat of 1818 was different. Though the king insisted on the appointment of the bishops, the abolition of the fiscal exemptions of church lands and the limitation of the jurisdiction of church courts, on the other hand the restored status of Catholicism as the sole religion of the state, the re-establishment of church censorship and financial support for the clergy seemed a return to the *status quo ante* (i.e. before the French Revolution).[41] It was probably the Kingdom of Piedmont-Sardinia that provided the greatest concessions to the Church: here, as well as the restoration of some church lands and the re-entry of the Jesuits, the privileges and property of the Church and its ministers was protected to such a degree that it came to be regarded as the most 'clerical', not to say 'priest-ridden', state in Restoration Italy.[42] But in none of the states could the institutional church be said to find itself in difficulties. Thanks to the concordats a degree of stability had finally been achieved in those arrangements, and this afforded the Church the space and freedom to renew itself and grow.

The Restoration papacy

There was no need of concordats in the Papal States of central Italy, for here the Church *was* the state, the government being a theocracy from the pope down. Cardinals and other leading prelates of the Roman Curia, the Vatican's governing elite, acted as 'legates' or governors in the various regions and provinces of the Papal States and sometimes combined their secular role with the spiritual, i.e. serving as local bishops as well. While laymen could accede to positions in the papal administration, to rise to the top required some clerical status, but not much: Secretary of State Cardinal Consalvi was not ordained a priest until a very few years before the end of his career, and his successor in Pius IX's reign, Cardinal Giacomo Antonelli, never did rise above the rank of deacon.

Consalvi was undoubtedly the outstanding papal secretary of state in the Restoration period, and his greatest triumph was to negotiate successfully the restoration of the Papal States, at the Vienna Peace Congress, when none of the many church states inside the former Holy Roman Empire abolished by Napoleon was treated thus.[43] The theory behind the restored temporal power, which would be advocated by the popes and their spokesmen long after it had been finally swept away in 1870, was that some sort of territorial sovereignty was absolutely indispensable if the papacy was to maintain its spiritual independence. The restored Papal States under Consalvi's guidance experienced some legal and administrative reforms, but these were largely reversed after the election of Leo XII in 1823. Under Leo, the power of the feudal aristocracy and that of the church courts was restored. Altogether, the popes of the Restoration period, Pius VII (1800–23), Leo XII (1823–29), Pius VIII (1829–30) and Gregory XVI (1831–46), were good and holy men, and not incapable administrators, but they seemed to lack a strong sense of realism. They adamantly demanded the restoration of *all* of the Church's privileges, prerogatives and property lost in the revolutionary period and manifested their hostility to any kind of reform. They put their trust in the new style of 'throne and altar' alliances to protect the interests of the Church in the peninsula, and indeed throughout Europe generally. In an age of growing political unrest, especially in the Papal States themselves, this was storing up a great deal of trouble for the future.

Liberalism and nationalism in Restoration Italy

The great threats to the Church in Restoration Italy came from the political legacy of the French Revolution, the movements of liberalism and nationalism, and their adherents. The French Revolution and the French invasions had left behind a rich humus of radical and revolutionary ideas and organisational forms modelled on those of the French Jacobins.[44] In the thirty years between the restoration of Italy's rulers and the 1848–49 revolutions, a variety of competing political programmes emerged for the future of Italy. In particular, after the failure of the old-style revolutionary societies, such as the Carbonari, in the 1820 and 1830–31 revolutions, the Genoese activist Giuseppe Mazzini announced the formation of his 'Young Italy' organisation with a programme of radical, republican nationalism seeking the achievement of a unitary, independent Italy by revolutionary means.[45] Other republicans, such as the *milanesi* Carlo Cattaneo and Giuseppe Ferrari, were less revolutionary in their methods and objectives, and the former urged the necessity of *economic* development as the key element in Italy's future.[46] More moderate (i.e. conservative) liberals, such as the Piedmontese aristocrats Camillo Cavour and Massimo D'Azeglio, eschewed revolution altogether, preferring the survival of monarchy, especially their own Piedmontese monarchy, as a guarantee of social and political stability. Cavour, like Cattaneo, was also keenly interested in Italy's future economic development. What they all shared, whether revolutionary, radical or moderate, was a belief in the need to reform the Church, that the Church and especially the papacy as then constituted were serious cultural and institutional obstacles to the achievement of progress in Italy. Thus ecclesiastical reform was at the heart of the 'Liberal Revolution' that would take place in Italy in the later part of the Risorgimento.

The Liberal Ecclesiastical 'Programme'

The programme of ecclesiastical reform promoted by the liberals varied according to the overall radicalism of the individuals and groups concerned, but in its essentials it can be reduced to the following elements: freedom of religion; secularisation of education and marriage (including the establishment of civil marriage and divorce); state supervision of clergy appointments, especially to the episcopacy, limiting the control of the papacy over the Church in Italy; limitation of the legal privileges of the clergy, including their exemption from the jurisdiction of the state courts; confiscation of church property and restricting the right of the clergy to own property (mortmain); and dissolution of the 'useless'(i.e. contemplative or mendicant) religious orders.

With regard to the last two items, it is interesting to note the essentially *utilitarian economic* motivation. The liberals regarded the tendency of the Church to amass, through donations and legacies, a large landed estate that, they alleged, was badly managed, as a major impediment to economic development through capitalist accumulation and technological improvement. It is significant that during a debate in the Piedmontese Chamber of Deputies in 1855, Cavour used the utilitarian argument on a bill to dissolve the mendicant orders, claiming that the legalised begging of mendicant friars encouraged the poor to follow suit, instead of working.[47] So modernisation, political and economic, demanded drastic reform of the Church. Given this strongly interventionist stance, it is hardly surprising, therefore, that when Cavour officially espoused the slogan 'A Free Church in a Free State' to describe and justify his policy towards the Church from 1855 onwards that it was received with scepticism and scorn by the pope and his supporters.

But the ecclesiastical programme of the liberals was not solely concerned with the financial, legal and social position of the Church in Italy. Given their strong *nationalistic* aspirations, it was bound to encompass the future status of the papacy was well. The temporal power of the popes had long been seen as an impediment to Italian national independence. Both Dante and Machiavelli had alluded to the divisive presence of the Papal States in Italy. Over the centuries, unable to unite Italy under some sort of hereditary, rather than elective, papal monarchy (although the Borgia popes had come pretty close to succeeding in that endeavour), the popes carefully sought to prevent anyone else from doing so, as a means of preserving their territorial sovereignty over the central Italian regions. The success of Consalvi's diplomacy at Vienna was therefore a problem for those seeking to free Italy from foreign (Austrian) rule and hopefully create a united Italian nation state. Apart from Mazzini's resolute unitary republicanism, most liberals and nationalists envisaged some sort of federal Italy, which would also solve the problem of what to do with the other (native) Italian rulers.

A tentative answer to the problem of the papacy and the Papal States in a united Italy along these lines came, not surprisingly, from a Catholic. At this point it should be said that there was much enthusiasm among Italian Catholics for liberal reforms and Italian independence. Liberal Catholics in Italy were probably less numerous, important and influential than their French counterparts, such as the Abbé Lamennais and Count Montalembert, but they could be vocal, even defying the pope during the actual processes of unification between 1859 and 1870. They endured Pope Gregory XVI's put-down of Lamennais and his journal *L'Avenir* in his encyclicals *Mirari vos* and *Singulari nos* in 1832 and 1834 respectively.[48] It was almost inevitable that Gregory – a man so reactionary that he disapproved of even the mildest reforms in the government of the Papal States suggested by Metternich and had once banned the building of railways in his dominions on the grounds that 'Chemin de fer, Chemin d'Enfer' – would condemn democracy and the liberal principles that Lamennais and his supporters espoused.

In fact, despite all of this and the Church's rejection of the eventual outcome of the Risorgimento, Catholics played an important, influential role in its politics, above all as formulators of ideas and opinion. For, despite the thunderous denunciations of liberal Catholicism by the pope, men such as the great novelist Manzoni continued to express support for liberal reform and nationalist objectives, and Rosmini in his *Five Wounds of the Church* did not spare even the papacy from his reforming zeal. A Catholic historian, Cesare Balbo, in his *Speranze D'Italia* ('The Hopes of Italy'), typified the Italian liberal Catholic belief that liberalism, nationalism and Catholicism were not incompatible.[49] The identification of Catholicism with nationalism in Ireland and Poland and the success of conservative Catholics and conservative liberals in creating, in 1831, an independent Belgian state that was also a parliamentary, constitutional monarchy seemed to bear out these hopes. But it was a Piedmontese priest, Vincenzo Gioberti, who, in his book *Del Primato Morale e Civile degli Italiani* ('On the Moral and Civil Primacy of the Italians'), squared the circle by transforming the papacy from being a major obstacle to the achievement of Italian unity into a potential force for its realisation.[50] In *Del Primato*, Gioberti argued that the papacy was a quintessentially *Italian* institution, an oracle, but that unlike the other Italian rulers, the pope had no personal, dynastic interests to pursue. Consequently, Italians should unite around and under the leadership of the pope. Gioberti more specifically called for the creation of an Italian federation under the presidency of the pope and defended by the sword of Piedmont, or, as he himself put it, a unity of 'the holy city and the warrior province'. Seeking a wide-based support, he tried to attract even sceptical, anti-clerical opinion to his banner by attacking their bêtes noires, the Jesuits.[51] Gioberti ignored the fact that the Papal States were probably the worst-governed of all Italian dominions and that Charles Albert, King of Piedmont-Sardinia, was extremely ambitious and committed to the age-long tendency of the House of Savoy to expand and conquer. Perhaps even more staggering is the fact that in *Del Primato* he totally failed to address the problem of how the Austrians were to be evicted from Italy. Would it be by persuasion or force? And what would happen to the Italian Church under such a regime? Would it have to submit to reform from above? Yet, for all its omissions, its unasked or unanswered questions, its contradictions and superficiality, Gioberti's blueprint was plausible: it offered lots of advantages as a way forward. Above all, it offered the prospect of progress without the dangers of violent social revolution or necessarily substantial changes to the position of the Church. So *Del Primato* was a winner. It succeeded in offering a moderate national programme acceptable to most Italian patriots, except republican revolutionaries such as Mazzini. Gioberti's ideas were potent enough to create a 'neo-Guelph illusion'(the Guelphs had been the Italian supporters of the pope against the emperor in the Middle Ages), the myth that the papacy would head the national cause in Italy, which exercised a powerful influence on educated, patriotic opinion in most Italian states between 1845 and 1848.

The events of 1848–49 in Italy

Indeed, such was the strength of the neo-Guelph myth that it helped to precipitate the dramatic events of 1848–49 in Italy. In particular, when Cardinal Giovanni Mastai-Ferretti was elected as Gregory XVI's successor in 1846, taking the name Pius IX, popular opinion hailed him as the 'liberal', 'neo-Guelph' pope predicted by Gioberti who would lead Italy to freedom. In fact, Mastai-Ferretti was not a liberal, though whoever succeeded Gregory XVI would have looked like one. The enthusiasm generated by Pius IX's election helped propel Italy's rulers, including the pope, along the path of constitutional reform, and when Pius, as a matter of form, protested against the Austrian occupation of Ferrara in the northern Papal States, this was interpreted as an indication of his commitment to the national cause. But peaceful change in Italy was soon overshadowed and overtaken by events in France. The Paris revolution of February, which overthrew Louis Philippe's July Monarchy, and which was then followed by revolts in Berlin and Vienna, excited hostility towards the Austrians. Soon the armies of Italian rulers, including that of the pope, were being sent off to fight in the war declared by Charles Albert against Austrian domination in northern Italy.

This was the final straw for Pius IX, who had become increasingly alarmed by the consequences of the constitution he had granted to the Papal States, which had encouraged all manner of radical, even revolutionary, political activity. In March 1848 he spoke out against the Italian national cause in his Allocution, which declared, not unnaturally, that the pope could not lead one Catholic people, the Italians, in a war against another, the Austrians. The incompatibility between Italian nationalism and the essentially international role of the papacy, which was henceforth to govern the policy of the papacy, was at last clearly revealed. As Hales puts it, 'So the Allocution, which censured the extremists of 1848, was published on April 29th, 1848, and the Pope and the Risorgimento parted company.'[52]

After the April Allocution, the situation in Rome could only deteriorate as the revolutionary groups got the upper hand in secular politics. In November, the papal prime minister, Count Pellegrino Rossi, was brutally murdered, and shortly afterwards Pius IX fled to Gaeta in the neighbouring Kingdom of Naples where a counter-revolution had been carried out by Ferdinand. In February 1849, Rome once more became a republic, this time under the rule of Giuseppe Mazzini. The reforming efforts of the republic, which were rational, measured and particularly beneficial to the poor, included the abolition of the temporal power, though 'The Head of the Catholic Religion' was guaranteed the free exercise of his spiritual power. But the republic did not last long. Pius threw in his lot with the reactionary forces, with the result that a French army besieged the Eternal City and took it despite the heroic resistance of Garibaldi and volunteers from all over Italy. The Venetian Republic was crushed in August, and Pius returned to Rome in 1850.

Religious minorities in the Risorgimento

The events of 1848–49 had significant consequences for the religious minorities in Italy.[53] The liberal principle of freedom of religion was enforced, though not universally and not absolutely. The constitutions granted by the rulers of Modena and Parma established the political and civil rights of both Protestants and Jews, and as did that in Piedmont-Sardinia, though in this case it also declared that 'the Catholic religion is the sole religion of the state'.[54] The severity of this statement was modified by subsequent legislation that permitted non-Catholics access to all professions and granted them full civil and political rights: thus the royal house of Savoy finally turned its back on a long history of religious repression.[55] No such emancipation was granted in either the Papal States or the Kingdom of Naples.[56] It seems likely that the refusal of these governments was more consonant with popular mood, which showed itself hostile to the Jews in several parts of Italy during 1848–49 and to the attitude of the Catholic clergy and hierarchy.[57] When Pius IX returned from his self-imposed exile in Gaeta in 1850, he reversed the emancipation granted by the short-lived Roman Republic and ordered the Roman Jews back to the Ghetto on the banks of the Tiber.[58] More clamorously, in 1858 he ordered a boy from a Bolognese Jewish family, who had been secretly baptised by a Christian servant-girl, to be taken away from his parents and brought up as a Christian. The resulting Mortara affair caused almost as much of a scandal throughout Europe as L'Affaire Dreyfus 36 years later.[59] Given this kind of atmosphere in the Papal States, it was not until after the conquest of Rome in 1870 that Italy's religious minorities were granted full parity with their Catholic compatriots. The consequent building of Waldensian, Methodist, Anglican and other non-Catholic churches in the Eternal City would generate much fear of 'Protestant propaganda and proselytism' on the part of the Roman Curia in the ensuing decades.

Ecclesiastical legislation in Piedmont-Sardinia

The neo-Guelph illusion (delusion) was thoroughly shattered by the events of 1848–49 and reaction triumphed almost everywhere in Italy, except Piedmont-Sardinia, where the Statuto (Constitution) of 1848 survived precariously under a new monarch, Victor Emmanuel II. The Statuto was by no means democratic – the eventual electoral law gave the vote to less than 2 per cent of the population – and it did not even guarantee a parliamentary system of government, though thanks to a succession of moderate liberal prime ministers, including Gioberti, Massimo D'Azeglio and Count Cavour, it had evolved in that direction by the end of the 1850s.[60] In that process, the state's prime ministers had to balance between a reactionary (and clerical) right and a democratic left. Ultimately, Cavour managed to stabilise the situation by an alliance of the centre-left with the centre-right in the lower house of Parliament, the Chamber of Deputies, the first example of what was to become the classic winning coalition in Italian politics. Both D'Azeglio and Cavour committed their governments to reform programmes that would 'modernise' Piedmont-Sardinia.[61] This was undoubtedly the first stage of the 'Liberal Revolution' that would transform not only the kingdom but eventually the whole peninsula. And at the heart of the programme was a series of reforms aimed at the Church, which, as Woolf remarks, 'underlined the determination of the Piedmontese ruling class to achieve a level of secular control befitting a modern, western state'.[62]

The ecclesiastical reforms carried out by first D'Azeglio and then Cavour were quite far-reaching in the Piedmontese context, for the Church, despite the depredations of the French invasions and occupations, had been a wealthy, powerful and privileged force in the kingdom. Between 1850 and 1852, legislation was passed that abolished the Church's power of censorship, established freedom of worship for Jews and Protestants, reduced the number of feast days, abolished the right of sanctuary on church property, the jurisdiction of church courts and the Church's monopoly of education. Further laws restricted the acquisition of property by ecclesiastical bodies and dissolved numerous contemplative and mendicant orders: in all, 334 out of 604 religious houses with a total population of 4,050 out of 5,506 monks, friars and nuns were closed down.[63] The Siccardi Laws, as they were known, constituted the major issue in Piedmontese politics at the time, as they were intended to be. The disputes over them polarised politics between liberals and 'clericals' (Catholic conservatives) in a way that had not been so hitherto and thus also effectively isolated the clericals in Parliament. In 1857, when the clericals managed to win over a third of the seats in Parliament, several of their number, plus a few members from the extreme left were unseated on what even Cavour's friends admitted were illegal grounds.[64] As Owen Chadwick has argued, this corruption of Piedmontese politics did not encourage Catholic confidence in the parliamentary system: even before the Holy See forbade Catholics from participating in Italian parliamentary elections as a protest against annexation of parts of the Papal States, one of those Catholics who lost his seat, the priest Margotti, in protest coined the phrase 'neither electors nor elected', which would become the slogan for later Catholic abstentionists from Italian national politics.[65]

The Siccardi Laws also outraged the pope, who broke off diplomatic relations with Victor Emmanuel's government. Piedmont-Sardinia emerged in the mid-1850s as the leading state in Italy, and it did so because its reform programme, not least the laws against the Church, marked it out as the major modernising, progressive force in the peninsula. The battle lines were thus being drawn between Turin and Rome, between the more explicitly secularising liberal forces that had emerged from the events of 1848–49 and the papacy.

The papacy and the unification of Italy, 1859–61

Between 1859 and 1870, Italy was unified in a series of stages under the Savoyard royal house. As the process developed, it looked increasingly like a political struggle between Piedmont-Sardinia and the papacy, between Prime Minister Cavour and Pope Pius IX. Very quickly the struggle also took on an international dimension. Cavour's intuition from the events of 1848–49 that Italy could not *farà da se* ('do it by herself', as the popular catchphrase had it), that to solve the 'Italian Question', i.e. to achieve independence from foreign (Austrian) rule, would necessitate a resort to high diplomacy, meant seeking a foreign ally to play off against Austria. This he found in the ambitious and adventurous new French emperor, Napoleon III. In the secret Treaty of Plombières of 1858, Napoleon agreed to go to war against Austria and thus acquire Lombardo-Venetia for Piedmont-Sardinia, in exchange for financial commitments and the cession of Nice and Savoy, both largely French-speaking territories but nevertheless traditional domains of the Savoyard dynasty. Given the presence of the French garrison in Rome, clearly that city was not on Cavour's agenda, so at this stage at least, Napoleon was not presented with any conflict between his new commitments and the longer-standing one of defending the pope in Rome. Certainly, at this stage of his plans, Cavour was not contemplating unification, in large part because of the inevitable conflict it would have precipitated not only with the papacy, but with the European powers.

In the third Italian war of independence in 1859, Austria was defeated on the field of battle, with the terrible carnage of Magenta and Solferino, but not sufficiently to win Venetia as well as Lombardy for Piedmont-Sardinia in the Treaty of Villafranca signed between the Austrian and French emperors. In the meantime, Cavour had used the patriotic, but loyal and conservative, National Society to engineer nationalistic revolts in support of Piedmont-Sardinia in the central duchies (Parma, Modena and Tuscany) and also in the ever agitated and volatile northern territory of the Papal States, Emilia-Romagna. In the spring of 1860, Napoleon reluctantly allowed the National Society to organise plebiscites in favour of unification to the newly formed 'Kingdom of Upper Italy' to take place in these territories in return for the cession of Nice and Savoy to France. Later in 1860, two more territories of the Papal States, Le Marche and Umbria, were lost to the pope, as the indirect result of Garibaldi's expedition of the Thousand Redshirts to exploit yet another revolt in Sicily.

What is especially significant about Garibaldi's conquest of the island from the Neapolitan Bourbons was the amount of enthusiasm it generated among elements of the lower clergy in Sicily, especially religious such as Fra Pantaleo, a reminder that, despite Pius IX's condemnations, the unification was a process that aroused much support among Catholics.[66] As Chadwick has demonstrated, in Italy as a whole there were lots of clergy, including a few bishops, who supported unification, and the strongest enthusiasm was to be found in the north.[67] Garibaldi's expedition was also a reminder of the still powerful influence of Mazzini on events, and in consequence, Cavour was confronted by a situation that was developing out his control. In order to recover the situation, Cavour sent Victor Emmanuel II with his army, both to prevent Mazzinian republicans from gaining the upper hand in Naples and to forestall Garibaldi, fresh from his triumphs there, from attacking Rome. Victor Emmanuel managed to persuade Garibaldi to disband his armies and return home to Caprera, handing over Naples and Sicily. Also to be incorporated were Le Marche and Umbria, which Victor Emmanuel had seized from the papal forces thanks to his victories at the battles of Ancona and Castelfidardo, on his march across central Italy to encounter Garibaldi. All of the newly conquered/liberated territories would be incorporated by popular plebiscite into the Kingdom of Italy, proclaimed in March 1861, under Victor Emmanuel's crown. All of Pius IX's entreaties and remonstrances to Napoleon III against the despoliation of his dominions were in vain: the French emperor was restrained from intervening in Italian affairs by Austrian and British pressure. The pope was now only left with the so-called 'Patrimony of St. Peter', the city of Rome and surrounding provinces, which was more or less coterminus with the present-day region of Latium.

Pius IX and Italian unification

Before his death in June 1861 Cavour had tried to seek some sort of permanent settlement with Rome. By means of the Jesuit father Passaglia and Dr Pantaleoni, he entered into secret negotiations with Pius IX.[68] The attempt failed for a variety of reasons, but not least because in contrast to Cavour's sweet words of a 'Free Church in a Free State', his lieutenants in the newly annexed territories, including those formerly belonging to the Papal States, had begun ruthlessly applying Piedmontese ecclesiastical legislation there. In consequence, by the time of Cavour's death in June 1861 it was clear that nothing could modify Pius IX's intransigent resistance to the loss of most of the Papal States and the confiscation of church property throughout unified Italy.

The circumstances surrounding Cavour's death throw some interesting light upon the position of those Catholics who supported unification. On his deathbed, Cavour asked for the last rites of the Church, and these he was duly given by the local parish priest. The assumption was that he must have recanted his actions against the Church in order for the excommunication imposed by the Holy See upon those who had set violent hands on church property and its rights to be lifted and for him thus to have received the last sacraments.[69] The initial refusal of the Church to give the last rites to Cavour's friend and colleague, the agriculture minister, Santa Rosa, in 1851 had aroused serious anti-clerical passions in Turin.[70] Why did these sceptics, with a rather 'minimalist' Catholic faith, seek reconciliation in the end? Was it that the Italian liberals, unlike their contemporary French or later Spanish counterparts, were not really anti-clericals, that they wanted to have their cake and eat it? That would seem to be the answer, and probably it was precisely this unwillingness on the part of the leading Italian liberals of the Risorgimento period to make a decisive, personal break with the Church, and the decision of the local ecclesiastical authorities not to ask too many questions of the dying, that helped prevent the conflict with the Church from becoming as bitter and violent as it became in France and Spain.

But Pius IX did not see things in that light and punished the priests involved.[71] And as ecclesiastical legislation was enforced more and more rigorously in the new Italian kingdom, he reiterated his condemnations of the 'sub-alpine usurper'(King Victor Emmanuel II) and his ministers and other agents who had assisted the advance of the forces of national unification. His intransigence was partly prompted by a suspicion that the new Italian State was fragile in the extreme and that there was absolutely no guarantee that it would last. Certainly until the mid-1860s, the new State was threatened by serious rebellions in the south, especially Calabria. The 'Great Brigandage' of the early 1860s was a mixture of deep-seated criminal activity (hence the term 'brigands'), peasant resistance to the demand for new taxes, especially the hated tax on the grinding of corn, conscription and the loss of benefits from church property, and rebellion deliberately stirred up by the supporters of the deposed Bourbon king of Naples, Francis II.[72] There were even allegations of papal involvement.[73] By 1866, hundreds of thousands of Italian troops had been used to crush successfully the rebellions on the mainland and the revolt in Sicily.

Pius IX's major response to the events in Italy was to publish, in 1864, the encyclical *Quanta Cura*, to which was appended the 'Syllabus of Errors', listing eighty propositions condemned by the Holy See, including the notorious rejection of the proposition that 'The Roman Pontiff can and ought to reconcile himself to, and agree with, progress, liberalism, and civilisation as lately introduced'.[74] The Syllabus has long been regarded as Pius IX's declaration of war upon the 'modern world', upon liberalism and secularism, and thus as marking the high point in the 'culture wars' of the nineteenth century.[75] Hales has very convincingly argued that it was the situation in Italy in the early 1860s that prompted the Syllabus:

The Syllabus was widely regarded as a gesture of defiance hurled by an outraged pope against the nineteenth century . . . Actually, as reference to the Encyclical from which it is drawn shows, it was the Piedmontese government's idea of what constituted progress and civilisation with which the pope was declining to come to terms.[76]

Nearly 60 of the 80 propositions dealt with issues at stake in the conflict between the pope and the new Italian State, as the titles of sections V to X demonstrate:

V.   Errors Concerning the Church and her Rights . . .
VI.   Errors about Civil Society, considered both in itself and in
        its Relation to the Church . . .
VII.   Errors concerning Natural and Christian Ethics . . .
VIII.   Errors concerning Christian Marriage . . .
IX.   Errors regarding the Civil Power of the Sovereign Pontiff
        . . .
X.   Errors having regard to Modern Liberalism.[77]

While liberals in Belgium, France, Germany, Spain and other European and Latin American countries were proponents of the errors condemned in these sections of the Syllabus, Italy in the early 1860s was *the* battleground in the latest phase of the struggle in the nineteenth-century 'culture wars'. The reference to 'the Civil Power of the Sovereign Pontiff' clinches the argument: only in Italy was the temporal power being seriously challenged and indeed had been substantially undermined already. One wonders whether the Syllabus would have been published at this point or at all, had it not been for the Italian situation.

The Syllabus seriously embarrassed the Catholic hierarchy in many countries until Bishops Dupanloup of Orleans and Ketteler of Mainz intervened to publish a reasoned analysis of its content and context that helped explain away its worst elements.[78] It could also be argued that another development in the Italian situation that helped to prompt the publication of the Syllabus was the September Convention between the French and Italian governments. The Convention got Napoleon III off the hook by allowing him to withdraw his garrison from Rome in return for an Italian commitment to make Florence the permanent capital of Italy and not to attack Rome or allow other Italian forces to do so. The Convention infuriated Pius IX, of course, but it certainly did not resolve the 'Roman Question', the hope among Italian patriots that one day Rome would be their capital. 'O Roma O Morte!'('Or Rome, or

Death!') had long been the watchword of those patriots bent upon complete Italian unification, and so it remained after September 1864. Indeed, Garibaldi sought to take advantage of the withdrawal of the French garrison to make yet another attempt to seize the Eternal City (the first had been defeated at Aspromonte by Italian troops in 1862) but was defeated by French troops at Mentana in 1867. Eventually, Napoleon III, under pressure from French Catholics, was forced to send back the French garrison to Rome.

The Council of the Vatican, Papal Infallibility and the fall of Rome

Following the September Convention, Pius and his secretary of state, Cardinal Antonelli, sought to defend papal possession of Rome through diplomacy and also the establishment of a substantial military force. The seizures of papal territory at the beginning of the 1860s had aroused much sympathy among Catholics throughout the world for Pius's plight, to the extent that to compensate for his financial losses the traditional collections of 'Peter's Pence' from the faithful was revived.[79] As the 1860s wore on, Peter's Pence offerings sent to Rome were directed towards the support of Belgian Monsignor (Mgr) De Merode's papal Ministry of War.[80] Once again it can be argued that the Italian situation was having a profound impact upon the development of the Catholic Church as a whole. It would not be going too far to say that this same situation also affected the pope's decision to call the (first) Council of the Vatican in 1870 and led to the decision by that council to proclaim the dogma of Papal Infallibility, that is, that when speaking *ex cathedra* (by virtue of his office as bishop of Rome) the pope can make no error in pronouncements upon matters of faith and morals. With such a massive reinforcement of his moral and spiritual authority, a further centralisation of power in the Church, Pius IX hoped to be able to better confront both liberalism throughout Europe, but above all the machinations of Italian liberalism as represented by the new state in particular. Certainly, in the decades to come, Infallibility would massively strengthen the hand of the papacy in its relationship with the Italian episcopate, clergy and laity.

As in previous stages of the process of Italian unification, the making of Rome into the capital was the result of events outside Italy. The outbreak of the Franco-Prussian War in 1870 obliged Napoleon to withdraw French troops from the city, and in September the Italian government seized the opportunity to attack the Papal States and besiege Rome. After token resistance, papal Rome finally surrendered and became a part of Italy on 20 September 1870.

Conclusion

The Liberal Revolution had dramatically and drastically changed the context in which the Church would henceforth operate in Italy. Unification had swept away the collection of pre-national states, and with them the differing arrangements for relations between church and state. This was the beginning of the end of the Italian 'churches'. The Italian ecclesiastical authorities now had a single state structure to contend with, and the tendency of the new Italian nation-state to homogenise the system of church–state relations, using the ecclesiastical legislation of Piedmont-Sardinia and early 1860s Italy, meant the beginning of the emergence of an Italian 'national church'. That process would be accentuated by Pius IX's response to the absorption of the Papal States into the unified Italian State and his consequent attempts to win back the temporal power.

The Liberal Revolution had also cast into doubt the future role of Catholics in Italian politics. Given the strictures of the Syllabus, 'Liberal Catholic' seemed almost a contradiction in terms. How could Italian Catholics play an active role in the parliamentary system of the new Liberal State, particularly since both Catholic journalists and even the Vatican itself seemed to negate the legitimacy of such participation? It would take the reigns of three successive pontiffs, Leo XIII, Pius X and Benedict XV, before a satisfactory answer to that question would be arrived at.

Chapter 3

THE CATHOLIC RECOVERY (1870–1914)

Introduction

THE 44 YEARS BETWEEN THE FALL of Rome in 1870 and the outbreak of the First World War in 1914 were a period of recovery and revival for Italian Catholicism. The roots of that revival undoubtedly lay in earlier periods, and the first 'shoots', so to speak, were visible during the Restoration period, but in the last three decades of the nineteenth century and the first of the twentieth, the recovery was strong, indeed sometimes spectacular. But it should be stressed that the Italian phenomenon was not unique: all over Europe, and a few isolated parts of Latin America, a resurgence of Catholic religiosity was evident.[1] As in Italy, it was closely connected with the Church's response to liberalism and secularism. Many of the trends in devotional practice, such as the intensification of devotion to the Sacred Hearts of Jesus and Mary, and Eucharistic devotions outside the Mass, were very specifically part of a conscious intent to reassert and reinvigorate Catholic identity and morale in the face of the dangers that loyal Catholics encountered in all walks of life, and as the basis for the mass mobilisation of Catholics against 'the enemy', liberalism and all its works.[2]

The institutional church after the Liberal Revolution

The most serious impact that the Liberal Revolution had upon the institutional church in the period of unification and after was on its property and revenues. The extension of Piedmontese ecclesiastical legislation to the various territories incorporated into the Kingdom of Italy between 1859 and 1870, and the further ecclesiastical laws of 1866–67 and 1873 (Rome and the surrounding provinces), meant the confiscation of all church property except that attached to parochial benefices (glebe lands). Chiefly, this meant the property of bishoprics (the *mensa*), the cathedral chapters and religious orders, male and female.[3] The ban on ecclesiastical bodies from making further acquisitions of property (including bequests and donations), as well as from alienating (selling or giving) it, and thus acquiring more liquid assets, meant an impoverishment of some benefices. The confiscation of the property of lay confraternities and congregations, whose objectives were usually liturgical or charitable, reduced the financial independence and room for manoeuvre of the average parish priest. Henceforth, the proceeds of the sale of all confiscated church property was to be held and administered by government bodies, most importantly the Fondo per il Culto established in 1866 and the Fondo per l'uso di religione della città, which was established for Rome in 1873, both of which were under the control of the Ministry of Justice.[4] From the returns on the investment of 60 per cent of the church lands sold, plus a special tax on the income of surviving ecclesiastical benefices which varied from 5 to 20 per cent, a stipend would be paid to the poorer benefices in order to equalise incomes.[5] Over the years, these payments had to be supplemented by a direct grant from the Italian treasury, partly because the 'administration of the funds was costly and inefficient'.[6]

Globally speaking, there were fewer clergy in mid-nineteenth century Italy than a century before, and in some dioceses of the northern and central parts of the peninsula the shrinking of financial resources after unification had a serious effect upon the parochial clergy.[7] In Mantua, for example, the number of clergy was literally halved between 1868 and 1887. In a report to Pius IX, the bishop of Mantua complained that:

> the career of the priesthood appears to have become exclusively restricted to the poor . . . the clergy of the diocese of Mantua are in a deplorable condition in relation to the means of subsistence, in large part reduced to the most abysmal penury and in danger of becoming beggars . . .[8]

A similar story was true of much of the Abruzzi and Calabria.[9] Though the situation was better in most areas of northern and central Italy, the effects of the loss of revenue on the clergy would be felt over the longer term in Lombardy, where numbers fell significantly in the 1880s and 1890s.[10]

But the impact of the 1867 laws was felt most keenly in the south, where its effect was the complete confiscation of the property of the *chiese ricettizie*;

thus these churches were left without even the income from the glebe lands, which had survived in the north.[11] In effect, the southern clergy were paid a miserable pittance by the State, over and above what they could exact from the tithe and the *diritti alla stola*, the customary fees charged for the celebration of Masses for the dead, baptisms, marriages and funerals. Given the fact that this put many of the clergy at odds with the desperately impoverished peasantry, one seriously wonders whether this wasn't the deliberate intention of the Liberal 'reformers'.

The difficulties experienced by the secular diocesan clergy after unification were compounded by the government's treatment of the religious orders and congregations. In the Catholic Church, regular clergy, those belonging to religious orders and congregations, have always supplemented the work of the secular clergy in providing pastoral care of parishes: indeed, many city centre parishes in Italy were staffed by friars or monks. The governments of United Italy came down very hard on the religious orders and congregations, male and female. Thousands were ejected from their houses, and in cities and towns these premises were frequently converted to government use, as prefectures (provincial governors' offices), military and police barracks, prisons, schools and town halls: in Rome they were used to house sections of the state bureaucracy, and other state institutions such as the National Library, as well.[12] The property of the orders was put up for sale, though some income from the proceeds was made available, and henceforth religious orders, like other ecclesiastical bodies, were forbidden to make further acquisitions of property.

The broader social consequences of the massive divestment of the Church's property were serious. In many areas, the confiscations led to a deterioration in the living conditions of the poor, especially the peasantry. The latter could rarely afford to buy the land put on the market, so the land was snapped up by existing landowners. On the other hand, this often led to uprooting of the former leaseholders of church lands, who had formerly enjoyed advantageous terms. These people now swelled the ranks of the *braccianti* and *giornalieri* (hourly and day labourers), categories of agricultural proletariat hitherto rare in most regions of Italy, especially southern regions such as Calabria, and added to the numbers of those who joined the 'brigands'. The reduction in landowning by the religious orders and the charitable congregations and confraternities of the parishes also inevitably reduced their capacity to serve the needs of the poor. 'Modernisation' in this sense, the redistribution of land into the hands of groups committed to a more capitalistic and intensive system of farming, was clearly not beneficial to the weakest strata in rural society who had for centuries been able to find a haven in times of difficulty in the ample bosom of Mother Church.[13]

The Catholic revival

Whatever limitations government legislation imposed on the institutional church in Italy, it emphatically did not prevent Catholicism from flourishing. Indeed, it is clear that from mid-1800s onwards there was a veritable Catholic 'revival' in Italy, as indeed there was in other countries. At the heart of the Catholic revival were, naturally, the clergy, and equally naturally, as has been seen, there was concern at all levels of the hierarchy, including the papacy itself, about their recruitment and training. According to the authoritative *Storia della Chiesa*:

> at the middle of the nineteenth century, a substantial minority of priests were well educated, energetic, intelligent and open-minded, [whereas] the majority were not up to the job, very often lacking a solid vocation or one at all . . . On the other hand, history in most cases is made by a decisive and energetic minority.[14]

In Italy, this 'active minority' were to be the chief agents of a Catholic revival. Men such as San Giovanni Bosco and Mgr Franzoni in Piedmont and Mgrs Marrioni and Ramazzotti in Milan, for example, set a high standard of personal sanctity and pastoral care.[15]

A key component of this minority of good priests were male religious; indeed, the clearest evidence of the Catholic revival in Italy in the second half of the nineteenth century is to be found in the massive expansion in the numbers of religious, male and female. Though the late nineteenth century witnessed a growth in the numbers of religious throughout the Catholic Church in Europe,[16] the conditions for such a development in Italy were unpropitious, given the legal restrictions upon the ability of religious to acquire property. Yet there was a resurgence in Italy, and significantly, it was chiefly among new congregations, not old orders. Whereas the old orders (i.e. those whose members professed solemn vows) did not reach pre-French Revolution levels of membership in this period, new congregations (whose members professed simple vows) recruited in large numbers. A total of 77 new congregations of male religious were founded in the Catholic Church in the nineteenth century, of which twenty were Italian, and if one adds in those of female religious, then the number of new foundations in Italy between 1866 and 1920 reaches the impressive figure of 100.[17] The actual numbers of religious began to grow significantly from the 1880s: the 28,000 female religious identified in the national census of 1881 were almost all members of new orders; by 1901 their numbers had risen to 40,000, by 1911 to over 45,000, and in 1921 they had reached nearly 72,000.[18]

Whereas there was a fall in the numbers of those religious dedicated to the contemplative and mendicant life, the work of religious, male and female, became increasingly diversified in this period, i.e. among emigrants, convicts, workers (especially female workers), the sick, the old, orphans and the disabled etc., and not just in the usual teaching and nursing fields of apostolate. This was an apt, appropriate response to an Italy that from the 1880s onwards was beginning to change in an industrial, urban direction. Consequently, these religious increasingly provided the new face of the Church in Italian society. The new religious congregations had less need for elaborate churches and conventual buildings; hence they were more easily financed. In any case, the old religious orders and new congregations got around the ban on the acquisition of property by all sorts of stratagems – registering property in the name of the religious superior or third party laymen or transferring it to commercial companies controlled by reliable laymen, or to diocesan bodies.[19] These *pie frode* ('pious frauds'), as they were called, were practised on a wide scale, and though the governments of Crispi and other premiers of the Sinistra (Left) threatened further confiscatory legislation, they were largely left alone by the State. By the turn of the century, the religious orders and congregations had assumed a powerful, multifarious role in the life of Italian society: it is a tribute to their influence that even children of the liberal-conservative political elite were often educated in the schools of the Jesuits and other religious.

Italian Catholicism shared in other aspects of the European Catholic revival of the second half of the nineteenth century. Devotion to the sacred hearts of Jesus and Mary was encouraged as a form of reparation for the 'carnevalesque' follies of February in particular and the iniquities of the secularising Liberal State in general. In 1856 Pius IX had established a feast day for the Sacred Heart of Jesus and in 1864 the French Visitandine nun, Margaret Mary Alacoque, who had helped popularise the cult of the Sacred Heart, was beatified: in 1889 Leo consecrated the whole of mankind to the Sacred Heart. Marian devotion, intensified by Pius IX's declaration of the Immaculate Conception of Mary in 1850, was as strong as elsewhere in Europe, though there were no major apparitions like Lourdes in France, Marpingen in Germany or Fatima in Portugal. Probably the reason was that Italy already possessed flourishing, long-standing centres of Marian devotion and pilgrimage, Loreto in Le Marche, the Santuario D'Oropa in Piedmont, the Madonna Della Guardia near Genoa, Monte Berico near Vicenza in north-east Italy, and countless other provincial shrines. A new one was developed in this period at Pompei near Naples.[20] The importance of Marian devotion in the Catholic revival is underlined by the fact that Leo wrote no less than eleven encyclicals on the rosary (but only one on the Eucharist) during the course of his 25-year pontificate.[21]

The celebration of local saints' feast days continued unabated, despite the financial assault upon some of the ecclesiastical corporations that organised them. Devotion to the greater saints of Italy, such as St Francis of Assisi, St Anthony of Padua and St Catharine of Siena was expanded by the increasing use of railways to transport vast numbers of pilgrims. And Leo XIII strongly encouraged pilgrimages to Rome/the Vatican as a way of challenging the Italian State's re-moulding of Rome from a papal city to the city of a new national monarchy, by driving new thoroughfares through medieval and renaissance quarters and constructing new palaces and other monuments of state power; in addition, pilgrimages helped to solve the Vatican's intermittent financial difficulties.[22] They also served a very important purpose in helping to build an Ultramontane papal 'personality cult' around the charismatic figure of Leo himself.[23] There is, therefore, a wonderful irony in the fact that the Italian State's encouragement and financing of railways as a form of nation-building – 'to stitch up the boot' – also benefited its 'enemy' the papacy in its efforts to re-assert its authority and influence vis-à-vis Unified Italy and its king . . .

The emphasis placed on gatherings at Eucharistic congresses, to celebrate the presence of Jesus in the Blessed Sacrament, in major national and regional centres was another manifestation of Catholicism's determination to fight 'the culture war' with liberal democracy on its own terrain, mobilising the Catholic masses in great celebrations of traditional religious identity. As in other Catholic countries in the late nineteenth century, in Italy there was an increasing stress on the centrality of the Eucharist in Catholic worship, accompanied by efforts to encourage Eucharistic devotions outside the Mass – Benediction and Exposition of the Blessed Sacrament. There are no statistical sources to give a picture of patterns of attendance at Sunday Mass in this period, so we can only guess how the ecclesiastical legislation of the new Italy affected religious observance. It is in fact likely that the legislation and the generally 'secular' atmosphere created in official circles had little or no impact upon religious practice, apart, possibly, from among elements of the middle classes, especially those in government employment who felt obliged to conform to the new 'secular' state. Then there were those who bought church lands, usually but not always wealthy landowners, both noble and bourgeois, who were in theory automatically excommunicated, although those who had purchased the landed property of the Holy See itself were able to elude the penalty by promising to return their property when the pope's temporal power was restored.[24] Again, in theory at least, all those who had collaborated in the ecclesiastical measures of the liberals, including the destruction of the Papal States, were automatically excommunicated, from King Victor Emmanuel II downwards: politicians, prefects, army and naval officers and civil servants.

How these people reconciled their consciences is unclear. Many would, at the very latest, have been reconciled on their death beds, like, most notably, King Victor Emmanuel II and Camillo Cavour. In any case, these people constituted a tiny minority of Italians, the inner elite of 'Legal Italy'. 'Real Italy', the mass of the population, and especially the peasantry, were probably largely unaffected by the changes. They would have gone on, in the time-honoured way, living, often starving, and dying, but with the sacramental comforts of the Church available to them. But their closeness to the Church, which effectively meant the parochial clergy, varied enormously from north to south.

The papacy, meanwhile, was equipping itself with the instruments and agents to conduct its war against the 'modern world' that it had denounced in the Syllabus of Errors, and especially so in Italy. In 1861, the Vatican bought the Rome daily newspaper *L'Osservatore Romano*, which soon became its official organ, as did *La Civiltà Cattolica*, the Jesuit fortnightly, which would become the authoritative voice of the papacy to bishops and clergy throughout the world. As in France, Germany and other Catholic countries, clergy and Catholic laity in Italy were encouraged to develop the *buona stampa*, literally the 'good press', periodical publications of every kind, as a means of combating the lies and temptations of the 'enemy' press at national, regional and local levels.[25] But the diffusion of a Catholic press was slower in Italy because of high levels of adult illiteracy. Another weapon of crucial importance in the papacy's battle versus liberal Italy was the development of new forms of Catholic associationalism that, though by no means superseding the confraternities, congregations and other traditional parish-based organisations, would be much more effective in mobilising the Catholic masses. In 1867, Pius authorised the formation of GIAC (Gioventù Italiana dell'Azione Cattolica), a national Catholic youth organisation with parochial groups; hence it could claim to be the earliest form of what would become in the twentieth century Catholic Action. As Catholic organisations, both adult and youth, male and female developed, their activities, and other Catholic initiatives like the press, were brought together under the umbrella of the Opera dei Congressi e Comitati cattolici, founded in 1872.[26]

The Opera became the key lay agency for the implementation of the Vatican's policy in post-unification Italy, and against the policies and pretensions of the Liberal State. Among the most impressive demonstrations of the vitality of the Catholic revival in Italy in this period, and of the growing strength of the developing Catholic movement, were the campaigns against the introduction of cremation, civil marriage and divorce, and in the case of divorce, it was a very successful one. Divorce was first introduced into Italy by Napoleon's Code of Civil Law in 1808, but it was roundly condemned by the clergy and almost entirely ignored by Italians of all classes and then swept away with other Napoleonic reforms in 1814.[27] In 1865, the first serious breach in the Church's monopoly of the regulation of matrimonial matters came with the adoption of civil marriage in the new Italian civil code.[28] In the 1870s, the precedence of the civil marriage ceremony over the church ceremony was debated, causing anger in clerical circles and perplexity and dismay among the poor unable to afford two ceremonies. Though the same law permitted legal separation and court authority over the custody of children, it still left intact the principle and practice of the indissolubility of the marriage bond.[29]

Between unification and the advent of Fascism to power a total of no less than nine attempts were made to change this situation by passing a divorce law through the Italian Parliament. Each one was a failure largely because of Catholic opposition. If there was ever an example of the successful mobilisation of Catholic opinion, this was it. The Opera organised very effective campaigns against all the divorce bills introduced into Parliament under the liberal regime. In the battle against the divorce bill of deputy Villa in 1898 it managed to collect 637,000 signatures to an anti-divorce petition in three months, and 10 years later it amassed a total of 3.5 million signatures against the attempt to introduce divorce as part of a reform of the civil code by the government of Giuseppe Zanardelli.[30]

The failure of divorce also points to another interesting aspect of Italian society under the liberal regime: that it remained essentially *Catholic* in so much of its private morality and behaviour. Bourgeois Liberal Italy was a very conservative, patriarchal society, more so than Republican France. In 1878, Francesco Crispi's political career had nearly been destroyed by allegations (essentially true) of bigamy.[31] And during the parliamentary debates of 1882 on divorce Antonio Salandra, later prime minister, warned that the law was simply not desired by the overwhelming mass of the population.

Pius IX, the fall of Rome and the Law of Papal Guarantees 1871

On the 20 September 1870, Italian troops entered Rome and made it the capital of Italy. Pius IX's response was to excommunicate the 'subalpine usurper' and the other perpetrators of this final act of 'despoilation' and to withdraw into the Apostolic Palace of the Vatican. Henceforth, he would describe himself as 'the prisoner of the Vatican', a concept that was only partly true in fact but which would be promoted by intransigent Italian Catholics, ecclesiastical and lay, in their future battles with the liberal regime, and would be used by Ultramontanists everywhere in the Catholic world as an especially potent image with which to extract Peter's Pence, financial sustenance of the papacy from the faithful.[32] In practical terms, this intransigent policy as far as the Vatican was concerned meant a reiteration of the 1864 *non expedit*, the ban on Italian Catholics from voting in parliamentary elections and persuading them, especially the clergy, to have as little contact with governmental authorities as was practically possible.

Within a year of the occupation of Rome, the Italian government made a genuine attempt to resolve both the 'Roman Question' and some issues in church–state relations within the Italian peninsula. The Destra Storica (Historic Right), the party who were then in power, in principle followed the Cavourian maxim of 'A Free Church in a Free State', but in practice this meant both the separation (and secularisation) of the state from the church, and the latter's subjection in essential matters to the jurisdiction of the State. As far as the 'Roman Question' was concerned, there was really little they could concede to the papacy. No government after 1870 could have retro-ceded even a square metre of the sacred national territory so recently won with Italian blood. Therefore, a resurrection of the temporal power in whatever shape or form was simply not possible. But, of course, it was restoration of the temporal power that Pius IX desired and demanded in numerous encyclicals and other public documents, even if Cardinal Secretary of State Antonelli regarded the abolition of the Papal States as a blessing in disguise.

The Law of Papal Guarantees, which the Destra Storica managed to push through the Italian Parliament against the opposition of both the Left and some of its own followers, became law in 1871. It provided for the recognition of the sovereign status of the pope by granting him the honours, privileges and immunities due to a monarch, including the diplomatic privileges of ambassadors accredited to him as guaranteed by international law; it granted him the free 'enjoyment' of the Vatican and its dependencies, the Lateran Basilica (the cathedral of Rome) and Palace, the papal villa at Castelgandolfo and an annual 'civil list' of 3.25 million lire in compensation for the loss of the Papal States and the property of the Holy See within them.[33] In addition, the Italian government guaranteed the free and undisturbed meeting of councils and conclaves. As far as the wider issue of the relations between church and state were concerned, the Italian State guaranteed free communication between the Holy See and the Italian clergy and the free assembly of members of the clergy; it pledged the abolition of the *placet* and *exequatur*, i.e. state consent to the actions of the ecclesiastical hierarchy, and it abandoned the necessity for bishops to take the oath of allegiance to the king and promised to review legislation dealing with ecclesiastical property.[34]

Pius rejected the law, on the entirely justifiable grounds that: a) it did not restore the temporal power that had been unlawfully taken away from the papacy; and b) it was a unilateral act of the Italian Parliament that could just as unilaterally be abrogated by the same parliament. Indeed, there were real fears in the Vatican that the more anti-clerically inclined Sinistra (Left) opposition would do just that after it came to power in 1876.[35] The Law had many other defects, not least in the section dealing with relations between church and state, chief of which was that relating to property. It was inconceivable that the Italian State would return property to the Church, because it had been largely financial necessity (as in the case of the French Revolution) that had led to the confiscation of church lands. Indeed, within two years of the passing of the Law of Guarantees, the Italian government extended the laws on the confiscation of ecclesiastical property to Rome and its surrounding territory (see above, pp. 29–30). The rejection of the Law meant the rejection of the financial subsidy to the papacy.

The Vatican's failure to accept the Law of Guarantees also meant that the promised legislation on ecclesiastical property never materialised, so the *exequatur* and *placet* remained in effect. In consequence, the Italian Church henceforth faced a particular difficulty over the filling of vacant episcopal sees. Newly appointed Italian bishops still needed to seek confirmation from the king before they could accede to their 'temporalities', i.e. the revenues of their sees: 33 bishops were expelled from their temporalities because they had failed to apply for the *exequatur*.[36] Local police chiefs and prefects carried out checks on the probity of episcopal candidates and, above all, on their attitude towards the government and its ecclesiastical policies.[37] Pius IX forbade this, with the result that he was obliged to subsidise dozens of bishops from the coffers of the Vatican itself to the tune of half a million lire a year.[38] In some difficult cases, the State refused the *exequatur* on political grounds, leaving large and important Italian bishoprics, such as Genoa, for instance, vacant for several years.[39] A further consequence of Pius's intransigence was that the State asserted the regalian rights of direct appointment to some bishoprics in the former Habsburg territories, Sardinia and Sicily continued, leaving the Holy See little control of nominations to important sees, including the metropolitan see of Palermo and the patriarchal see of Venice.[40]

In the decades after the death of Pius IX in 1878, the Vatican increasingly sought the path of compromise so that more and more nominees to Italian sees obtained the *placet* from the local representative of the king, the procurator, with the result that Italian bishoprics were increasingly filled by clergy more amenable to state policy, the most prominent of whom were 'Conciliatorist', such as Bonomelli of Cremona and Scalabrini of neighbouring Piacenza. This compliant attitude would also make it possible for Italian bishops to adapt to the change of regime from liberal democracy to Fascism in the mid-1920s.

The longer-term effect of Pius's intransigence was a tightening of the grip of the Holy See on the institutional church in Italy. Financially sustained by the pope, some Italian bishops felt a deep sense of direct loyalty to him and his successors. The Vatican Secretariat of State now increasingly exercised effective control of the Church in Italy, acting on behalf of the pope as primate. Thus a truly 'Italian Church' began to emerge, rather than the 'churches' of the regions and former states of the peninsula. As long as those states had existed, bishops anxious to keep papal interference at arm's length could find some protection by exploiting the natural tendency of their secular rulers to do the same. Now those buffers and barriers against papal power had gone, and the Italian episcopate and clergy were more closely subject to the decrees not only of the Secretariat of State but of the other dicasteries (departments) of the Roman Curia. It should be said, however, that the case of the Italian Church was not unique; this process of Roman centralisation was one that increasingly affected all parts of the Catholic Church in the late nineteenth and early twentieth centuries.

Church and state in the reign of Leo XIII (1878–1903)

By the end of Pio Nono's reign, the Italian political situation had taken a turn for the worse from the Church's point of view. The essentially conservative Destra Storica had been replaced in the parliamentary 'revolution' of 1876 by the more radical Sinistra, to which was allied the Estrema (Extreme Left) of radicals and republicans. While the leading exponent of the Sinistra, and many times prime minister, Agostino Depretis may have been more pragmatic in his attitude to the Church, as indeed he was on virtually every major policy issue, others were more hostile. In particular, Francesco Crispi, former lieutenant of Garibaldi in the invasion of Sicily, was a fire-eating anti-clerical, a veritable *mangia prete* ('priest eater'). The reign of Pius's successor, Leo XIII (Gioacchino Pecci) began well enough.[41] Francesco Crispi, who was the minister of the interior at the time of Leo's election, by the use of very careful police measures was able to prove to both the Church and the world that Italy would enforce the Law of Guarantees and ensure the freedom and safety of the Conclave, an interesting portent of his later attempts as prime minister to pursue a more pragmatic, less dogmatic policy in church–state relations. But despite this good augury, and Leo's willingness for better relations, his pontificate was punctuated by a series of serious disputes with the Italian State: in 1881, after a Roman mob had tried to tip the coffin of Pius IX, in procession to its final resting place at San Lorenzo, into the Tiber; in 1887, after a further series of legislative measures against the Church; in 1889 following the debacle of the 'Tosti affair' (see below, p. 41) and the unveiling of a monument to the heretic and 'free-thinker' Giordano Bruno in Rome; and in 1891 after a riot by French pilgrims.[42] On at least four occasions Leo threatened to leave Rome and was only dissuaded by the threat from Crispi that if he did so, he would not be allowed to return.[43]

Leo saw the machinations of Freemasonry behind the restrictive ecclesiastical legislation of the governments of the Sinistra. It is no coincidence that of the four encyclicals that he published against Freemasonry, three of them were addressed to Italy, condemning Freemasons as disciples of Satan and claiming that they were committed to nothing less than 'the destruction of the Holy Church, publicly and openly'.[44] There was undoubtedly some truth in Leo's accusations against the lodges, but there was also an element of paranoid conspiracy theory: Italian Freemasonry was never as strong or as organised as the clericals claimed. Anti-clericals, however, were just as prone to conspiracy theories. As Jemolo has written:

> Every sign of unrest, every popular disturbance, every national setback, great or small, evoked the cry 'behold the hand of the priest.' The Vatican was behind everything . . . on the morrow of the first, desultory uprisings of the Sicilian *Fasci* [see below, p. 43] – clearly the unorganised, planned protests of men driven to desperation by poverty – Crispi accused the leaders of the movement of having acted in collusion with clerical associations of other European countries.[45]

Governments of the Sinistra pursued their legislative campaigns against the Church for two main reasons: first, they were afraid of being outflanked by the Estrema; and second, especially under Crispi who became prime minister for the first time in 1886, they sought to reduce the influence of Catholicism in Italian society and politics, which they judged to be dangerously excessive. Certainly, in the 1880s, despite the depredations of the Liberal Revolution, the Church remained the major institutional force in Italian society, especially rural and agrarian Italy, where the parish priest exercised a powerful moral and political influence through the confessional and the pulpit. This was probably less true in the south, but even here the priest possessed the advantage of often being the local elementary school teacher in those areas where levels of adult illiteracy were high and the ability to speak Italian as well as dialect was restricted to a few in the educated elite. Everywhere, the parish remained the centre of the organisational activity surrounding the chief forms of local entertainment – the celebration of local saints and other religious feasts.[46] And as in the time of the *ancien régime*, the Church in Italy still played a key role in the provision of education and welfare relief for the poor. In addition, even before Leo's encyclical *Rerum Novarum* of 1891 (see Chapter 4, pp. 61–5), which laid down how Catholics should respond to the social consequences of industrialisation, the Italian Catholic movement was already developing a new, more modern dimension to the Church's presence in Italian society. Individual priests concerned about the condition of the rural masses in the 1880s began to found small savings banks and credit unions (*casse di risparmio*), mutual insurance societies (*società di mutuo soccorso*) and agrarian cooperatives, in large part, it has to be said, as a response to the activities of their radical and even Socialist enemies.[47]

The Sinistra sought to counter and combat this influence of the Church with measures that would help to create a more secular, 'national' Italian culture, particularly after Crispi succeeded Depretis as prime minister in 1887, when he launched a legislative assault that would clip the Church's wings. It was not simply a change of prime minister that opened the way for legislation against the Church. A key part of the background was the Tosti affair, a rather half-baked and ultimately unsuccessful attempt to achieve some measure of reconciliation between Italy and the papacy by Fr Tosti, the Vatican's deputy archivist and Abbot of Monte Cassino, who published a best-selling pamphlet on the subject. Both Leo XIII and Crispi encouraged Tosti's efforts, but they were effectively sabotaged by the French and the intransigents in the Vatican.[48] Crispi managed to prevent his involvement in the affair from damaging his reputation, and he exploited Vatican intransigence to whip up parliamentary support for his measures to protect the country against 'clericalist domination'. In 1887, in part as a response to popular demands, Crispi as minister of the interior abolished church tithes, thus intensifying the financial difficulties of some of Italy's lower clergy; a year later, his own government passed a law making access to religious instruction in state primary schools more difficult (the day-to-day administration of the schools was provided by the municipal councils), and in 1889 Crispi as prime minister sought to counter the influence of the parochial clergy by inserting into the new Code of Criminal Law drawn up by Zanardelli a clause punishing clergy for preaching, or even speaking, against the Italian State, its institutions, laws and officials.[49] But the biggest blow that Crispi struck against the Church was the 1889 law on the *opere pie*, the vast network of endowments and trust funds that financed both religious and charitable works. A 'congregation of charity' was founded in each commune to coordinate the activities and accounts of these bodies, under the overall supervision of the prefect and other provincial authorities, thus effectively removing the clergy from the major role that they had played in the distribution of charity for centuries.[50]

The threats posed by the laws on religious instruction and the *opere pie* stimulated a partial Catholic re-entry into the politics of the Liberal State. Though the *non expedit* forbade Catholic participation in parliamentary elections, it said nothing about those conducted at a local level, the elections of communal (municipal) and provincial councils. It was these bodies that had the effective responsibility for implementing both laws. Catholics, therefore, felt obliged to reclaim control over charity and education by seeking election to these councils. As a result, endless battles were fought in council chambers over the future of *opere pie* and the purposes to which they should be devoted. Despite the machinations of the anti-clericals, the Church was able to claw back some control over what had previously been a virtual monopoly. As far as religious instruction was concerned, Catholics sought to use their place on councils to prevent attempts to stop the teaching of the catechism. When their anti-clerical opponents were joined by Socialist Party activists from the 1890s onwards, this in turn prompted more conservative liberals to join forces with Catholics in 'clerico-moderate' alliances to oppose these policies. As a result of the clerico-moderate alliances, the catechism continued to be taught in the overwhelming majority of Italian schools and Catholicism remained the essential component in the culture of both the agrarian and industrial masses.

These battles over the catechism demonstrate the inherent weakness of the Liberal State and its ruling class, in particular their failure during the four decades since unification to establish hegemony over Italian society and thus inculcate a national culture and morality, and a sense of Italian identity into the Italian masses. They had certainly tried. The grand building projects in the capital in the 1870s and 1880s, the elaborate panoply of Victor Emmanuel's funeral in 1878 and the construction of the vast, and ugly, monument to his memory in Piazza Venezia in the centre of Rome were all part of an attempt to create a new national culture; in addition, the history curriculum in secondary schools had been revised in order to emphasise the glories of the Risorgimento period, all to little effect.[51] It was not even possible to emulate the Third French Republic by rooting loyalty to the new state in the peasantry, because of the deep class tensions in the countryside, especially in the south. The feebleness of Depreti's extension of the franchise in 1881 – from 2 to 7 per cent of the population – demonstrates that the Italian ruling class were profoundly afraid of what they regarded as the semi-barbarous and savage rural masses, in thrall to the Church. And the attempts to generate popular pride in colonial greatness in the late nineteenth century ended in the humiliating military disasters of Dogali (1887) and Adowa (1896). Though both these incidents generated some upsurge of national feeling, which also affected Catholics, it could hardly be said to have penetrated to the masses.[52]

Whatever other interests were at stake for the liberals in these municipal battles, an important consideration was indeed the preservation of the catechism because, as Antonio Gramsci, one of the founders and chief theoretician of Italian Communism, pointed out, the Italian ruling class was forced to fall back on the Christian religion as a means of insulating the masses against the 'virus of Socialism', implicitly accepting the Catholic claim that the catechism would teach children 'to obey their parents, to love them and to honour their family and the fatherland, and to respect other people and their property and to obey the authorities'.[53] Gramsci obviously had an axe to grind, but he was essentially right. In the longer term, the battles had an outcome of wider importance; they created the precedent for clerico-moderate alliances, which provided ruling coalitions for cities as large and diverse as Milan, Bologna and Rome between 1890 and 1914, and were yet another practical form of cooperation between Liberal and Catholic Italy.

The end of century crisis

The crucial turning point in relations between Catholic and Liberal Italy came in the 1890s, during the so-called 'end of century crisis'. Against a background of economic difficulties of different kinds, including harvest failures, and the growth of working class organisations, Italy was wracked for nearly a decade by sporadic outbursts of spontaneous agitation and violence, including the agitations of the *fasci* in Sicily in the early 1890s and a full-scale insurrection in Milan in 1898.[54] In 1900, King Umberto I was assassinated by an anarchist. Catholic activists, especially intransigent opponents of the Liberal State, were branded as 'subversives' and treated accordingly. The rationale for this policy was that by their hostility to the State, they were just as much a threat to law and order as anarchists, Socialists and other radicals; the increasingly violent, spontaneous expressions of the discontent of both rural and urban poor and the simultaneous the rise of the working class movement, under various ideological standards, gave rise to all sorts of paranoid conspiracy theories on the part of a terrified ruling class. The intransigent priest Don Davide Albertario – who in his newspaper, *L'Ossevatore Cattolico*, insistently lambasted the Liberal State and all its works, and any softness displayed towards it by fellow Catholics – was a particular target of this paranoia. After the events in Milan, Albertario was arrested and imprisoned along with the cream of the Socialist Party; Albertario's newspaper was shut down and hundreds of Catholic organisations with it.[55] But once the dust had cleared, it became clear to Catholics and conservative liberals alike that they had more in common than that which divided them: combating their common enemies, Socialism of various kinds and, to a lesser extent, anarchism, required a united front.

Pius X and Italian Catholicism in the new century

The new century more or less coincided with the accession of a new monarch, Victor Emmanuel III, in 1900, and two years later a new pope,

Pius X. The cardinal elected to succeed Leo XIII was Giuseppe Sarto, patriarch of Venice, the very epitome of a revivified Catholic Italy, so much so that he was canonised in 1954.[56] The Veneto and eastern Lombardy were already becoming the heartland of the Catholic sub-culture and the motor of Italian Catholicism. They would produce five out of the seven Italian popes of the twentieth century: Pius X, John XXIII and John Paul I (all patriarchs of Venice) and Pius XI and Paul VI (archbishops of Milan). Geographically, Papa Sarto's ecclesiastical career straddled the border between Lombardy and the Veneto (Angelo Roncalli, later John XXIII, would go in the same direction, from Bergamo in Lombardy to Venice). Born in Riese, Treviso province, in 1835, Sarto served as a country curate and parish priest, then as a seminary teacher and finally as chancellor of his diocese. He was appointed to the bishopric of Mantua in Lombardy in 1885, and returned to his native region in 1894 when he was translated to Venice and made a cardinal. Mantua was, as has been seen, a diocese with serious problems: some notoriously restless priests defected in the 1880s; an impoverished parochial clergy was not being replaced by sufficient ordinations; and a rising working class movement was drawing away many poor peasants from the Church. Sarto tackled all of them with a pastoral, reforming zeal that would become his hallmark.

He was no less vigorous in his pastoral activity in Venice, and not for nothing would he later be called 'the parish priest pope'; certainly his pastoral activity at the Vatican was all-encompassing. Pius brought several concerns and objectives to the papacy, which were absolutely central to the character of the 'new' Italian Catholicism that had emerged since unification. In the first place, he was a firm believer in the centrality of the Eucharist, of the sacramental life of clergy and laity, to the pursuit of salvation. This trend culminated in 1907, when St Pius X called upon Catholic clergy to ensure that lay people should be encouraged to confess and communicate as frequently as possible and not just once a year and that children should receive communion at an early age.[57] On the other hand, he was a little tepid towards other aspects of religious observance that he thought peripheral, such as the Marian cult, for example, though he did issue an encyclical celebrating the fiftieth anniversary of Pius IX's promulgation of the dogma of the Immaculate Conception.[58] He abhorred superstition and even the secondary ornamentation of religious practice, such as the intrusion of fads and fashions into the music that accompanied the Mass. Thus he sought the restoration of the Gregorian Chant to a central place in church music.[59] He was also a great exponent of the need to train teachers of the catechism, especially in those areas where municipal administrations still obstructed its teaching in state schools: at the first National Catechistic Congress in Piacenza in 1889, his proposal for a single national text of the catechism was agreed and sent to Rome for approval.[60]

The pope's attention was particularly focused on the training of priests: new, and stricter, regulations were issued on priestly formation, and as far as Italy was concerned, he encouraged the re-grouping of institutions of sacerdotal education into regional seminaries, especially in the south where, in the generally small dioceses, seminary provision was inadequate, or even in some cases, completely lacking.[61] Along with his reform of the Roman Curia in 1907, he sought to rationalise the distribution of Italian dioceses, especially between north and south, but he failed.[62] Also dating from 1907 was his decision to set up a commission to codify canon law, the working rules and regulations of the Church, which was a further step in the direction of the centralisation and 'Romanisation' of the Catholic Church as a whole. His policy of appointing northerners to southern Italian sees was another element in the process of creating a truly Italian church, as was the despatch of inspectors to visit all of Italy's seminaries during the course of his reign (see below, p. 47).

Being a cardinal and the spiritual head of a great city had given Sarto an opportunity to move onto the Italian national stage, and consequently gain some understanding of politics. Thus though his was an intensely pastoral pontificate, he did not shy away from 'political' decisions as well. He gave strong support to the emerging agenda of Italian social Catholicism, including the work of Giuseppe Toniolo (see Chapter 4, p. 61). It was under his auspices that the Catholic Union of Social Studies came into being in 1889, somewhat later, it has to be admitted, than its counterparts in Belgium, France and Germany. But those countries were, after all, rather further down the path of industrial modernisation than Italy. He also gave his blessing to the clerico-moderate political forces, which defeated the anti-clerical radicals and won control of Venice city council. He would become the great patron of clerico-moderate alliances, effectively sponsoring their adoption at a national parliamentary electoral level, which, coupled with a relaxation of the *non expedit*, would permit Catholics to ally with conservative liberals to fight the rising Socialist menace at a national political level (see Chapter 4, pp. 65–6).

Pius X and the Italian State

Papa Sarto's support of clerico-moderate initiatives carried over into his more general attitude towards the Italian State. He shocked the faithful members of Rome's black aristocracy by welcoming all into the Vatican, including the deputies and ministers of the liberal regime and even members of the royal family: he is known to have received the Queen Mother, Margherita, a devout Catholic, in private audience.[63] As his secretary of state, Cardinal Raphael

Merry del Val, once confessed to a foreign diplomat, the Vatican had no desire to exercise significant temporal power again.[64] This relaxed pragmatism was, however, accompanied by a principled, public reiteration of the injured rights of the Holy See in relation to Italy.

Despite Pius X's relaxation of the *non expedit* and other conciliatory gestures, he, too, had his run-ins with the governmental authorities. Like Leo, he worried about the machinations of the Masonic lodges, though probably with more justification. From 1907 onwards, Rome city council's ruling group, the 'Popular Bloc', containing strong elements of the Estrema, was led by Mayor Ernesto Nathan, who was a Jew and a Freemason and another veritable *mangia prete*. That the mayor of Rome should have been a Jew was anathema to many Catholics, though the fact that in 1910 the prime minister of Italy, Luigi Luzzatti, was also of the Jewish faith does not seem to have excited any opposition.[65] The new ruling group quickly moved to wrest control of the city's many charitable foundations from Catholic control, using the terms of the 1898 act. Nathan's 1910 speech commemorating the breach of Porta Pia on 20 September was especially insulting to the papacy and the following year the mayor attempted to turn the celebrations of the fiftieth anniversary of Italian unification into a major anti-clerical demonstration, without much success.[66]

The activities of Nathan were the tip of the iceberg of an anti-clerical 'revival' that was typical of Italy in the new century, which in turn was the result of a certain unease among elements of the Italian political class about a perceived 'cozying up' between church and state. Giovanni Giolitti, the statesman of Piedmontese origin who was the overwhelmingly dominant personality in Italian politics between 1903 and 1914, may have coined the famous formula of church and state as 'two parallels that should never meet', but in practice things were different. Government officials turned a blind eye to 'clerical abuses' with greater frequency; Ernesto Pacelli, president of the Banco di Roma and the principal financial adviser of the pope, was able to negotiate behind-the-scenes deals, and he resolved several disputes between church and state, including a settlement of a row between the Vatican and Nathan's municipal administration.[67]

'The modernist crisis' and Italian Catholicism at the end of Pius X's reign

Pius X's obsessions with the so-called 'modernist heresy', and his campaigns to root it out, were to have important effects upon Italian Catholicism. For him, 'modernism' was the 'synthesis of all heresies', and was to be found in new thinking about ecclesiastical history, theology and exegesis (the interpretation of biblical texts), which chiefly emanated from Britain, France and Germany, but especially France whose most important exponent was the biblical scholar, Alfred Loisy.[68] In 1907, Pius issued two major public statements condemning 'modernism', *Lamentabili* and *Pascendi*, the former containing another veritable 'syllabus of errors'.[69] He followed them up by a witch-hunt against clergy suspected of being infected with the heretical ideas and the imposition of the 'anti-modernist' oath on all priests.[70] He then sent apostolic visitors to inspect dioceses, and especially seminaries, suspected of harbouring infection. Not even those dioceses that were the responsibility of leading Italian cardinals were spared; thus cardinal archbishops Della Chiesa of Bologna (later to be elected Pius's successor as Benedict XV), Ferrari of Milan and Maffi of Pisa were suspected of dangerous opinions.[71] These visitations and the humbling (some would say 'humiliation') of the archbishops concerned marked a reinforcement of the Vatican's control over the Italian Church.

The 'modernist' crisis of Pius's reign inevitably affected the Italian Catholic movement. Charges of modernist infection were laid against several of its leaders, clerical and lay, most notably Romolo Murri, the head of the Christian Democratic group, which had played such a prominent role as the most advanced, reforming element in Italian social Catholicism.[72] But the modernist 'crisis' had wider negative effects in the Italian Church. An atmosphere of suspicion and fear was created by the activities of Vatican under-secretary of state, Mgr Umberto Benigni, and his spies in the Sodalitium Pianum, or La Sapiniere, an 'anti-modernist international', whose job was to inform anonymously on anyone even remotely suspected of 'heresy'. With the support of Pius X, Benigni had free rein: his activities were only curtailed, and eventually stopped completely, when Cardinal Della Chiesa ascended the papal throne in 1914.[73] But in the last years of the pontificate of Pius X, Benigni and the ultra-integralists had the upper hand and used it ruthlessly and brutally, like the Scotton brothers, three ultra-integralist priests in the Vicenza diocese who published an intransigent newspaper, *La Riscossa*.[74] Another journal of this ilk was *L'Unità Cattolica* of Florence, and the editors of mainstream, 'clerico-moderate' Catholic newspapers were warned that their general attitudes were 'not in conformity with pontifical directives'.[75]

There were several notable Catholic priests and laymen who were victims of the anti-modernist witch-hunt. The first was Ernesto Buonaiuti, priest, author and editor of the *Rivista storico-critica delle scienze teologiche* (Critical Review of the Theological Sciences): the *Rivista* was placed on the Index and Buonaiuti was eventually excommunicated.[76] Andrea Fogazzaro was a novelist, the author of *Il Santo* (The Saint), which proposed the reform of the Church, and the editor of the journal *Il Rinnovamento*. Both his novel and the journal were put on the Index.[77] Finally, there was Padre Giovanni Semeria, a biblical scholar. He and Salvatore Minocchi had introduced the works of foreign 'modernist' writers to Italy. [78] Pius X may not have turned the Italian Church into an intellectual desert, but the effective silencing of all these men, and more, left Italian Catholicism intellectually crippled at the end of his pontificate in 1914.

Chapter 4

ITALIAN CATHOLICISM AND THE CHALLENGES OF ECONOMIC DEVELOPMENT (1880–1914)

Introduction

DURING THE LAST TWO DECADES of the nineteenth century and the first 15 years of the twentieth, Italy underwent unprecedented processes of economic development. While the changes in agriculture were very limited, nevertheless in these years Italy was equipped with a modern industrial manufacturing base, albeit limited and localised. Another major development in this period was the massive migratory flows of the Italian population. The first, an internal pattern of migration from countryside to town, mainly in northern Italy, was a corollary of industrialisation and urbanisation, and the second, from rural, especially southern, Italy, went overseas, to other parts of continental Europe, to Britain, and to the Americas. Italian Catholicism had to respond to these important demographic shifts, with their social/cultural consequences. In addition, it had to face the political consequences of momentous economic and social change – the rise of a revolutionary working class movement, dominated in turn by republican, anarchist and Marxian ideologies. On the whole, it can be said that Italian Catholicism responded to these challenges positively and successfully.

Italian industrialisation and the emergence of new classes, 1880–1914

By comparison with the USA and Britain, and even other parts of western Europe – such as Belgium, France and Germany – Italy was a latecomer to industrialisation.[1] Thus, at its unification in 1861, Italy was still an over-whelmingly rural, agrarian society with only a few pockets of industry. The emergence of a large-scale manufacturing industry was a phenomenon of the 1880s, 1890s and the early years of the twentieth century, hence the description of this period as that of the *prima industrializzazione*, the first industrialisation. It is with this period that we are concerned here. Thereafter, Italian economic development took place in fits and starts, with the years of the First World War, the Fascist period and above all the late 1950s and early 1960s witnessing further major phases of industrial growth.

The pattern of Italian economic development in the period of the *prima industrializzazione* was characterised by various forms of dualism, in the first place by the coexistence of a modern industrial sector alongside 'backward' forms of production, i.e. the artisan sector. Dualism also developed on a geographical basis, the localisation of major centres of manufacturing industry in north-western Italy, the industrial 'triangle' of Milan, Turin and Genoa, as against the limited growth in the centre and the extremely marginal development in the south. In the latter, the economy remained overwhelmingly agrarian, and that agriculture was characterised by the survival of semi-feudal forms of landholding and backward methods of agriculture. Dualism also persisted within the agricultural sector itself, between small-scale subsistence farming virtually everywhere in Italy and large-scale capitalist farming, especially on the dairy farms of the Po Valley but also, exceptionally, in a restricted area of Apulia in the south.[2]

In these circumstances, during the period of the *prima industrializzazione* the characteristically fragmented structure of the Italian working class quickly established itself. Alongside the burgeoning factory-based working class and workers in transport industries, large groups of artisans continued to survive and often played a key role in the development of the working class movement. Of equal if not greater importance was the emergence of a rural, agrarian proletariat, most especially on the big farms of the Po Valley and in Apulia. This proletariat consisted of large numbers of *braccianti*, *salariati* (labourers with more stable employment) and *mezzadri* (sharecroppers) whose standard of living was often as precarious as that of the *braccianti*. In addition, there was a bewildering variety of small tenant farmers, leaseholders and even small landowners.[3]

It was also frequently the case that seasonal migration to towns, and seasonal or even permanent employment in manufacturing based in the countryside, especially of women, were essential to the family economy.[4] To faithfully reflect the complexity and diversity of this picture, it also needs to be emphasised that patterns of landholding, cultivation and employment varied between north and south, and from region to region, and from province to province, but also within individual provinces. A final and very important point: for obvious reasons the bulk of the first generation of the industrial proletariat was recruited from a largely rural and agrarian background.[5]

The Church's response to industrialisation

The attitude of the hierarchy and the parochial clergy to the rise of industrial capitalism in Italy was a broadly uniform but essentially ambivalent one. The social problems thrown up by the new industrial system were quickly denounced. Capitalism was seen to be the evil child of philosophical and political liberalism and was condemned as the unfortunate result of the 'Manchester (School) of Economics' and as the fruit of an 'unrestrained thirst for profit'.[6] In the eyes of some clergy at least, it was also associated with Jews and Protestants.[7] John Davis argues that 'in denouncing the self-centred materialism of Liberal dogma, as the cause of these evils, the mainly Catholic conservative critics of the new Italy gave their *imprimatur* to the language of class'.[8] In fact, the 'language of class', and especially the Socialist concept of class struggle, were emphatically rejected by the ecclesiastical authorities who urged on the victims of the industrial system the virtues of accepting their lot, obeying their social superiors, and resigning themselves to their earthly destiny. Thus in 1899 Cardinal Ferrari, archbishop of Milan, and a noted Catholic leader in the social field, reinforced the Church's traditional message that the parochial clergy, 'Should make the poor understand that everything is ordained by God, that it is God who makes some rich and some poor . . .'[9] The constant reiteration of this message undoubtedly assisted industrial entrepreneurs in their efforts to transform the rural immigrants into docile and disciplined industrial workers.

But the Church's first practical concern was to respond to the consequences of demographic change, in other words, industrialisation, urbanisation and migration. There is no Italian equivalent of the Victorian census of church attendance that might provide some kind of statistical basis for a picture of the impact on religious practice of industrialisation, migration, urbanisation and proletarianisation. On the other hand, papal pronouncements, the deliberations of assemblies of the ecclesiastical provinces of bishops, diocesan synods and episcopal visitations of parishes provide considerable evidence of the effects of these processes in alienating elements of the working masses from the Church and of the reaction of the Church to this phenomenon.[10] Certainly, at the highest levels of the ecclesiastical hierarchy there was a strong belief that such processes of change were having a deleterious effect upon both religious practice and personal morality. Pius X (1903–14) in particular was deeply concerned about the effects of these changes, going so far as to make it policy to appoint bishops of northern extraction to southern dioceses in order to apprise the southern clergy of the perils of industrial-isation.[11] In reality, the scope for industrial development in the south, apart from the Neapolitan hinterland and a few other areas, was minimal, despite the efforts of Giolitti's governments in the early 1900s. As we shall see, the only area in which economic and social changes posed a serious threat to church allegiance was in western Apulia.

In the industrialising cities of the north, such as Milan, Turin and Genoa, and minor centres of industry such as Bergamo, Brescia and Vicenza, the clergy were quick to note any decline in the performance of religious duties. In Turin, for example, the chief problem was seen to be a situation in which existing ecclesiastical structures and resources were being outstripped by demographic pressures, particularly in the new industrial suburbs. Immigration from the country areas of Turin province and the rest of Piedmont, with the consequent aggregation of large numbers of 'un-churched' poor, was perceived as being the major cause of alienation of the new industrial working class from religious practice: a situation that, in some ways, was not very different from that of industrial cities in Britain or the USA or the rest of Europe in the same period.

If we continue with the example of Turin, which was becoming Italy's industrial city *par excellence*, it is clear that in the 1890s and early 1900s numerous requests were being made by local parochial clergy and leading lay people for the building of new churches and the establishment of new parishes.[12] The Turin ecclesiastical authorities were slow to respond to these requests: in the period 1878–1906 only six new churches were built, with another seven constructed by 1916.[13] The interminable delays of the diocese's curial bureaucracy and the corporatist mentality of the city's clergy who, as incumbents, feared loss of revenue from the splitting of parishes would help to explain this slow, inadequate response.[14]

Research carried out on Milan gives a very clear picture of how the Church sought to respond to the alienation of the working masses from religion. A similar picture of a 'slow dechristianisation of factory workers' also emerges here, but a major obstacle to an effective response on the part of the ecclesiastical authorities to the problems thrown up by industrialisation and immigration lay in the lack of manpower.[15] Between 1805 and 1895, the numbers of parochial clergy in the Milan diocese declined from 2,071 to 1,895, and a similar decline was recorded for other industrialising Lombard dioceses such as Bergamo, Brescia and Como.[16] And this could only be partially offset by the activity of the regular clergy. Nevertheless, it should be noted that Milan was to see one of the first experiments in 'worker priests' in the history of the Church, the *capellani del lavoro*.[17] How far Lombardy's clergy manpower shortage was typical of a more general phenomenon in northern and central Italy is difficult to ascertain, but what was undeniably common to all these areas was a scarcity of the means to pay the clergy, thanks to the partial expropriation of ecclesiastical property carried out by Cavour and his successors (see Chapter 3, p. 37).

A not entirely dissimilar story from that of Turin and Milan can be told about Italy's other major industrial and commercial centre, the port city of Genoa, the one in which the Italian Socialist Party was founded in 1892. From 1899 onwards, Archbishop Tommaso Reggio began building a series of new churches to meet the needs of the rapidly growing population.[18] This process was continued by his successor, Mgr Pulciano, to meet the needs of the new suburbs, working and middle class alike.[19] But in the Genoese case, there was an aspect of the solution to the demographic growth of the diocese consequent upon industrialisation that was more drastic than elsewhere. In 1892, the area of Genoa province to the east of the provincial capital was detached from the jurisdiction of the archbishop and erected into the new diocese of Chiavari, something that has very rarely happened in the modern history of the Church in Italy.[20]

The need to provide adequate facilities for the spiritual needs of migrant populations was not the only problem thrown up by the effects of industrialisation. The parochial clergy in industrialising areas (and some rural ones, too) often lamented the fact that due to the new patterns of work and production, many workers were unable to attend Sunday Mass, a phenomenon that was noted elsewhere in industrialising Europe.[21] Remonstrations with employers, often practising Catholics, about the need for the *riposo festivo* (Sabbath rest) were to no avail despite pastoral letters of bishops and the sermons of parish priests. The gravity of the situation in Turin led to the foundation of the Pia Opera per la Santificazione delle Feste, a sort of Italian equivalent of the British Lord's Day Observance Society.[22]

Also of concern to both bishops and local clergy were the alleged effects of industrialisation upon personal morality: in particular, female and child labour were seen as posing a threat to health and sexual mores.[23] Women's work was, of course, nothing new, but in rural, agrarian society it was usually carried out at home, or on the farm, under the supervision of male family members. In some rural areas, out-work for local textile factories continued at home, but now, increasingly, female labour actually took place away from the home, in silk, cotton or woollen mills that offered work to which women transferred naturally and easily from domestic modes of production. In some areas, the solutions adopted for these problems involved the establishment of organisations specifically designed to supervise them, the engagement of nuns to supervise the unmarried female factory workforce and the provision of female residential hostels.[24]

In broader terms, clergy deplored the fact that the necessity of migration from countryside to town in search of work often destroyed religious faith and devotional habits, and warned against the decline in the moral behaviour of uprooted populations.[25] The perception of the city as a centre of decadence and degradation, in contrast to the healthiness and morality of country living, was a leitmotif of ecclesiastical discourse in this period.[26]

Overseas migration

Even more serious alarm was generated by overseas migration. It has been estimated that between 1881 and 1910 close to 11 million Italians migrated overseas, mainly to North and South America, and nearly 3.5 million of them never returned to their motherland.[27] The Italian Church responded with a number of initiatives to give material and spiritual support to emigrants at all levels: there were even cases of local parish priests leading the emigration of whole villages.[28] Facilities were set up both at their points of departure from Italy – mainly Genoa, Naples and Palermo – and in their countries of destination.[29] The two leading conciliatorist bishops, Scalabrini of Piacenza and Bonomelli of Cremona, set up new organisations for Italian emigrants in 1887 and 1900 respectively. Italian members of existing religious congregations and orders – Jesuits, Franciscans, Servites, Conventual Friars, the Pallottine Fathers, the Passionists and Augustinians and the Salesians of Don Bosco, as well as new orders founded by Scalabrini, such as the Cabrini and Scalabrini Sisters, followed emigrants to the Americas, and in the case of the USA 'national parishes' were founded for Italian immigrant communities.[30] In 1912 the Consistorial Congregation of the Roman Curia established a special office to oversee the work of Catholic organisations among Italian immigrants.[31] The Church's concern for the spiritual welfare of Italian immigrants was not unjustified: in the 1920s and 1930s, Italians returning from America would bring with them the seeds of the first serious Protestant dissent in Italy in modern times, nuclei of Baptist, Jehovah's Witness, Pentecostal and Seventh-Day Adventist organisations, especially in the south (see Chapter 7).

Migration, whether to the city or overseas, was not the only new phenomenon that exercised the minds of the clergy in this period. The processes of immiseration and proletarianisation in the countryside were a source of similar concern. The lamentations of rural parish priests about the degradation of members of their flocks who had lost their land – either owned or tenanted – and had been reduced to the status of *braccianti*, the lowest of the low in the rural social hierarchy, were legion and usually evinced a charitable response on the part of the diocesan authorities and leaders of Catholic organisations.[32] The starkest example of the effects of rural proletarianisation comes from the south. In his study of the rise of agrarian Socialism in the Apulian provinces of Foggia and west Bari, the rich agricultural lands of the Tavoliere, Snowden paints a picture of alienation on the part of the rural poor from the Church, and outright hostility to the clergy.[33] The factors seen elsewhere, the brutal, inhuman demands made upon on the workforce by a ruthless new capitalist class, were all present, but this time in a rural, agrarian setting. The abysmal levels of attendance at Mass that he records would have horrified even the most besieged and desperate parish priest in the northern industrial towns.[34]

Part of the problem in Apulia lay in the inadequacies of ecclesiastical organisation in the south, and in the small, poor dioceses, much smaller than in the north and centre of Italy, rather than in the results of demographic change (see Chapter 3). In the areas that Snowden describes, the rural proletariat were concentrated in 'agro-towns' that were not lacking in churches. What was lacking, however, was clergy; the national average of inhabitants per parish priest in the early 1900s was 1567; in the diocese of Trani, Barletta and Bisceglie it was ten times that number.[35] A further problem was the abysmal quality of the clergy, who were often poorly educated, semi-literate, superstitious, greedy and usurious:[36] these defects were the result of poor or non-existent seminary training. The heavy dependence of the clergy on the local (landed) elites was also a factor in alienating the masses from the Church. This was the result of the *chiese ricettizie* system of paying local clergy, which had entered into crisis as a result of Liberal ecclesiastical legislation (see Chapter 3, p. 11). In northern and central provinces, the rural parochial clergy were generally better educated, better behaved and less financially dependent upon the local landowning class. Moreover, in most areas they were recruited from the middle ranks of the peasantry itself and were thus natural leaders of their parishioners.[37] The fact that in some cases the priest cultivated the 'glebe', alongside the rural proletarians, helped consolidate the relationship between parishioners and clergy. The burden of the tithe did sometimes sour relations between the peasantry and the cure of souls, and the *diritti alla stola* – the fees that the parochial clergy charged for baptisms, marriages and funerals – were often resented by the poor, but in the end some sort of balance seems to have been achieved.[38]

The strength of the Church's standing among the lower classes of Italy is testified to by no less a person than Mikhail Bakunin. According to the Russian anarchist leader who lived in Italy from 1880 to 1900, Italian peasants were often superstitious, but 'they loved the Church because of its dramatic dimensions and because it interrupted the monotony and misery of country life with its theatrical and musical ceremonies'.[39] There is probably a great deal of truth in Bakunin's observation and it might suggest that the decline of religious practice among migrants usually began in the alien conditions of urban industrial society rather than in the countryside itself.

The rise of the Italian working class movement

A rapidly developing feeling among Italy's Catholic clergy from the 1890s onwards was that it was not only economic and demographic changes that were 'dechristianising' sectors of the population but that the actively anti-clerical propaganda of the emerging working class movement played a huge role in this unfortunate development. The militant anti-clericalism of the working class movement, which in some areas campaigned against the Church, was blamed for the loss of religious belief and practice among both urban and rural proletarians. Priests in Turin, for example, declared that 'here the Socialist element has taken control' and claimed that as a result 'the religious spirit is being lost in local parishes', and in the Milan diocese the major justification for founding the *capellani del lavoro* was given as the 'urgent need to protect religious faith from the Socialist propaganda that is spreading in this region.'[40]

The impact of the anti-clericalism of the working class movement could also be observed in a rural setting: in Emilia-Romagna, the rise of agrarian Socialism among the *braccianti* and *mezzadri* soon posed serious problems for the bishops and parochial clergy of the region. According to Albertazzi, 'In 1906 Mgr Trebbioli was appointed bishop of Imola to halt the abandonment of traditional religion'.[41] There were also serious problems in the next-door diocese of Bologna, which was ruled after 1907 by Mgr Giacomo Della Chiesa, later Pope Benedict XV. According to another local historian, Sauro Onofri, 'The agricultural area of the plains was almost completely "red", on the other hand, the success (of the Socialists) in the hill area was modest, while in the high Apennines, the Bolognese "Vendee", Socialism was almost unknown.'[42] The record of the pastoral visitations conducted by Archbishop Della Chiesa confirms the accuracy of this picture. In the diary entries for the parishes of the plain such reports as 'small number of faithful present, few communicants', 'lots of women, few men', and 'only a few WOMEN were present in church' are found repeatedly.[43] The classic pattern of dechristianisation was largely confined to parishes of the plains where agrarian Socialism had taken strongest root. It must have been particularly galling for Della Chiesa that the diary entry written by his chaplain for his visitation to the parish of San Giorgio in Panigale, just outside the walls of his see city, read as follows: 'Returned to Bologna . . . with the painful impression of the religious conditions of this populous village, which has demonstrated itself not so much hostile to the Archbishop, as indifferent.'[44]

The anti-clericalism of the Italian working class movement had its origins in Mazzinian republicanism and the Garibaldinian democratic movement, which had been its nursing mothers in the 1860s and 1870s. While some Democrats, most notoriously Francesco Crispi, became conservatives in later life, many others, such as the followers of the *La Plebe* newspaper in the Lombard town of Lodi, passed over to Socialism, taking with them a lively anti-clerical tradition.[45] In some parts of Emilia-Romagna and Le Marche, both formerly part of the Papal States, the militantly anti-clerical republican movement (to which, among others, Mussolini's blacksmith father belonged) enjoyed lingering working class support down to the outbreak of the First World War.[46] Republican anti-clericalism was also transmitted elsewhere through the culture and organisations of the artisan class, an element that played a very important part in the creation of the working class movement.[47] And the Italian experience of anarchism also ensured that anti-clerical ideas would be planted in Liguria, Tuscany and even in remote areas of the south.[48] Thus the establishment of the ideological hegemony of Marxian Socialism over the Italian working class movement in the early 1890s served merely to reinforce with atheistic materialism an already strong anti-clerical tradition.

A characteristic feature of the handling of the religious question by the Italian working class movement was the attempt by some Socialist intellectuals to construct an alternative set of religious myths and values to Catholicism. This attempt, which was in part inspired by Garibaldi's concept of 'religion without the priests',[49] bore some resemblance to the ideas espoused by John Trevor's Labour Church and the 'ethical Socialism' of Keir Hardie.[50] The anti-clericalism of turn-of-the-century Socialist intellectuals such as Turati was seen to be too abstract, and that of Mussolini too crude and vulgar, to be an effective way of combating the residual Catholic values of the working population. Indeed, some working class leaders sought to avoid anti-clerical propaganda altogether for fear of offending religious susceptibilities; for example, Antonio Labriola, though forever warning of the use of religion as an instrument of repression by the ruling classes, argued that for tactical reasons it was probably best to treat it as a 'private matter'.[51] Others, such as Prampolini, sought to construct a kind of de-mythologised, de-clericalised version of Christianity with which he hoped to be able to attract the new proletariat. Appealing to a notional 'primitive Christianity', Prampolini elaborated an evangelical Socialism that appropriated the values of charity and solidarity inherent in a perceived 'social gospel', built around the figure of Christ the Worker.[52] It is no accident that the rise of Catholic modernism in Italy (see Chapter 3) caused alarm in Socialist circles not only because it was associated with Romolo Murri and the Christian Democrats etc., the militantly reforming wing of the rival Catholic movement, but also because of its perceived tendency to demystify and 'de-clericalise' the Catholic religion.[53]

Another prominent Socialist leader, Andrea Costa, also urged the necessity of offering a complete system of values to the working classes:

> We should not believe that it will be enough to offer the people bread in order to make them revolt. The people are by nature idealistic and they will not rise up until Socialist ideas have the prestige and force of attraction religious faith once had.[54]

It is difficult to gauge the success of either Costa or Prampolini's efforts, but the iconographic evidence, that is, the popularity of pictures of Christ the Worker, and Marx and the Madonna side by side in working-class homes, suggests they had limited impact.[55]

The anti-clerical stance of Italian Socialism manifested itself in a number of ways in the ordinary life of the Italian working classes. In some places it took the form of a purely nominal attendance of workers at Sunday Mass: Rinaldo Rigola, one of the early leaders of the trade union movement, for example, remembered that during his youth artisans attended church but that they treated the proceedings in a perfunctory and sceptical manner:

> [During the Mass] they remained standing at the back of the church, and spoke among themselves more or less as if they were in the piazza. At the end of the service they crossed themselves, and they departed fixing as they did so the place for the afternoon's festivities.[56]

Male abstention from religious practice also became common, and at Biella, a northern Piedmontese textile town, at the end of the 1890s it was said that 'Only women go to mass.'[57] There thus developed what might be called the 'Berlinguer syndrome', that is, men accompanied their wives to Mass but remained outside the church to converse with comrades until it was over.[58] The religious sensibilities of women were a matter of great concern to the leaders of the working class movement: in Cremona, a major agricultural centre in the Lombard plain, for example, the organisers of the peasant leagues were urged to treat them kindly because 'in the confessional they are warned of the threat of family breakdown as a result of the introduction of new ideas'.[59] But working women were not always as passive in the face of clerical power as this quotation suggests; in Cene, Bergamo, in 1895, several women textile workers hit back when their bishop and their parish priest excommunicated them for joining a Socialist trade union by denouncing them both in an open letter to the local Socialist paper.[60]

The abandonment of religious duties never became universal. As in other parts of Europe, most working people continued to demand and to receive the rites of baptism, marriage and burial, though as tensions arose between unionised workers and the Church, refusal of the last rites became frequent.[61] The celebration of religious rites could be divisive, especially at funerals. At Bologna, in 1905, the police reported the case of a young member of the bricklayers' union, killed in an accident, who was given a religious funeral because 'he had always led a Christian life'.[62] When the priests arrived at the funeral parlour his Socialist comrades abandoned the procession, and one of them delivered an oration outside the church in which he declared that 'the presence of the priests and of members of the young Catholic association had defiled the body of the worker'.[63]

As it consolidated its presence in Italian civil society the working class movement began to institute secular equivalents of the services of the Church in the matter of 'rites of passage'. In particular, as in France, there developed a veritable cult of the secular, civic funeral, modelled on the 'Republican' funeral already widespread in areas such as Emilia-Romagna and le Marche.[64] These celebrations of life rather than death became the distinguishing mark of the new secular, Socialist culture and its leaders.[65] Working-class organisations in particularly strong Socialist centres sought to build a comprehensive counter-culture to that of the Church, using *Case del Popolo* (Houses of the People) and *circoli operai* (workers' clubs), social centres for workers and their families, to provide a whole range of facilities, including theatrical and musical associations, crèches and cheap restaurants, in competition with the facilities of the Catholic parish. A striking example of this development is to be found in Sesto San Giovanni, an industrial satellite town to the north of Milan, where the organisations and activities of the working-class movement have been studied in detail for the period 1880–1922. In its definitive form, this culture was characterised by the adoption of all manner of secular events and heroes to contest the public demonstrations of Catholic piety and loyalty, particularly the celebration of local saints.[66]

The Church's response to the rise of the working class movement

The rise of the Socialist working class organisations in the 1880s and the 1890s, with their explicit anti-clericalism and their strategy of class struggle, elicited a determined response from Italian Catholicism. As Howard Bell points out in his study of Sesto San Giovanni, the creation of Catholic trade unions, peasant leagues, cooperatives and other economic and social organisations was largely a response to prior Socialist initiatives, although there is some evidence of earlier Catholic initiatives in these fields.[67] The first Catholic organisations for workers and peasants were created in the 1880s and 1890s, essentially as charitable and philanthropic institutions, with a strong educational element for often illiterate young workers as well. [68]

In its battle with Socialism, the Italian Church disposed of two valuable assets. The first was the existing parochial structure. As Gabriele De Rosa has noted, the parish had long operated as a social centre, and provided a reference point for artisan groups in its confraternities and other pious associations; as a result of industrialisation and the other processes of economic and social change, the parish became the key organisational element in many areas of Italy in a new and growing campaign of Catholic social initiatives,[69] so long, that is, as priests heeded Leo XIII's call to 'come forth from the sacristy and go among the people'.[70] The second asset was the existing Catholic movement, the Opera Dei Congressi. In this organisation the Church already possessed a flourishing network of Catholic associations, and with it cadres of trained and combative lay leaders.[71] The Opera was essentially the product of Catholic intransigent opposition to the Liberal State and abolition of the temporal power. On the basis of the cultural, youth and recreational organisations of the Opera, it would prove possible to build specifically economic and social institutions with which to challenge Socialism.

On the other hand, two factors initially inhibited the growth of those institutions. The first was the established concentration of the efforts of the Opera on the 'Roman Question' – the struggle to restore the temporal power – and on battles against the ecclesiastical policies of the Liberal State. As has been seen (Chapter 3), the crucial turning-point came during the end-of-century crisis in the 1890s when Italy was wracked by economic difficulties, resulting in social distress and violent disorders such as the *fasci siciliani* (1893–95) and the Milan insurrection of 1898, culminating in an anarchist's assassination of King Umberto I at Monza in 1900, and bitter conflicts within the ruling elite.[72] The emergence in precisely this period of the Italian Socialist Party (PSI – Partito Socialista Italiano) and the Socialist trade union movement (CGL – Confederazione Generale del Lavoro) and peasant leagues prompted a change in the strategy of the Opera, the emphasis shifting away from the 'Roman Question' to the 'Social Question', that is the condition of the working classes and the threat of Socialism. The change found its clearest expression in the formation of 'clerico-moderate' electoral alliances between Catholics and Liberal conservatives at a local and later national level (see Chapter 3, pp. 42–3), which seemed to confirm the Socialist allegation that the Church had become a part of the Italian establishment.[73]

A further problem was the nature of the principles underlying Catholic social initiatives. As has been seen, the first Catholic organisations in the social field were essentially charitable and *paternalistic* in inspiration, mostly of the 'mutual benefit' type, i.e. providing social insurance – similar, in fact, to the earliest organisations of the working-class movement. Like them, they were eventually to develop into *società di resistenza*, full-blooded trade union associations by category. Catholic paternalism also manifested itself in the activities of some industrialists who in areas such as Venetia provided an array of facilities such as cheap workers' canteens, crèches and hostel accommodation. The most typical of these industrialists was Alessandro Rossi. This kind of paternalism was both a practical manifestation of the Christian precept of charity and a method of keeping a stable, contented workforce.[74]

Paternalism was also the essence of the solutions to the 'Social Question' proposed by the Pisan Catholic sociologist Giuseppe Toniolo, whose various social programmes were to have a formative influence on emerging social Catholicism in Italy.[75] Foreign influences, the examples of Catholic social movements in Belgium, France and Germany, also played an important part in the development of the Italian movement in the late nineteenth century.[76]

Leo XIII, *Rerum Novarum* and the development of Italian social Catholicism

Part and parcel of Toniolo's paternalism was the idea of mixed unions of workers and employers, an essentially neo-Thomist re-evocation of the guilds of a mythical, medieval golden age of European Catholicism.[77] This idea was also to be found in *Rerum Novarum*, the great social encyclical of Pope Leo XIII (1878–1903), which was published in 1891. It was taken as the founding charter of social Catholicism and thus provided the main impetus to the creation of Catholic economic and social institutions in Italy. In general terms, *Rerum Novarum* repeated previous solemn denunciations of Communism and Socialism on the grounds that the collective ownership of goods was against nature and the Divine Law. On the other hand, it earned its sub-title, 'On the Conditions of the Working Classes', by deploring the working and living conditions of many sections of Europe's new industrial proletariat, by advocating the workers' entitlement to a fair wage, to legal and peaceful collective action in defence of their economic interests and also the duty of the State to intervene in defence of those rights.[78]

In practice, paternalism, or inter-class 'solidarity' as it was officially described, meant that the first Catholic trade unions, the Unioni del Lavoro, were dominated by wealthy Catholic notables and by the clergy, though the Turin experience suggests that Catholic industrialists were unwilling to participate.[79] Paternalism, and the autocratic control of parish life by the clergy, which was sanctioned by both canon and civil law, also had the effect of discouraging the emergence of leadership cadres among the workers themselves.

At the turn of the century it was the newly emerging Christian Democratic movement of Don Romolo Murri and Don Luigi Sturzo, with its programme of radical economic, social and political reform, that gave real impetus to the formation of true Catholic trade unions, especially in Milan and its agricultural and industrial hinterland. The effects of their recruiting activities were reinforced by all manner of Catholic charitable and welfare institutions operating among the peasantry, including soup kitchens.[80] The success of these efforts may be judged by the rash of strikes of mainly agricultural workers in the 1890s and early 1900s, and it was also the Christian Democrats who provided much of the moral and material support for the *capellani del lavoro* referred to above.[81] But the election of Pius X in 1903 signalled a setback in the development of Catholic trade unionism. Papa Sarto's innate social conservatism and consequent fears about the influence of the Christian Democrats, coupled with his anxieties about the 'modernist' heretical tendencies of Murri and some of his followers, led him to dissolve the Opera, over which they had established such a strong influence, in 1904 and effectively outlaw the Christian Democrats.[82] For the next ten years, the efforts of the ecclesiastical authorities to protect their flocks from the 'modernist contagion' would cause bitter divisions inside the Catholic movement and undermine the credibility of Catholic peasant and trade union leaders.[83]

Much time and effort was also wasted by the Catholic movement in sterile controversies over the nature of Catholic economic and social organisations: whether they should be 'mixed' or include only employees, and whether they should be strictly 'confessional', requiring a declaration of religious allegiance (and often proof of good character from a parish priest), or be open to all.[84] On the eve of the outbreak of the First World War, organisations of all types continued to exist – though the tendency was still towards confessional organisations – but the overwhelming majority of Catholic trade unions were exclusively made up of employees.[85] Towards the end of his reign, Pius X came close to banning Christian trade unions altogether. The Jesuit, Padre Monetti, wrote a series of articles and published them in his order's journal, *La Civiltà Cattolica*, between February and May of that year. In them he inveighed against the 'excesses' of existing Catholic trade union organisations and challenged their moral legitimacy, intending to prepare the way for their eventual condemnation.[86] In all probability, only the death of Pius X in August 1914 prevented a blanket condemnation of Christian trade unionism, which would have had serious effects upon the social action of Italian Catholics.[87]

Another problem that exercised Catholic trade union leaders was the morality of the use of the strike. It was permitted by union rules and implicitly condoned by *Rerum Novarum*, but it was still considered a weapon of last resort and regarded with disapproval by the ecclesiastical authorities.[88] It is significant in this regard that when the bishop of Bergamo actually gave his moral and material assistance to a strike of textile workers at Ranica in his diocese, in 1909, he did so without the support of the Vatican.[89] The Ranica strike encapsulated so many of the difficulties facing Italian Catholic trade unionism as it emerged in the early 1900s, as well as exposing the contradictions from which most of these difficulties sprang. A price was paid for the official support of the diocesan leadership of the Catholic movement, in particular its president, Rezzara: the subordination of the union strike committee to the diocesan leadership, who effectively took over the direction of the negotiations with the employers. Rezzara's moderation, and increasing fears among the clergy of the subversive effects of strike action, meant that the outcome of this long and bitter dispute fell far short of the workers' demand and led to a decline in the position of the Catholic unions.[90] The fundamental conflict within the Catholic trade union movement between the ideal of interclass solidarity on the one hand, and the imperative of class struggle on the other, was left unresolved.

Other important factors in the relative failure of the Ranica strike were the lack of cooperation with the Socialists (although these were sympathetic to the strike) and the hostility of the Catholic middle class and aristocracy, the latter represented by the very influential Count Medolago Albani.[91] Indeed, the Ranica episode highlights a general lack in the historiography of the Catholic movement in Italy, that is, a clear understanding of the relationship between the Catholic trade unions and peasant leagues and the Catholic plutocracy of industrial manufacturers, large-scale (mainly aristocratic) farmers and financiers, which emerged in northern and central Italy in the two decades before the outbreak of the First World War.[92]

Notwithstanding the problems outlined above, Catholic economic and social organisations grew rapidly in the era of Prime Minister Giovanni Giolitti's dominance of Italian politics, 1903–14, creating a network of not only trade unions and peasant leagues but also workers' mutual aid societies, *casse di risparmio* and workers' and peasant cooperatives. This development provoked the resentment and rivalry of the Socialists. In a speech to the Socialist-dominated trade union movement, CGL, in 1911, its secretary general, Rinaldo Rigola, denounced Catholic trade unionism as 'systematic blacklegging' and denied that the Catholic organisations were 'true unions'.[93] Catholic organisers hotly denied this, and even another Socialist trade union leader, Montemartini, declared that they were 'genuine class organisations'.[94] The rivalry deepened when Giolitti admitted representatives of the Socialist trade unions to his National Council of Labour in 1904, while excluding Catholics and discriminating against Catholic cooperatives in the awarding of government contracts.[95]

At the heart of the Catholic network of economic and social institutions was the Ufficio del Lavoro, an organisation operating at city, diocesan and national level to bring together Catholic workers in opposition to the Socialist Camera del Lavoro (which was modelled on the French *bourses du travail*). Every initiative of the Socialists was soon matched by the Catholics, so that the Catholic movement quickly equipped itself with cultural and recreational organisations specifically aimed at the workers, including libraries, bands, concert halls and canteens.[96] But in 1910 the membership of the Socialist trade unions still outstripped their Catholic rivals by a factor of six to one:

Socialists (reformists and syndicalists)	650,000
Catholics	104,000
Independents	60,000

The official surveys of unionised labour carried out by the Ministry of Agriculture, Industry and Commerce at this time, and two years later, confirm that the Socialist unions were very much stronger among the workers in heavy industry and among the *braccianti* than their Catholic rivals. The latter's major recruiting success was in textiles, and this was largely due to the support of women who formed two-thirds of the workforce. Membership of Catholic trade unions in the metal and metal-mechanical and building industries, and among railwaymen and miners, was slight by comparison with the Socialist unions. Equally, clerical workers were represented in the ranks of Catholic trade unionists.[97] In agriculture, Catholic trade union membership was chiefly to be found among sharecroppers, small tenant farmers and even small landowners, but there were also significant pockets of support among *braccianti* and other agricultural labourers in Cremona province, the stronghold of Catholic deputy (member of Parliament) and peasant leader Guido Miglioli, and in other provinces of the Lombard plain.[98] The particular strength of the Catholic organisations in the agricultural sector may be attributed to a number of factors: the appeal of the Catholic ideal of the small peasant landowner to marginalised groups (as opposed to the Socialist aim of collectivisation); the idea of the 'co-management' of large farms adopted by Miglioli; and possibly the feeling among some peasants that the Socialists were not fundamentally interested in the agrarian question.[99]

Lombardy was the geographical stronghold of Catholic labour, with 62.5 per cent of the membership of agricultural unions and 43 per cent of the agricultural ones: 55 per cent of the total membership of all Catholic unions.

Apart from Lombardy, the only other region with a significant proportion of Catholic unionised labour was Venetia with 18.3 per cent of total membership, and south of Rome, support for Catholic unions was exiguous.[100] These figures confirm that the Catholic trade unions and peasant leagues and their other social and economic organisations, despite their minority role, were now a firmly established presence in Italian society. They also demonstrate that a Catholic sub-culture had emerged by 1914, and that it was predominantly localised in what were now to be called the 'white' provinces of north-eastern Italy, whereas the Marxist sub-culture had established itself in industrial cities such as Milan, Turin and Genoa, and their hinterlands, and in the 'Red Belt' of the Po valley and central Italy, especially among the rural proletariat of those areas.

The Catholic political response to Socialism

The existence of the *non expedit* precluded Catholic involvement in Italian national politics after the Risorgimento. But in the last three decades of the nineteenth century, divisions emerged in the Italian Catholic movement on precisely this issue. Thus, while the intransigents remained rigid upholders of hostility towards the Liberal State and consequently absolute political abstentionism, conciliatorists such as bishops Bonomelli and Scalabrini sought some sort of accommodation with liberalism (see Chapter 3, p. 38). There had also emerged an influential lay movement that, in journals such as *Annali cattolici*, *Rivista universale* and the *Rassegna Nazionale*, struggled against the restrictions imposed by both the *non expedit* and the Syllabus of Errors in an attempt to insert Catholics into the political life of Italy by means of a 'national, conservative party' that would embrace both Catholics and liberals of goodwill.[101] The national conservatives were drawn in the main from the Catholic *haute bourgeoisie* and landed aristocracy, especially, but not exclusively, of northern and central Italy. During the period of the *prima industrializzazione*, the Catholic bourgeoisie built up powerful interests in the financial sector of the economy, especially banking and insurance, in agriculture and, to a lesser extent, in manufacturing industry. In addition, they acquired a controlling influence over the Catholic press and therefore the Catholic movement as a whole.[102] They also became the leaders in those political activities permitted by the *non expedit*, notably local government.

As has been seen (Chapter 3, p. 42), in the communes (municipal districts) and provinces of Italy, major Church interests were at stake in the decades after unification, in particular, control over charitable and educational facilities. The Catholic notables became the leaders in this sort of politics, and when the *non expedit* was relaxed at the national political level in 1904, they were

among the first Catholics to enter Parliament. Committed to alliances with
the less avowedly anti-clerical elements of the Liberal establishment, they were
to become, as Capitani D'Arzago, a Milanese political Liberal conservative
leader described them in 1908, to all intents and purposes merely the Catholic
wing of the conservative Liberal ruling class.[103]

The patriotism of Italian Catholics had already been demonstrated by their
response to the Italian colonial setbacks at Dogali and Adowa. The Italian war
against the Ottoman Empire in 1911–12, which involved the invasion and
occupation of Libya as a colony, as well as the occupation of the Dodecanese
Islands in the Aegean, was strongly supported by Catholic financial interests
clustered around Ernesto Pacelli and the Banco di Roma and through the
newspapers that they controlled, which brought some clerico-moderates, as
these Catholics were now called, close to even the extreme right-wing
Nationalist Association of Corradini, Rocco and Federzoni.[104] When the
majority of the clerico-moderate MPs voted for Italian intervention in the
First World War in May 1915, all the ideological pre-conditions for the later
Catholic conservative alliance with Fascism had been fulfilled.

Catholic intransigence, on the other hand, took a different turn. Those
intransigents of a social reformist bent founded the Christian democracy
movement. They were inspired by *Rerum Novarum* and by Pope Leo's other
major encyclical *On the Christian Constitution of States*, which abandoned the
Church's hostility towards liberal parliamentary democracy.[105] Further
influences were the writings of Giuseppe Toniolo, whose Milan *Programme of
Catholics vis-à-vis Socialism* was predictably paternalistic, stressing the dignity
of work, the social function of property, supporting the formation of labour
unions but condoning the use of the strike only as a weapon of last resort.
Led by two priests, Murri and Luigi Sturzo, the Christian Democrats eventually
elaborated a programme of economic, social and political reform that, in the
event of a Catholic entry into national politics, aimed at a radical transformation
of the Liberal State. The Turin programme of 1899 advocated proportional
representation, the need to encourage small-property formation and
administrative decentralisation – all policies that were to be the hallmarks of
political Catholicism in Italy until long after the Second World War.[106] In the
short term, the Christian Democrats concentrated on the further development
of Catholic economic and social organisations, especially the trade unions and
peasant leagues as part of direct action to help the Catholic masses (see above,
pp. 60, 63).

If the Christian Democratic programme was different from that of the
clerico-moderates, then so was their membership, which broadly represented the Catholic small-town and rural middle classes – small businessmen
and professionals, parochial clergy, and organisers of Catholic trade unions

and peasant leagues, with a sprinkling of prominent Catholic intellectuals.[107] By 1903 they had captured effective control of the Opera, but the new pope, Pius X, feared both their radical reform programme and the heretical, 'modernist' tendencies of Murri. This induced him to break the hold of the Christian Democrats by dissolving the Opera and reorganising the Catholic movement into various associations more directly dependent upon the ecclesiastical hierarchy.[108] After this setback, the Christian Democratic leadership dispersed: Guido Miglioli continued to work for his beloved peasants and Don Sturzo moved over to head the major organisational legatee of the Opera and forerunner of the inter-war Catholic Action, the Unione Popolare. Murri, after an unsuccessful attempt to keep political Christian democracy alive in the National Democratic League, drifted further and further into disobedience, becoming a radical member of Parliament in 1909.[109]

The advent to the papal throne of Pius X marked an important milestone in the history of Italian political Catholicism in another sense. Impressed by the success of Catholics in defending the Church's interests through clerico-moderate alliances in local government in his native Veneto, and concerned about the growing Socialist threat, whose militancy reached its peak in the general strike of 1904, the pope decreed the suspension of the *non expedit* on a limited basis for the general elections of 1905. Catholics in some key northern constituencies were permitted to vote for acceptable Liberal conservative candidates or even stand for Parliament themselves, in order to keep out Socialists. The result was to establish a pattern of clerico-moderate alliances with the Liberal conservatives, the 'party of order', and to permit the entry of Catholics into national, parliamentary politics. Catholic candidates stood and were elected in 1905 and 1909, and in 1913, following the introduction of virtual universal male suffrage, 29 Catholics were elected to Parliament.[110]

These developments did not, however, signify the emergence of a Catholic political party in Italy. From the outset, the Vatican, which controlled Catholic political activity through the Unione Elettorale, stressed the distinction between *deputati cattolici*, that is, deputies who happened to be Catholics, and *cattolici deputati*, i.e. deputies who saw themselves as officially representing Italian Catholics: the latter were emphatically ruled out. In any case, the disparate nature of the Catholic parliamentary group, which included both clerico-moderates and others of a more Christian Democratic orientation, meant that they rarely voted as a block. Nevertheless, their participation in the parliamentary process was to prove a useful experience for the post-First World War Catholic Partito Popolare. Even more significant for the future was the outcome of the 1913 general elections. As a result of the pact between Giolitti and Count Gentiloni, the president of the Unione Elettorale, dozens of Liberal conservative candidates sought and obtained Catholic electoral support according to a set of conditions laid down by the Unione, in order to protect their seats against an expected Socialist onslaught. Gentiloni actually claimed that, in fact, over 200 Liberal conservative MPs owed their election to Catholic support.[111] Certainly, Giolitti's majority was saved thanks to Catholic support, and it is clear that a mass electoral base existed for a future Catholic party even before the outbreak of the First World War.

Following 'Red Week' in June 1914, when parts of northern and central Italy were convulsed by strikes, riots and seizures of town halls and churches, and even that of a whole city, Ancona, for a week, by anarchist and socialist militants, the municipal elections were effectively a showdown between the working class movement and the rest of political Italy in which Catholics were decisively on the side of the conservative forces, including the newly founded right-wing Nationalist Movement of Enrico Corradini.[112]

Conclusion

In his article, 'The Dechristianisation of the Working Class in Western Europe (1850–1900)', Hugh Mcleod states:

> There were several parts of Europe where the Roman Catholic Church had considerable success in resisting the movement towards Socialism and building up its own network of political, trade union and benefit organisations.[113]

McLeod goes on to list Germany, the Netherlands and Flanders. Had his timescale extended to 1914, he would have been able to add Italy to that list. By then the Church had clearly demonstrated its ability to maintain the allegiance of a substantial part of the working class that had emerged in the first period of industrialisation in the peninsula, not only in the rural areas, but in the cities, and not only in the classically 'Catholic' provinces of Como, Milan (mainly the rural hinterland), Brescia, Vicenza and Padua, but in nearly all the major industrial centres. It had managed to create nothing less than a Catholic 'sub-culture' alongside the Marxist one, thus laying the foundations for the brief period of success of the Catholic political party, the Partito Popolare Italiano, from 1919 to 1926, and more importantly, for that of the Christian Democratic Party from 1944 to 1994. But already the essential lines of an ambivalent relationship with the Church hierarchy had emerged along with premonitions of the clashes of policies and interests within the Catholic movement, which would erupt with disastrous consequences in the early 1920s.

Chapter 5

ITALIAN CATHOLICS, THE GREAT WAR AND THE RISE OF FASCISM (1914–29)

Introduction

THE PERIOD RUNNING FROM THE OUTBREAK of the First World War in August 1914 to the signing of the Lateran Pacts between Italy and the papacy in February 1929 was characterised by two divergent features. First, the war, and especially the transition from a neutralist stance to interventionism on the part of the Italian government between October 1914 and May 1915, revealed the fundamental conflict between the international, diplomatic interests of the papacy on the one hand, and the domestic priorities of the Italian Church and the essentially national loyalties of the Catholic movement on the other. Second, Italy's experience of the First World War significantly narrowed the gap between Catholics and the rest of Italian society, and between the Italian State and the institutional church.

The post-war period saw the emergence of Christian Democratic hegemony over the Italian Catholic movement, sanctioned by Benedict XV's tacit acceptance of the establishment of both the Catholic Partito Popolare Italiano (PPI) and the Confederazione Italiana del Lavoro (CIL), the Catholic trade union confederation, in 1919. But this experiment was to be of short duration because the Christian Democrats were caught between the weakness of the Liberal State, the violence of the rising Fascist movement and the hostility of Benedict's successor, Pius XI. Eventually, that pope managed to 'reconcile' the interests of the papacy with those of Italian Catholicism by exploiting the enormous improvements in church–state relations achieved in the intervening 15 years to reach a general settlement of outstanding disputes and arrive at a *conciliazione* with the Fascist regime of Benito Mussolini.

The papacy, Italian Catholics and the Intervention Crisis of 1915

The outbreak of the Great War in 1914 coincided almost exactly with a change of pope. Pius X died three weeks after the outbreak of war, and on 2 September Cardinal Giacomo Della Chiesa, archbishop of Bologna, was elected pope as Benedict XV. That election was to be a very significant one for the Italian Church. Della Chiesa, who was always front-runner in the balloting, had been opposed by the curialist and most fanatically anti-modernist elements in the conclave from the start.[1] Not surprisingly, he departed from or even entirely reversed a number of his predecessor's policies. Thus, in his first encyclical, *Ad Beatissimi*, he implicitly condemned the anti-modernist witch-hunt; he wrote to French president Poincare to announce his election, an obvious reversal of Pius X and Merry Del Val's intransigent policies towards France; and along with his secretary of state, Cardinal Pietro Gasparri, he took up a much more active and high-profile form of peace diplomacy than previously pursued by the papacy.[2]

The Vatican's consequent declaration of impartiality and neutrality suited the Italian government, which had also declared its neutrality at the outset of the great struggle. Though a member of the Triple Alliance along with Germany and Austria-Hungary, after the latter's rejection of Giolitti's *parecchio*, the proposal to give Italy substantial territorial concessions in Trento and Trieste, Italy had little to gain from fighting on their side against the Entente powers, Britain, France and Russia, particularly when the first two were the main naval powers in the Mediterranean.[3] But the Italian government, now led by two conservatives, Salandra as prime minister and Sonnino as minister of foreign affairs, did not give up its efforts to exploit the conflict for Italy's great cause, 'sacred egoism', as they called it. Thus negotiations continued with Germany and Austria-Hungary, and were also opened with the Entente, in the latter case culminating in the secret Treaty of London of April 1915. By the terms of the Treaty, Italy agreed to enter the war against its former allies on condition that she received Trento, Trieste, Gorizia, most of the Istrian peninsula and parts of Dalmatia, with a vaguer commitment to a share of the colonial possessions of the Central Powers (which now included Turkey).[4]

The Italian government's decision to go to war prompted a serious political crisis in May 1915. On one side of the divide were ranged the monarchy, the government (in a parliamentary minority) and a curious 'liquorice allsorts' of interventionists – the Nationalists, the Futurists led by Filippo Marinetti, Gabriele D'Annunzio, the nationalist novelist, playwright, poet and poseur, and, more surprisingly, Benito Mussolini and other assorted revolutionary Socialists and revolutionary syndicalists, republicans and anarchists who were convinced that war would lead to revolution. Most surprisingly of all, among the 'democratic interventionists' were not only liberals such as Francesco Nitti and Bissolati but also Christian Democrats, most notably Romolo Murri, Luigi Sturzo and Filippo Meda, all of whom hoped, not for revolution, but radical reform as a result of a 'people's victory'.[5] Other Christian Democrats such as Guido Miglioli stayed true to their neutralist instincts, following the mass of the peasant population and the Socialist Party. On the other hand, the majority of the clerico-moderates followed their increasingly nationalistic instincts and voted for war.[6] In the middle lay Giolitti and the majority of liberal-conservative members of Parliament. Giolitti backed off from openly opposing the ratification of the Treaty of London because he feared that since King Victor Emmanuel III had signed the draft, rejection would oblige him to abdicate. Giolitti's inaction and the massive and vociferous street demonstrations organised by the interventionists cowed Parliament into voting for war.

The Vatican took a decisively neutralist line. Indeed, in the months leading up to the Intervention Crisis Benedict and his secretary of state, Cardinal Gasparri, used all diplomatic means to keep Italy neutral, pleading with Austrian Emperor Franz Josef and his ministers to make territorial concessions to their former partner in the Triple Alliance. A genuine horror of armed conflict and the hope that it was possible to prevent the war from spreading, the desire to keep Italy out of the war for fear of its economic and political repercussion, worries about the capacity of the Habsburg Empire (the papacy's only reliable great power ally and its perceived bulwark against Russian/ Orthodox expansion in the Balkans) to survive, and concern about its own international position in an Italy at war all put Vatican diplomacy at variance with Italian foreign policy at this point. But this policy of impartiality and neutrality, while in accord with the instinctive feelings of the Catholic peasant masses who would have to provide the war's trench 'fodder', also put the pope at odds with the bulk of the Italian Catholic political elite, clerico-moderate and Christian democratic alike.[7]

With Italian Catholics deeply divided by the war, Giuseppe Dalla Torre, the president of the Unione Popolare, the main organisation of the Italian Catholic movement, took his instructions from the Vatican and laid down the official Catholic line: 'All support for the war, but no responsibility for it.'[8] This did not make the pope popular with the interventionists, particularly the likes of Benito Mussolini and his newspaper *Il Popolo D'Italia*. Equally, Benedict XV was not happy with the markedly patriotic, pro-war tone of some Catholic associations, clergy and press.[9] It was a very difficult, confused situation: Italian intervention had undermined his peace hopes and the patriotic enthusiasm of Italian Catholics could easily compromise the Vatican's neutralist stance in the eyes of the Central Powers. *L'Osservatore Romano* displayed a predictable coolness to the announcement of the entry of Filippo Meda and other Catholics into the Boselli government in 1916. Meda's appointment was obviously meant to signify the inclusion of even the Catholics in a government of 'national solidarity', but Benedict insisted that 'Meda only represents Meda', a rather unrealistic attitude in the circumstances.[10]

Fighting the good fight, 1915–19

The Italian episcopacy was also seriously divided over attitudes to the war: very few were really committed interventionists, even fewer were 'dyed-in-the-wool' neutralists, the vast majority giving their support to the war *effort*, rather than the war itself, with varying degrees of enthusiasm.[11] But the importance of the role of bishops and clergy in helping to maintain national morale, during a war that was not generally popular in Italy, should not be underestimated. The government certainly did not underestimate it; indeed, in April 1918 during a crucial battle on the Piave river, Sacchi, the minister of justice (responsible for ecclesiastical affairs) sent a circular to the country's more than 300 bishops requesting that the clergy 'intensify their cooperation in the task of reinforcing the (popular) spirit of resistance and sacrifice, especially in rural districts, among the families of soldiers . . .'[12] Two months later, he sent another circular expressing his gratitude for the bishops' support.[13]

For his part, despite his opposition to the war, Benedict complied when asked by the Italian government to mobilise the support of the bishops and clergy for the war effort, and in particular for war loans. By the end of the war and into the peace, the Vatican itself had subscribed several million lire of its own funds to government bonds.[14] Some 2,000 priests were mobilised as medical orderlies, including Angelo Roncalli, the future Pope John XXIII, and thus were enabled to carry out an unofficial role as chaplains to the men at the front. Later this was institutionalised, and the Vatican appointed Angelo Bartolomasi as Chaplain General of the Italian armed forces, to oversee what had become a major pastoral responsibility.[15]

Ironically, the contribution of Italian Catholics, and especially the clergy, to the patriotic cause was never enough to satisfy some interventionists, and especially their press. Their hostility to the papacy, and Vatican policy generally, reached its height in November 1917 following the cataclysmic Italian defeat at Caporetto when, paradoxically, Catholic commitment to the war was most obvious and complete.

Within the space of less than three weeks in late October and early November, the Italian armies were driven back from their positions on the

Isonzo river, on the far side of the Austro-Hungarian frontier, over 120 miles west to the river Piave (a few miles east of Venice), and they only managed to stabilise the northern end of their new front line with great difficulty. In the rout they lost nearly 300,000 men, not to mention precious guns and equipment.[16] In this great national crisis, the Church and especially the rural clergy of Veneto region were called upon to play a vital role in restoring morale. On 12 November, the new Italian prime minister, Vittorio Emanuele Orlando, asked Benedict to order the bishops to tell the people of the front-line areas to stay put, in order to diminish the stream of panic-stricken refugees who were hampering the efforts of the Italian armies to re-group.[17] In fact, information reached the Vatican that in areas on the line of retreat of the Italian forces, both Italy's civilian and military authorities had behaved badly, often abandoning their posts. In the resulting chaos, and amidst widespread looting by Italian soldiers, the local bishops and clergy were the only focus of authority.[18] Behind the lines, bishops and clergy were often the main providers for those refugees, church property being used for these as well as military purposes. Benedict showed great patriotic concern, and noted with a certain irony that the same Italian ministers and officials who had been responsible for obstructing his humanitarian efforts for prisoners of war were now besieging the Vatican with requests for information about their sons or nephews taken prisoner by the enemy.[19]

Yet some Italian officials still showed scant appreciation of the Church's involvement in the war effort. In early 1918, both Prime Minister Orlando and the Vatican were contacted by bishops in the front-line areas about numerous cases of their clergy being prosecuted for defeatism, spying or contacts with the enemy.[20] Another victim of Italian suspicion and hysteria in the wake of Caporetto was Giuseppe Dalla Torre, head of Italian Catholic Action, who was investigated by the 'Commission of Inquiry into Caporetto' for encouraging defeatism.[21] More seriously, the interventionist and anti-clerical press, returning to their longstanding accusation that the pope and the Vatican were the pawns of the Central Powers and in search of a scapegoat for Caporetto, cited Benedict's 'Peace Note' of August 1917 as having spread defeatism among the Italian troops at Caporetto. The more malicious changed Benedict's regnal name to 'Maledetto XV' (literally 'Cursed XV: Benedetto can also mean 'Blessed' in Italian) and the pope was depicted as Pontius Pilate in a cartoon in Mussolini's newspaper.[22]

Despite the dark side of the story described above, as Pietro Scoppola has observed, the war radically altered the position of Catholics in Italian society and politics.[23] The support of at least some Catholic politicians for intervention, and the participation of the Italian Catholic masses, especially the peasantry, in the war, combined with the patriotic mobilisation of both the Catholic clergy and lay organisations in the war effort, helped remove the anti-patriotic, anti-Italian stigma that had been attached to Italian Catholics since the Risorgimento. Also, in a very real sense, as a result of the war the Italian Church had virtually become a part of the establishment, a sort of 'national' church. Two incidents illustrate this very poignantly. On 9 November 1918, the cardinal vicar of Rome celebrated a solemn Te Deum for the Italian victory over Austria in the church of the Ara Coeli (the 'municipal' church) in the presence of not only the mayor of Rome and government ministers, but also HRH the Duke of Genova, the Lieutenant General, or Regent, of the kingdom in the absence of the king who was still at the front. And in the following month a meeting in Rome celebrated the arrival of Mgr Endrici, bishop of Trento (which remained under Austrian control until 1918), whose internment by the Austrians for defiance of their orders had made him a national hero, the very symbol of Catholic, patriotic Italy. The meeting closed, appropriately enough, with cries of 'Long live the King!', 'Long live Italy!' and 'Long live the Pope!'[24]

The war was also a revelation for the 24,000 priests and seminarians who were called up during the course of the conflict and thus came into contact with millions of men drawn from all parts of Italy. It revealed 'a traditional religion that was almost superstitious and was especially widespread among soldiers from the South . . . a religious sentiment without a religious consciousness. Our people are not as religious in a Christian sense as many think.'[25] This was the first warning about the superficiality of the religious beliefs of many Italian Catholics, but that would not become a matter of serious concern until the 1950s and 1960s (see Chapter 8, pp. 147–8). On the other hand, according to Traniello, the war also offered military chaplains an opportunity to experiment with new liturgical and para-liturgical forms, such as the consecration of priests to the Sacred Heart of Jesus.[26] These rites, organised on a more massive scale, would become an increasingly important characteristic of Italian Catholicism from the 1920s onwards.

The Vatican, Italy and the 'Roman Question' after the First World War

The First World War had also transformed the relationship between the papacy and the Italian State. Relations had been extremely strained at certain moments between 1915 and 1918, over such disputes as the Italians' occupation of Palazzo Venezia, the Austro-Hungarian embassy to the Holy See, the Gerlach spy affair and Article 15 of the Treaty of London, which resulted in the Holy See being barred from the Versailles Peace Treaty.[27] But the assiduous diplomacy of Baron Carlo Monti, senior Italian civil servant and friend of Benedict XV, who had performed the very difficult task of intermediary between the Italian government and the Vatican in the war years, smoothed away many problems.[28] In consequence, relations were generally cordial in the post-war period, giving rise to frequent suggestions that the two sides would short-circuit the 'Roman Question' by establishing diplomatic relations on a 'without prejudice' basis. This new state of affairs made it much easier for Benedict and Gasparri to protect the essential financial interests of both the Italian Church and the Holy See itself.[29]

Such was the goodwill prevailing between Benedict and Italian premier Vittorio Emmanuele Orlando in particular that behind the scenes at the Versailles Peace Conference in Paris a very serious attempt was made to reach a settlement of the 'Roman Question' in the spring and summer of 1919. The negotiations, essentially directed at restoring some sort of territorial sovereignty to the Holy See, with international guarantees, and establishing relations between the Holy See and Italy, were carried out between Orlando and Mgr Kelley, an American prelate who happened to be in Paris, and then Mgr Cerretti, papal under-secretary of state, who was sent there precisely for this purpose. Though Cerretti and the Italian premier achieved a large measure of agreement on the issues discussed, Orlando's government fell at the end of June. In any case, it seems unlikely in the turbulent political atmosphere in Italy during the summer of 1919 that Orlando could have obtained the agreement of either the king or Parliament.[30] There were further secret discussions with both the Nitti and Giolitti governments in 1920, and Benedict helped to 'normalise' relations with Italy further through his encyclical *Pacem Dei Munus Pulcherrimum* of 1920, which relaxed the ban on Catholic sovereigns and heads of state visiting the Quirinale.[31]

The Catholic presence in Italian society and politics in the 1920s

By 1920, however, Italian politics had become further complicated by the emergence of a Catholic political party – the Partito Popolare Italiano (PPI) – and the creation of a Catholic trade union confederation – CIL. Both were emblematic of the new-found confidence of Italian Catholics after the end of the war. Indeed, in 1919 the Catholic movement in broader terms was arguably at the peak of its power and influence in Italy. In addition to networks of peasant cooperatives and mutual help societies, there also existed a growing Catholic banking sector ranging from the smallest local *cassa di risparmio* to big players on the national financial scene such as the Banco Ambrosiano, the Banco di Roma, and Credito Nazionale.[32] There was a substantial Catholic press and publishing sector, complete with 25 dailies and many weekly and other periodical publications, with a readership of millions. And under the umbrella of the Unione Popolare, renamed 'Catholic Action' after the emergence of the PPI, there were networks of Catholic sporting, recreational and cultural organisations, Federazione Associazioni Scautisti Cattolici (FASC – the Catholic Boy Scouts) and male and female organisations, adult and youth, in the latter case the Gioventù Cattolica Italiana (GCI) and the Gioventù Femminile Cattolica Italiana (GFCI), with hundreds of thousands of members between them. In addition, the Associazione Magistrale di Nicolo Tommaseo, the organisation of Catholic teachers, exercised a powerful influence inside the state school system.[33]

Both CIL and the PPI were dominated by men of an essentially Christian Democratic orientation, and the triumph of the Christian Democrats was due partly to their support of the war, but also to the support of the pope. Benedict had been close to a number of leading Christian Democratic figures while archbishop of Bologna: Angelo Mauri, who was later to become a leading member of the PPI; Luigi Sturzo; and G-B. Valente, an active trade union leader in his native Genoa, at a time when it was neither fashionable nor entirely safe for an Italian bishop to be so.[34] He was, effectively speaking, a 'closet' Christian Democrat on economic and social matters. It was hardly surprising that shortly after his election, in 1915, he appointed Mauri as secretary general of the Unione Economico-Sociale and Sturzo as president of the Unione Popolare.[35] Thus the Christian Democrats had returned in force to the leadership of the Italian Catholic movement after a break of 12 years. Though Gasparri showed some hesitation and perplexity when the PPI was founded in late 1918, and the CIL the next year, Benedict was more confident given the leadership provided by Sturzo and Valente to the two respective organisations. Papal approval was absolutely essential for such a radical change in the arrangements for Catholic participation in Italian politics, not least for the final abolition of the *non expedit*, which was necessary in order to permit all Italian Catholics to vote in general elections. The programme of the PPI contained no elements of which the Vatican might have disapproved; on the contrary, it was firmly in line with papal teaching on the family and freedom of education, and mainstream Catholic thinking on economic and social matters, though it was perhaps a little ambivalent on the 'Roman Question'.[36] What were perhaps a little more 'risqué' were its foreign policy, which was essentially based on US President Wilson's 'Fourteen Points', and the proposal to give votes to women – yet Benedict did not disapprove of even this.[37]

The emergence of the PPI onto the Italian political scene was quite impressive: within months of Sturzo's first appeal the overwhelming majority of the various elements of the wider Catholic movement, including all of the existing Catholic deputies in Parliament and the bulk of the parochial clergy had rallied to it. Only the bishops remained more cautious in their attitude.[38] Moreover, the results of the 1919 general elections, conducted under proportional representation and universal male adult suffrage for the first time, confirmed the strength of the Partito Popolare in the country at large – the party won 20 per cent of the votes and 100 out of the 508 seats in the Chamber of Deputies, making it the second largest party after the Socialists. The fact that the Popolare vote was largely concentrated in the classic 'white provinces' suggests that the party's electorate was essentially made up of Catholic 'loyalists'.[39] Ironically, the breadth of support for the PPI in the Catholic movement and electorate was to prove a weakness as well as a strength, for as an inter-class party whose lowest common denominator was a shared religious faith, the party was always going to be rather heterogeneous, spanning virtually the whole arc of the ideologies and interest groups to be found in the Italian Catholic world. In particular, it brought together in an unnatural and short-lived alliance great landowners (as well as financiers and businessmen) at one extreme and landless labourers at the other. This alliance quickly fell apart under the impact of the rise of agrarian Fascism in northern and central Italy in 1921 and 1922.[40]

The party divided into recognisable factions from the start. There was a group of intransigents gathered around Padre Gemelli, friend of Mgr Achille Ratti, later Pope Pius XI, and rector of the Catholic University of Milan, who were critical of Christian Democracy. On the centre-right were the clerico-moderate grandees such as Grosoli, Santucci and Crispolti who effectively controlled the Catholic press. The centre, led by Luigi Sturzo, was the dominant force in the party, including most of the torchbearers of early Christian democracy and the bulk of the Catholic trade union leadership.[41] And on the left were men such as Guido Miglioli, whose Socialist leanings had inspired him to suggest the name 'Party of the Christian Proletariat' at the founding Bologna congress. It is interesting to note that some men of Miglioli's inclinations could not accept the policy of the party and in the 1921 general elections these dissident Partito Popolare and the Cristiani del Lavoro won 30,000 votes between them in Lombardy and Venetia.[42] As time went on, not even the charismatic leadership of Sturzo, who as priest and last historic leader of the original Christian Democratic movement commanded unrivalled authority in the party, was able to hold these divergent factions together. Indeed, the fact that Sturzo was a priest became a source of weakness to the party, for as such he was forced to lead the party from outside Parliament, and hence could not become prime minister, and his priestly status was to prove the Achilles' heel of the Partito Popolare because he was vulnerable to canonical sanction by the ecclesiastical authorities.

The PPI in Italian politics, 1919–22

Despite the PPI's inherent weaknesses, not to mention its relative newness to parliamentary life, the party's emergence was to have a dramatic impact on post-war Italian politics and it would play a key role in parliamentary government between 1919 and 1923. While the party almost certainly robbed the Socialists of a greater victory than they actually achieved in 1919 (the Socialists won 150 seats and therefore became the largest party in Parliament), more significantly the PPI, by monopolising the Catholic vote, also deprived the liberals of their parliamentary majority. Given the fact that the Socialists refused to participate in 'bourgeois politics', i.e. parliamentary government, the PPI thus became central to the formation and survival of governing coalitions. Each of the six cabinets formed between July 1919 and October 1922, including Mussolini's first government, contained at least two Popolare ministers (usually more) and several under-secretaries of state. Finance and/or the Treasury, as well as agriculture, were usually in the hands of the Partito Popolare, and in 1921, in a move unprecedented in the history of Liberal Italy, a Catholic became minister of justice. In February and July 1922, as the parliamentary crisis of the Liberal State deepened, Filippo Meda, veteran Catholic politician and the leader of the parliamentary caucus of the PPI, was asked by the king to take the premiership. Much to Sturzo's dismay, Meda refused because of his unwillingness to shoulder the burdens of high office. Meda's refusal deprived his party of the opportunity to play a dominant role in politics, and probably also scuppered the last real chance to save Italian parliamentary democracy.[43]

The party's experience of parliamentary politics was not a happy one. The demands of a modern, mass party, with a fixed programme, did not square with the traditional, transformist tactics of the Liberal notables who continued to form governments in this period. Governments came and went with increasing rapidity, partly because of bitter rows between the Partito Popolare and a succession of conservative liberal premiers – Nitti, Giolitti, Bonomi and Facta – over the failure of the latter to implement policy commitments made when cabinets were formed. These structural problems generated by Italy's transition to a fully democratic political system in the post-war period were compounded by two complementary factors: working class militancy during the 'Red Two Years'(from 1918 to 1920); and the rise of the Fascist movement, which was very largely a reaction to that militancy. The PPI was caught between these unfortunate developments. The militancy of the Italian working class movement between 1918 and 1920 was by no means exceptional in Europe. On the contrary, it was largely a product of events elsewhere on the Continent, most notably the Bolshevik Revolution of 1917 and the other attempted revolutions and short-lived soviet republics in the Baltic States, Germany, Hungary and Romania. In Italy, during the war, the trade union movement had been largely repressed, yet at the same time it had grown in membership due to the expansion of industry and the promises of reform made by war-time premiers to sustain morale; Wilson's 'Fourteen Points' all added to expectations. In 1917, rioting, with the erection of barricades in Milan and Turin, gave some sign of the extent of popular discontent and a taste of the trouble to come.[44] The two years following the war were marked by militancy of all kinds: protests against rises in bread prices and rents, strikes, occupations of the land in various parts of Italy and the occupation of the factories during the summer of 1920. And these forms of working class militancy were often accompanied by violence, which sometimes fell upon the organisations and members of the Catholic movement: even churches were attacked in some parts of Italy.[45] But this militancy was not confined to Socialist organisations; even some of the Catholic peasant leagues adopted very militant tactics in their struggles with landowners over tenancy agreements and sharecroppers' contracts.[46]

The response of the PPI to this situation was regarded as inadequate, not only by local bishops faced with the apparent threat of 'Red revolution', but also by the Vatican. The latter condemned Catholic trade union militancy in Bergamo in March 1920,[47] and in August, at the height of the occupation of the factories, the pope issued a general condemnation of Bolshevism.[48] Meanwhile, in the local elections of the spring and autumn of 1920 the PPI disregarded demands and pleas from bishops to combine with local conservative liberal groups in those areas where the Socialist Party was strongest.[49] This intransigence on the part of Sturzo's party, which, it has to be said, actually reaped considerable electoral benefits, alarmed and outraged the hierarchy and the Vatican. By the end of 1920 it was clear that the Catholic party and the institutional church in Italy were drifting apart.

Benedict, the PPI and the rise of Fascism, 1919–22

Italian Fascism was a child of war, the First World War. The very disparate leading figures in the early Fascist movement, such as the ex-revolutionary Socialist Benito Mussolini, the ex-revolutionary syndicalist Edmondo Rossoni, the anarchist Michele Bianchi, the republican Dino Grandi and the Futurist Filippo Marinetti, were all supporters of intervention in May 1915 and all shared in Italy's ensuing experience of war. The first *fascio*, which they founded in March 1919 in Milan, was, like its National Socialist counterpart in Munich, heavily based on the support of ex-servicemen and therefore strongly paramilitary in character. Given the essentially leftist political past of most of its leaders, the early Fascist movement was inevitably marked by strong elements of anti-capitalism, anti-liberalism, anti-monarchism and anti-clericalism, as well as a desire for a vigorous foreign policy. But early Fascism remained a numerically small, marginal political movement, almost entirely restricted to the cities and towns of northern Italy; in the November 1919 elections, Mussolini and other Fascist candidates only managed to win 5,000 out of the 250,000 votes cast in the Milan constituency.

The dramatic expansion of the Fascist movement in Italy – particularly from the autumn of 1920 when it succeeded in exploiting the bitter agrarian conflicts in the countryside of northern and central Italy and turning itself into a violent form of class defence of the interests of the landowners and their allies – had an immediate impact on the Catholic movement. In the first place, many Catholic economic and social organisations in rural areas were as much victims of the violence of the paramilitary Fascist squads as their Socialist counterparts. As Filippo Meda argued in an impassioned attack on the clerico-Fascist collaboration with the Fascists in 1924:

> (But) it is entirely positive for the Christian people of our country – the people of the villages and the mountains, martyred and persecuted by their present rulers – governed often by the cudgel and the revolver, driven from their clubs and cooperatives, impeded from voting or forced by threats to vote for those whom they do not want – to ask you to account for this intolerable situation.[50]

As the violence of the squadristi against Socialists and Catholics alike spread in the provinces of northern and central Italy in 1921 and 1922, Mussolini used the carrot as well as the stick to advance his ambitions to achieve political power. After his entry into Parliament following Fascist participation in Giolitti's anti-Socialist National Block electoral cartel, the Fascist leader used his maiden speech to woo Italian Catholics, a small minority of whom were already to find the attractions of Fascism irresistible. In a cynically opportunist abandonment of his lifelong anti-clericalism and atheism – this was the man who had written a semi-pornographic novelette about a cardinal's mistress, who called for the abolition of marriage at the Socialist Party congress and who had declared in the pages of *Il Popolo D'Italia* in 1919 that 'there is only one possible revision of the law of Guarantees and that is its abolition followed by a firm invitation to his Holiness to quit Rome' – Mussolini eulogised Catholicism. In particular, he announced, rather brazenly, that 'Fascism neither preaches nor practises anti-clericalism', and went on to declare that the only universal values in Italy emanated from the Vatican.[51] Mussolini's speech cut little ice in the Vatican of Benedict XV.

But the civil war that the Fascist squads were waging in the provinces, and the apparent inability of the state authorities there to end it, had more and more serious repercussions at a national political level. By the end of 1921 Italian parliamentary democracy was entering into crisis as the ruling coalition was pulled apart by the spectacle of Italy's apparent un-governability. In the midst of this period of deepening political crisis in Italy, Benedict suddenly became ill and died.

The election of Pius XI

In the conclave of February 1922 Cardinal Achille Ratti, archbishop of Milan, was elected pope, taking the title Pius XI.[52] Ratti had had an unusual career: a scholar, he had been librarian of the prestigious Ambrosian Library in Milan, and then from 1912 Vatican Librarian. In 1917, he was suddenly plucked from his books by Benedict and sent off as Apostolic Visitor to Lithuania and Poland, that is, papal envoy in a confused end-of-war situation and in the absence of official diplomatic relations. Just as suddenly, he was removed from Warsaw, where he was becoming distinctly unpopular with the Polish government and the episcopate, and appointed archbishop of Milan in July 1921. He was thus in many ways Benedict's 'creature' and consequently was expected to follow in his footsteps. The fact that he continued to employ Pietro Gasparri as secretary of state and continued Benedict's policies in relation to the Eastern churches and the missions certainly made it seem that way in the early days of his pontificate. But he had taken the name 'Pius', which belonged to two recent 'hard-line' popes, Pius IX and Pius X, and he possessed a very independent, authoritarian temperament, which manifested itself quickly. In relation to Italy and its turbulent politics, he had, in any case, a very different stance from that of Benedict. He was very conservative on many social and economic issues, a stance which was derived in part from his circle of friends and acquaintances among the clerico-moderate bourgeoisie and aristocracy of Milan. During the time he spent as archbishop of the city from September 1921 to February 1922 his closest collaborators were the Caccia-Dominioni brothers – Pietro, who was deeply involved in the world of Catholic banks, Ambrogio, whom he appointed as head of Milanese Catholic Action, and Carlo, whom he took to Rome to fill the important post of papal *Maestro di Camera*, and who would become the leading spokesman of the clerico-Fascist interest inside the Vatican.[53]

Ubi Arcano Dei and the Christian restoration of society

Papa Ratti's new approach was quickly signalled by his first encyclical *Ubi Arcano Dei* of September 1922, which called for the Christian restoration of a society corrupted and enslaved by the evils of the modern world. Catholic Action was to be the instrument of that process of restoration and to this end the Vatican recommended bishops in many different countries to create organisations to ensure 'the participation of the laity in the apostolate of the hierarchy'.[54] Throughout the 1920s and 1930s, Pius and the Roman Curia would repeatedly exhort the episcopates of very diverse countries to implement his plans for Catholic Action as the best defence of the Church's interests and the propagation of its beliefs. The role that Pius XI assigned to Azione Cattolica Italiana in Italian society and politics is best understood in this broader context of the overall objectives and strategy of the pope's reign.

Three months after the publication of the encyclical, the papal Secretariat of State announced the decision to reorganise and revivify the Catholic movement, which arguably had languished somewhat following the emergence of the Partito Popolare and CIL. Of the organisations created by Pius X in his reforms at the beginning of the century, the Unione Elettorale had been rendered redundant by the abolition of the *non expedit*, the Unione Economica e Sociale had been weakened by the creation of a Catholic trade union federation and that left only the Unione Popolare, which was suffering a crisis of identity and confidence thanks to the emergence of the Partito Popolare.[55] As Italian politics became ever more turbulent, Pius and Gasparri sought to lift the Catholic movement above the fray and to firmly subject it to ecclesiastical control at every level, from the national to the parochial.[56]

Pius was to reveal a deep-seated distrust of 'Catholic' parties and politicians, especially 'priest-politicians' such as Luigi Sturzo, Ludwig Kaas, Ignaz Seipel, Hlinka and Joseph Tiso, the leaders of the Partito Popolare, the German Centre Party, the Austrian Christian Socials and the Slovakian People's Party respectively. So it seems likely that long before the March on Rome of October 1922 he had decided upon a policy of increasing distance between the Church and the Partito Popolare, which was, after all, Gasparri's instinctive feeling as well.

The increasing divisions emerging in the Partito Popolare as a result of Sturzo's intransigent parliamentary tactics during the long political crisis of the summer and early autumn of 1922, which led to the collapse of the first Facta government in June and the stillbirth of another Giolittian coalition in October, alienated increasing numbers of conservative Catholics. In June a short-lived secession of disaffected conservatives in the Unione Costituzionale failed to get off the ground, but in July the Roman aristocrat Prince Francesco Boncompagni-Ludovisi abandoned the *popolare* whip in the Chamber and joined the Nationalists, and in September, eight *popolare* Senators signed a letter to Sturzo protesting against the party's flirtations with the Reformist Socialists. The direction in which all of these elements was moving was that of *popolare* participation in a government of 'National Order' presided over by Orlando, Salandra or Giolitti, and including right-wing forces – the Fascist not excepted.[57]

On the other hand, Mussolini's policy towards the Church was now winning favour, as was demonstrated by *L'Osservatore Romano* and *La Civiltà Cattolica*, which in a very short period of time moved from blanket condemnation of the rising Fascist movement to more specific criticisms of its undesirable elements and their violent activities, coupled with a cautious recognition of the movement's merits as a patriotic force fighting Bolshevism.[58] Throughout 1922 the Vatican endlessly reiterated that Catholic Action was non-political and that the clergy should abstain from politics: since the only party they were likely to support was the Partito Popolare, it was clear that the Vatican was in every way seeking to dissociate itself from that party. All of these statements were repeated at the beginning of October as Italy's political crisis deepened.

The Vatican and Fascism from the March on Rome to the end of the Matteotti Crisis

When it came, the Vatican greeted the outcome of the March on Rome with relief and satisfaction.[59] Whether it could have anticipated it or not, Mussolini's appointment brought immediate benefits in the form of a series of measures to improve the position of the Church, which he announced to Parliament in early November, including a rise in the stipends of priests paid by the State and the re-introduction of religious education into secondary schools, which was possibly part of a deal to secure the parliamentary support of the Partito Popolare for Mussolini's government. Mussolini's measures were purely opportunistic devices to win further support in the Catholic world and, by stealing some of its policies, to isolate the PPI and make it appear redundant in the eyes of some Catholics. In January 1923, the first, secret, meeting took place between Mussolini and Cardinal Gasparri: the outcome was a commitment on the part of Mussolini's government to rescue the failing Banco di Roma, in which the Vatican had considerable deposits and a substantial shareholding, in return for which the bank would cut its ties with the Catholic party.[60] In the summer of 1923, as the Acerbo Law – legislation to change Italy's electoral system – was debated in Parliament, the Vatican ordered Luigi Sturzo to resign from his position in the Partito Popolare, thus depriving the party of his leadership at a most critical juncture. When the time came for elections under the new system, in March 1924, the Italian Catholic world was deeply divided politically. Fifteen Catholics, former *popolare* MPs and senators, stood in Mussolini's National Block of candidates along with other liberal-conservative camp-followers of Fascism.[61] The Partito Popolare, on the other hand, followed its usual policy of independence and emerged as the second largest opposition party.

The last chance for Italian democracy came in the summer and autumn of 1924, following the murder by Fascist thugs of Giacomo Matteotti, leader of the Reformist Socialists (PSU – Partito Socialista Unitario). This provoked a wave of revulsion against Fascism throughout Italy, and Mussolini's government tottered on the brink of collapse as many of his newly elected parliamentary supporters deserted him. In common with other opposition parties, the Partito Popolare withdrew from Parliament in protest against the crime and constituted an 'Aventine Secession'. In September, attempts were made to form an anti-Fascist government of opposition parties around the Partito Popolare and Reformist Socialists, but at this point Pius XI uttered a public denunciation of Catholic political collaboration with a Marxist party, despite the fact that such alliances had been made in Germany, Poland and Czechoslovakia.[62] The pontiff had made his choice; he had chosen an as yet authoritarian Fascist regime, which seemed to him the best defence against the threat of Bolshevik revolution and seemed to offer the best chance of resolving the 'Roman Question'. Another, not insignificant, consideration in his mind might have been the fear of violence, disorder and instability in Italy during the coming Holy Year of 1925.[63]

The decline of the Catholic movement

While the history of Italian Catholicism in the mid to late 1920s was dominated by the emergence of a new relationship between the Vatican and Fascism, an equally important development, and one that was largely a consequence of it, was the serious decline in the strength of the Catholic movement and its presence in Italian society. Within a decade of the Catholic movement's establishment of itself as a major presence in Italian society, the situation had dramatically changed. CIL and the Partito Popolare were gone, dissolved along with other non-Fascist trade unions and political parties in 1925 and 1926. Many of the Catholic peasant cooperatives had fallen victim to the squadrist violence of agrarian Fascism between 1920 and 1924.[64] In 1925, the Istituto Cattolico di Attività Sociale (ICAS) was created to replace the semi-moribund Unione Economica e Sociale. According to Brunori di Siervo, 'by founding ICAS, it was hoped to save the "saveable", to prevent the fruits of the fifty years of Catholic activity in the economic and social fields from being lost to Fascism'.[65] ICAS almost certainly did prevent more losses to the new Fascist Ente Nazionale per la Cooperazione. Catholic banks and *casse di risparmio* were also decimated: between 1926 and 1929 it is estimated that 74 Catholic banks and *casse* – 1,021 branches and a total loss of one milliard lire – either closed their doors or were taken over by more resilient institutions.[66] The Catholic banks were the casualties of the banking crisis that ravaged Italy in the late 1920s, thanks in part to Mussolini's monetary policy. Only the presence of clerico-Fascists on their boards of management saved other Catholic banks from the same fate.[67] The establishment of an Istituto Centrale di Credito to supervise and provide liquidity to Catholic banks – underwritten in part by a Vatican commitment of 1,000 million lire and with a leading clerico-Fascist senator, Stefano Cavazzoni, as governor and Luigi Colombo of Catholic Action as his deputy, to assure the future of the Catholic banking sector – was one of the behind-the-scenes deals agreed during the negotiations for the Conciliazione.[68]

The crisis of the Catholic banks could not have come at a worse moment for that branch of the Catholic movement that was so heavily dependent upon them – the press. Whereas in 1923 the Catholic movement could boast 21 daily newspapers, 90 per cent of which were to be found, as we would expect, in northern and central Italy, by 1929 that figure had been more than halved.[69] The central problem of the Catholic press had always been financial and the largest combine of Catholic newspapers, Grosoli's Trust, had lurched from one crisis to another from the beginning of Benedict's reign. The political divisions within the Catholic movement created by the defections of the clerico-Fascists from the Partito Popolare also caused problems and Fascist pressure to conform to the new press laws did the rest.[70] On the eve of the Conciliazione the Italian Catholic movement was much smaller in nearly all of its various forms and activities than it had been when Mussolini came to power in 1922, and the Catholic presence in Italian society was consequently diminished in size and effectiveness. Pius XI seems to have observed this process with relative equanimity, but at least what remained, with the possible exception of the Centro Nazionale Italiano, had been brought firmly and securely under the control of the hierarchy.

The negotiations for the Conciliazione of 1929

Whatever damage the rise of Fascism had done to the Catholic presence in Italian society in the early to mid-1920s, it had made it possible for the pope and his secretary of state to achieve what was for them the ideal situation, a direct interlocutory relationship with the Italian State without the complicating presence of a strong Catholic party in politics. In consequence, in 1926 secret negotiations got under way for a settlement of the 'Roman Question' and other related issues between church and state, which would culminate in the Conciliazione, the signing of the Lateran Pacts between Italy and the Holy See in February 1929.

The negotiations of 1926–29 cannot be properly understood, except within the broader context of Mussolini's process of consolidating power, by reaching accommodations with the various elements of what Alberto Aquarone has described as the 'block of consensus', the basic support structure of the Fascist regime.[71] Having won the support of much of the northern landowning class for Fascism in the early 1920s, Mussolini went on to achieve the support of the industrial, commercial and financial interest groups, and then the monarchy, the armed forces and finally the Church for the construction of his regime during the late 1920s. But, as Adrian Lyttelton has pointed out, part and parcel of the process of consolidating power was the elimination of resistance to his compromises with the establishment from within his own party.[72] Though he cleverly used Roberto Farinacci to bring the more the more dangerous loose cannons of Fascism to heel between 1925 and 1926, the eventual dismissal of Farinacci, himself one of the most anti-clerical, independent and violent of the local Fascist bosses, as party secretary signalled the subjugation of the party.[73] Similarly, the removal of anti-clerical philosopher Giovanni Gentile from the post of minister of education and the replacement of Oviglio as minister of justice by Alfredo Rocco, were absolute prerequisites for a settlement with the Vatican.

Yet in 1926 Mussolini was far too preoccupied with the crisis of the lira to be serious about negotiations, and at this stage Pius XI does not appear to have been very optimistic about the prospects of success either, with the result that both were content with the progress being made by the Ecclesiastical Law Reform Commission set up by Rocco.[74] Suddenly everything changed when Fascism turned from its demolition or absorption of Catholic economic and social organisations and started to lay violent hands on the Catholic youth. Pius tried hard to prevent the dissolution of the Catholic Boy Scouts (FASC), and this seems to have persuaded him and Gasparri that only by offering Fascism the glittering prize of a settlement of the 'Roman Question' as a bargaining counter could they salvage what remained of Catholic youth organisations.[75]

The secret negotiations conducted by Francesco Pacelli (brother of the later Pope Pius XII) for the Vatican and Domenico Barone for the regime encountered many difficulties, about religious marriage, the exact status of the Vatican in international law, financial compensation for the loss of revenue from the Papal States and last, but not least, the future of the remaining Catholic youth organisations.[76] The pope was able to ensure the survival of the GCI and GFCI but was unable to prevent a further restriction of their activities in the sporting and cultural fields; however, in broader terms, the Vatican did very well out of the negotiations. The Lateran Treaty provided for the establishment of Vatican City as a sovereign, independent and neutral state, thus realising what all popes since Pius IX had aspired to, a restoration albeit in minuscule form of the former temporal power, and the Financial Convention gave substantial compensation for previous losses, thus ensuring the Vatican's future financial independence.[77] The third agreement, the Concordat, established the framework for a new relationship between church and state in Italy, one that would, in the long term, be largely advantageous to the Church, ultimately providing for the rebuilding of the Catholic presence in Italian society.

Conclusion

By the end of the 1920s, the first attempt to make Italian political Catholicism into a parliamentary, governmental force had ended in failure. Fascism had taken over the political arena and in doing so had not only swept away Christian democracy, but Italian democracy itself. The PPI was not the only victim of Fascism; other branches of the Catholic movement had suffered as well. But through the Lateran Accords, the pope and Gasparri hoped to secure the future for this diminished Catholic presence in Italian society against the further encroachments of Fascism's increasingly totalitarian claims to control all aspects of the life of Italy and its citizens and even to expand it.

Chapter 6

FASCISM, WAR AND RESISTANCE (1929–45)

Introduction

FROM 1929 ONWARDS, ITALIAN CATHOLICS under the direction of the papacy had to learn to live under a new form of political regime. Though Fascism had espoused totalitarian claims to the loyalty of Italians since the mid-1920s, Pius XI and his collaborators were rather inclined to view Mussolini's rule as a conservative-authoritarian regime, not dissimilar from many others in Europe in the 1930s, and one that would conveniently assist in the reconstruction of that Christian, Catholic society that had been destroyed, or at least seriously weakened in some of its essentials, by the 'Liberal Revolution' of the preceding century.

Many of the policies of the regime, and most importantly its unremitting hostility to Freemasonry, Socialism and Communism, suited the Church's book exactly. Its destruction of the liberal democratic state was certainly not mourned by the majority of the Italian Catholic hierarchy, nor by some lay Catholics either, though significant minorities of both parochial clergy and laity remained Christian democratic at heart throughout. But as Fascism, after the success of the Ethiopian conquest and especially as it came increasingly under the influence exercised by Nazi Germany, moved towards more serious attempts to implement its totalitarian project, in particular the introduction of the Racial Laws, the underlying ideological differences between Catholicism and Fascism came to the surface. Mussolini's increasing efforts to 'sacralise' politics, as part of a totalitarian reorganisation and regeneration of Italy and the creation of the 'new' Fascist man, by the adoption of credos, decalogues and liturgies in an almost blasphemous imitation of Catholicism, meant

Fascism was contending for the natural terrain of the Italian Church. Yet the Conciliazione of 1929 of itself ensured that Fascism would have no victory over Italian Catholicism: the continued existence of Catholic Action ultimately made a mockery of Fascist totalitarian pretensions, and the very existence of the papacy as an essentially charismatic institution meant that even in that most characteristic of Fascist innovations, the cult of the Duce, Mussolini was challenged by a powerful rival.

The Concordatory regime

Since the Conciliazione was hailed as such a momentous event in the history of Italy, one needs to ask in what ways it changed the pattern of church–state relations in Italy after 1929. The key phrase in the Treaty's Article 1, 'Italy recognises and reaffirms the principle contained in the first article of the constitution of the Kingdom of Italy, March 4th, 1848, by which the Holy Catholic Apostolic and Roman religion is the only State religion',[1] was now, for the first time in the history of the Italian State, a reality. Hitherto, that clause of the Statuto Sabauda had, perforce, in a liberal, secularising state, been a dead letter, honoured more in the breach. The clearest sign of the special place of the Church in the Italian State was Mussolini's decision to abolish the 20 September holiday, which had commemorated the capture of Rome by troops in 1870. That, and other concessions to the Church, provoked criticism from anti-clericals in both the ranks of the Fascists and their opponents, such as the eminent senator, Benedetto Croce.[2]

Certainly, in legal terms, the Church had increased its power and influence, or, rather, it had recuperated a lot of the power that it had lost during the previous century, and it did so in some key areas: marriage, education and the legal privileges of the clergy. Furthermore, the supply of funds from the state to the Church was guaranteed, and, in addition, the Church was now free to acquire property at will.

As far as marriage was concerned, the Concordat effectively transferred jurisdiction over marriage questions, apart from legal separation, to the church courts, annulments being automatically ratified by the Italian Courts of Appeal.[3] The result was that there were now *three* types of marriage – civil marriage, marriage in the Catholic Church and civil marriage for the religious minorities. In addition, there was the extraordinary anomaly whereby any Catholic who had previously contracted a civil marriage could, notwithstanding, marry another partner in church. As Jemolo pointed out: 'In this way there was foisted upon the country the most chaotic and anomalous marriage law that could possibly be imagined . . . which left its regulation entirely in the hands of the Church.'[4] What was even more significant for Italian society was that under the Concordatory regime the dissolution of civil marriages was effectively impossible, and this remained the case until the position was successfully challenged by the Divorce Law of 1970.

The Concordat also signified a major gain for the Church in the field of education. Catholic (private) schools now had effective parity with those of the State, and religious instruction became obligatory in secondary schools, giving rise to fears about its impact on the teaching of philosophy. The unease in the Fascist Party about these measures was such that Mussolini felt obliged to state in his speech on the ratification of the Lateran Pacts that: 'You will note that I categorically rejected the demand that religious instruction be introduced into the universities.'[5] The Church's 're-entry' into the educational sector was paralleled elsewhere, by the setting on an official, state footing of the Military Chaplain General with an archbishop as 'Military Ordinary' and chaplains for the armed forces, as well as chaplains in state-run hospitals.

The year 1929 also saw a resurrection of ecclesiastical privileges and immunities that had not been seen in Italy for decades, including exemption of the clergy from military service in war-time: seminarians could delay it to the age of 26, by which time they were likely to be ordained anyway. According to Article 8 of the Concordat, in cases where clergy were prosecuted in state courts the local ordinary (bishop) was to be kept informed at all stages of the trial. But perhaps the most contentious element of ecclesiastical privilege was the ban on the public employment of 'apostate or censored' priests, which immediately gave rise to a row about probably the most notorious of them all, the writer Ernesto Buonaiuti.[6]

Both the Concordat and the Financial Convention were generous in the provision that they made for the Church in the areas of income and property: basically, the existing funding arrangements – i.e. ownership of former ecclesiastical property by Fondo per il Culto and subventions to episcopal sees (the *mensa*), chapter, collegiate and parochial clergy – continued, but ecclesiastical bodies, including religious orders, could now freely own property that, in theory at least, they had not been able to do in the past. Thus the secular state's attempts to limit the Church's property-owning, and therefore its capacity to extend economic, social and political influence, was abandoned. The growth of the role of the Church as property-owner would develop apace, most notably in the case of the Holy See itself, which by the terms of the Financial Convention received compensation for the loss of the Papal States amounting to 1,750 million lire in cash and government loan stock (nearly £20 million sterling or $91 million).[7] The investment of this money was entrusted by Pius XI to Bernardino Nogara, a Milanese banker, who chose both international financial markets – gold, currencies, foreign government loan stocks, public utilities and property – and banking, insurance, manufacturing and financial holding companies in Italy, with the result that the Vatican acquired a major stake in the Roman and Italian economies in the 1930s, which in the short term effectively tied it to the fortunes of the Fascist regime, and in the longer term helped create a joint Catholic–Fascist domination of the large sectors of the Italian economy.[8]

The 1929–30 and 1931 crises in church–state relations

Despite the euphoria of February, the honeymoon of 1929 did not last long. Mussolini's own anxiety to appease his anti-clerical Fascist followers was one factor in dampening the atmosphere. In the debates on the ratification of the Lateran Pacts in the Italian Parliament, the Duce's defensive mentality translated into an aggressive public stance when he declared that:

> Inside the State the Church is not only not sovereign it is not even free. It is not sovereign because that would be a contradiction of the concept of the State, and it is not free because it is subject to the institutions and laws of the State, and, indeed, to the terms of the Concordat.[9]

There was a real fear of the potential for Catholic *prepotenza* (bullying) on the part of some Fascists, which was publicly expressed by, among others, Ezio Garibaldi, grandson of the eponymous Risorgimento hero, but this fear was not widespread because the concordat was, after all, with the Fascist regime.[10] Mussolini was determined to contain Catholic expansionism, hence the crises of 1929–30 and 1931. (It was to be a different story during the years of Catholic 'triumphalism'(see Chapter 7)). The crisis of 1929–30, such as it was, essentially sprang from Mussolini's efforts to reassure his Fascist supporters that he had not sold out to the Church, hence his remarks minimising the significance of concessions made in the Concordat, and his heretical claim in the debates on the ratification of the Pacts that:

> We should be proud of the fact that Italy is the only European nation which contains the headquarters of a world religion. This religion was born in Palestine but became Catholic in Rome. If it had stayed in Rome it would have shared the fate of the many sects, like the Essenes or Therapeutae, which vanished without trace.[11]

Despite Pius XI's inevitably outraged response, the crisis passed over and the Lateran Pacts were ratified and came into force. But tensions flared up again in December 1929 when Pius XI published his encyclical *Rappresentanti in Terra* ('On the Christian Education of Youth'), which re-asserted the rights of the family and the Church in the matter of educating young people and in which the pope attacked many practices of the Fascist youth organisations and in particular their 'exaggerated nationalism' and the military training of young boys and girls 'contrary to the very instincts of human nature'.[12]

Youth organisations were once again at the heart of the conflict that flared in the late spring and early summer of 1931. Against the background of Vatican celebrations of the fiftieth anniversary of *Rerum Novarum*, which was commemorated by a social encyclical of Pius XI's own, *Quadragesimo Anno*, there was a full-blooded crisis in the relations between the Holy See and Italy. Mussolini's regime cracked down on the youth and occupational organisations of Azione Cattolica Italiana (ACI), which had grown apace since 1929, and this was accompanied by virulent anti-Church polemics in such Fascist newspapers as *Il Lavoro Fascista* and *Il Popolo D'Italia*.[13] The 1931 crisis was about more than a few thousand Catholic youth and quasi-labour organisations: it was also about bitter disillusionment on both sides over the outcome of *Conciliazione*. The Duce had hoped to be able to harness papal diplomacy to the objectives of his foreign policy, and the pope had hoped to use the regime as his secular arm for a Catholic restoration in Italy.[14] Neither had been successful.

The signing of the 1931 September Accords signalled an end to the conflict between the Holy See and the regime. The Accords were meant to be a clarification of Article 43 of the Concordat of 1929, recognising, but also regulating, the operations of Italian Catholic Action. The 1931 Accords reiterated the autonomy of ACI and the ban on priests from playing a political role, but also restricted Catholic Action's activities in the youth and labour fields.[15] Nevertheless, as will be seen, ACI recovered from the crisis of 1931 and continued to grow throughout the 1930s, particularly in its youth organisations.

Catholic anti-Fascism

With the dissolution of the Partito Popolare in 1926, there was little space left for autonomous political activity on the part of Catholic laymen. Even the clerico-Fascist supporters of the regime found it increasingly difficult to retain a place in the new political system. The Centro Nazionale Italiano, the major clerico-Fascist organisation, found its activities repudiated by the pope in 1929, and in the Plebiscite of 1929 it was allowed only four candidates in the single Fascist Party list. Apart from these elected MPs, the clerico-Fascists could count fewer than a dozen members of the Senate, thus henceforth the

'Catholic' presence and influence inside the Fascist regime was to be marginal to say the least.[16]

There was obviously even less space for Catholic anti-Fascism. Only a handful of popolare leaders followed Luigi Sturzo into exile: De Gasperi was caught trying to leave Italy, arrested, tried, imprisoned and eventually released into the custody of the Vatican who became responsible for his 'good behaviour'. De Gasperi, along with another exponent of *popolarismo*, Guido Gonella, found refuge and employment inside the Vatican itself, where they pondered on their experience of Italian politics in 1920s and contributed articles to several Catholic publications, including *L'Osservatore Romano*. In any case, the differences between the main exiled Popolare leaders, Sturzo, Ferrari, Donati and Miglioli – the latter's strange odyssey eventually took him to Moscow in search of the 'peasant international' – prevented the formation of a Partito Popolare in exile on the lines of the Communists and Socialists or the radical-reforming Giustizia e Libertà organisation. Sturzo's anti-Fascist activities in Belgium, Britain and finally America had a minimal influence on Catholics in Italy.[17]

The majority of ex-popolare politicians retired into a private life relatively undisturbed by police surveillance and harassment. Nevertheless, the voice of that 'silent minority' was occasionally heard. When Cardinal Schuster, archbishop of Milan, publicly claimed that 'From the beginning, Catholic Italy and even the pope himself, have blessed Fascism', this provoked the outraged condemnation of 300 Catholic laymen in his diocese.[18] But only two overtly anti-Fascist organisations succeeded in attracting significant Catholic support during the years of the regime: the Alleanza Nazionale (National Alliance) of Lauro de Bosis, which was not, in any case, strictly speaking Catholic in ideological orientation and was quickly crushed by the police in 1931, and the Movimento Guelfo D'Azione (Guelf Action Movement) of Piero Malvestiti. The latter was the only genuinely Catholic anti-Fascist movement to be tried by Mussolini's Special Military Tribunal.[19]

Pius XI and Italian Catholic Action

The only relatively 'free space' in which Catholic political activity of any sort could be carried on was inside the organisations of Italian Catholic Action. To understand the consequently important role of Catholic Action in Italian politics and society in the Fascist period, it is necessary to remember Pius XI's broader strategy of using Catholic Action organisations throughout the universal Church as means of fulfilling the objectives of his pontificate. Papa Ratti's motto was 'Restaurare omnia in Cristo', and the restoration of all things in Christ was also at the heart of his encyclical *Ubi Arcano Dei* of 1922 (see Chapter 5, pp. 81–2). Thus Catholic Action was to be the instrument of that Christian restoration of Italian society.

It would not be extravagant to compare Pius XI's determination to bring about a 'Christian restoration of Italian society in a Catholic sense' to the palingenetic mission of Fascism. Certainly, Mussolini and Fascism sought the regeneration of Italian society and the State from the 'decadence' into which they claimed it had fallen after the brief glories of the Risorgimento. They wished to create a 'new Fascist man' (and perhaps woman) and thus restore Italian national vitality and military strength in preparation for the next stage of the international social, Darwinian struggle.[20] Papa Ratti, for his part, proposed nothing less than turning the clock back, restoring to the Roman Catholic religion the position that it had enjoyed in Italian society prior to 1861 or, more realistically, prior to 1848, before, that is, the liberals had taken power in Piedmont and begun the introduction of ecclesiastical legislation.

As the principal instrument of Christian 'restoration', after February 1929 Italian Catholic Action endeavoured to operate as a pressure group on the Fascist regime in such matters as 'public morality', censorship and the activities of non-Catholic religious groups. Mussolini and other Fascist bosses resented and resisted this campaign, and it thus became a contributory cause of the crisis of 1931.

Obviously, the key to Catholic life under Fascism was the Church's massive and organisationally efficient network of 24,000 parishes, spread throughout the peninsula, to most of which were attached various Catholic Action groups, men/women and youth, and recreational/sporting facilities. In addition, there were separate and elite organisations of the Federazione Universitari Cattolici Italiani (FUCI), Movimento Laureato and various professional/ occupational groups.[21] Despite the scars left behind by the 1931 crisis, Catholic Action continued to operate autonomously and, by the mid-1930s, had begun to grow in numbers: the Catholic youth organisation alone grew from 250,000 to 400,000 members between 1930 and 1939. The ban on athletic and labour activities notwithstanding, Catholic Action found ways of reinforcing and expanding the presence of the Church in Italian society.[22] Finally, at the heart of Pius XI's plans for the 'redemption of Italian society' was the Catholic University of the Sacred Heart in Milan. Founded in 1921 in the reign of his predecessor, and presided over by Fr Agostino Gemelli, the Catholic University was intended by Pius XI to be the intellectual powerhouse of a new, Catholic Italy, providing the intellectual cadres for its 're-conquest' by the Church: to this end, a special school was established to train the cadres of Catholic Action.[23]

The Church was not slow to exploit new technology as a means of exerting influence on the masses. In 1931, Guglielmo Marconi inaugurated the Vatican radio station that would become a potent voice to many peoples, not just the Italians.[24] Despite Pius XI's strictures on the dangers of motion pictures in his encyclical *Vigilanti Cura* of 1936, the Church recognised the potential of the cinema, and the Italian Catholic movement thus provided itself with a crucial instrument of cultural control in the 'age of the cinema'. By the end of the 1930s, for example, there were 546 *sale parrocchiali* (parish cinemas), which according to Dunnage 'competed with the regime regarding control over what films the public should be allowed to see'. The Church also possessed parish theatres, in which plays of a thoroughly Catholic content were performed.[25] In addition, the 1930s saw a massive growth in the periodical publications of religious congregations. It was in this period, for example, that *Famiglia Cristiana* was founded by the Paulists: it would go on to become Italy's most popular weekly by the 1950s (see Chapter 9, p. 172).

In these and other ways, the Church was able to preserve the essential elements of the Catholic sub-culture in Italy under Fascism and, to some extent, even expand it. Moreover, it is clear that the Vatican under Pius XI did not necessarily assume that Fascism was there to stay; indeed, at times, especially during the Great Depression, it expressed serious doubts about its durability.[26] Thus Pius XI had contingency plans if and when Fascism fell, and Italian Catholic Action was at the heart of them. It was seen by the pope, and by some of its leaders, as the basis for a political alternative to the regime, with cadres being prepared for power in the youth movements, especially the FUCI and Movimento Laureato, under the tutelage of Mgr G-B Montini (later Pope Paul VI), who was working in the Vatican Secretariat of State.[27] In August 1943, after the collapse of the Fascist regime, ACI had become the largest and most influential mass movement in Italy, and its head, Luigi Gedda, offered to place the resources of this formidable organisation, which with its dependent groups numbered over 1.5 million members, at the service of Mussolini's successor, Marshal Badoglio, and his post-Fascist government.[28]

The Italian Church under Pius XI

From the beginning of his reign, Pius XI devoted considerable attention to the specific needs of the Italian Church. It is clear that he wanted to make it a more national church, and to ensure that it would be more Tridentine in its functioning and religiosity. In particular, he continued the efforts of Pius X to improve priestly education, chiefly by the formation of regional seminaries, especially in the south, following the publication of his encyclical *Deus Scientiarum Dominus* in 1931.[29] He also spent a significant part of the money acquired from Italy in the Financial Convention of 1929 in building clergy houses, again especially in the south and the islands, where they were frequently wanting.[30]

Ironically, given the emphasis in Tridentine reforms on the centrality of the parish, expressions of Catholic religiosity increasingly took place outside the parish in the 1920s and 1930s. Catholic priests now took on more official roles as chaplains to the armed forces and prisons, the Fascist youth organisations, and even the Fascist Militia, precisely at a time when their numbers were diminishing.[31] Various branches of Catholic Action, plus ONARMO (Opera Nazional Assistenza Religiosa e Morale agli Operai), an organisation providing religious assistance to workers, and the Opera dei Ritiri Operai, which organised spiritual retreats for workers, and sought to provide religious experiences of different kinds to different categories of the population, such as teachers, students, doctors, nurses and assorted groups of workers, outside the formal parish structure.[32] This was also the period in which mass liturgical and extra-liturgical celebrations increased in number with Eucharistic and Marian congresses at both a regional and national level and also ceremonies connected with the cult of Christ the King.[33]

Just as significant was the fact that Pius XI insisted on organising massive national and international events on a grand scale in Rome. Between 1922 and 1939, hardly a year went by without some great Catholic gathering in Rome, for example: in 1925 a Holy Year and Missionary Exhibition; in 1927 celebrations to mark the seven hundredth anniversary of St Francis; in 1929 celebrations for the pope's Sacerdotal Jubilee; in 1930 an International Exhibition of Sacred Art; in 1931 the fortieth anniversary celebrations of *Rerum Novarum*; in 1933–34 an extraordinary Holy Year; in 1935 the Exhibition of the Catholic Press; in 1936 the International Congress of Catholic Nurses; and in 1937 the International Congress of Catholic Doctors. Many of these events were, of course, designed for the edification and education of the whole Catholic world, but they were also intended to give Italian Catholics a stronger sense of national identity, a pride in living at the heart of Catholic civilisation. In addition, they were meant as a demonstration to Mussolini and the Fascists that whatever else, Rome was still the 'panting heart' of Catholicism.

The Church and Italian society under Fascism, 1929–38

Ironically, the first elements in Italian civil society to feel the effects of the Conciliazione were not Italy's Catholics, but arguably its Protestants and its Jews. In his anxiety to prove that truly he had not sold out to the Church, Mussolini introduced two pieces of legislation to protect and regulate the position of the religious minorities in Italy. The law on the *culti ammessi* (literally the 'admitted' or permitted denominations), which was approved shortly after the Conciliazione in 1929, recognised most of Italy's minuscule Protestant churches.[34] Whereas some of them, such as the Waldensians and the Methodists, were long-established, others represented one of the fruits of return migration from the USA, and were accordingly especially strong in southern Italy. Whether the law actually afforded greater protection in practice against the bigoted Catholic crusade against Protestant proselytism and the simple ignorance and prejudice of the average Italian state official is doubtful; some Protestant groups were regarded with suspicion by the police simply because they were of (recent) foreign origin, such as the Baptists, Seventh-Day Adventists, Salvation Army and the Jehovah's Witnesses, others because of Masonic links.[35] The Pentecostalists were never given official recognition and were outlawed in 1940 because many of them were conscientious objectors, and the same happened to the Jehovah's Witnesses, for similar reasons.[36] The harassment of some Protestant churches worsened in the late 1930s, but it was nothing compared to their treatment at the hands of the Christian Democratic 'regime' after 1948 (see Chapter 7, p. 118).

The Jewish communities of Italy also received official state recognition by the law of 1932.[37] Jewish leaders publicly expressed considerable gratitude at the time for the law, though, of course, the legislation did nothing to protect the Jews when Mussolini decided to introduce the Racial Laws in 1938 (see below, pp. 102–3). Arguably, the legislation on the Jewish and Protestant minorities was entirely politically motivated, a pragmatic move to assert the State's independence of the Catholic Church in matters of religion and an opportunity to enforce Fascist totalitarianism on groups that, precisely because of their uncertain minority status, had lain outside of the bounds of Mussolini's putative 'totalitarian state', no different, in fact, from the moves to bring cultural, social, sporting and youth organisations under the direct surveillance and control of the dictatorship.

From the end of the 1920s, an increasing convergence between the Church's teaching and certain key policies of the Fascist regime became discernible. In particular, Fascist policies on women, marriage and the family, as encapsulated in the Rocco Criminal Code of 1932 and labour legislation, seemed to enshrine the most cherished elements of Catholic social teaching.[38] In his encyclical, *Casti Connubi* ('On Christian Marriage') of 1930, Pius XI very forcefully stated the Church's traditional teaching on gender, about the subordinate, differentiated role of the woman in family life, to the virtual exclusion of a role in social, even less political life.[39] Considering that Mussolini had once supported a motion at the Socialist Congress of 1912 condemning marriage, that he himself had 'lived in sin' with Rachele and had had several children out of wedlock, his 'conversion' to Catholic morality in matters of the family was wholly opportunistic.[40] As the pro-natalist 'Demographic Campaign', which included the establishment of a national health service for mother and child – ONMI – got under way after 1927, Futurist misogyny and Fascist male chauvinism, for that is what it essentially was, manifested itself in the propagation of an ideal type of woman as 'Madre e Sposa esemplare', the exemplary mother and wife, which suited the Church perfectly. Equally, Fascism's consequent ban on both artificial contraception and abortion was welcomed by the Church, even if, as Perry Willson has pointed out, the state legislation against abortion was probably less strict than the Church's total ban as expressed in *Casti Connubi*.[41] But Fascism's policies on 'public morality' never seemed to satisfy completely Italy's most militant groups – especially Catholic Action – as Fascist ministers complained. They were forever inveighing against *tabarins* and other cabarets of doubtful taste and decency, against anything that remotely smacked of pornography in the cinema and even against public dances and female athletics – the latter was a particular bête noire of Pius XI.[42] Catholic Action was also responsible at a diocesan and parochial level for the campaign against blasphemy: no less a person than Mussolini himself was the national patron of the Anti-Blasphemy Committee, which must have caused not a little embarrassment in the Vatican and hilarity in Fascist circles since Mussolini was notoriously prone to the vice himself![43] In broader terms, it has to be said that Fascism was not very willing to play the part of the secular, long arm of the Church, enforcing its morality in Italian society.

Even Mussolini's rather half-baked policy of 'Ruralisation', which has to be understood in the context of long-term plans for wars of expansion and a consequent necessity of autarky (self-sufficiency), which emphasised the 'sound' moral values of the countryside against the decadent ones of the city, chimed in with Italian Catholicism's cultural values.[44] The heartlands of Italian Catholicism *were* in the rural, agrarian and small town milieu of, especially, northern, eastern, and to a lesser extent, central Italy. The peasantry and lower middle classes of those areas, as we have seen, had a strong loyalty and attachment to the Church. So it is not surprising that the participation of the Catholic rural parochial clergy in the Battle for Grain, the attempt to make Italy self-sufficient in the production of cereals, its absolute staple, was strongly encouraged by the Fascist authorities.[45] When the Fascists began to mobilise rural women, in the *massaie rurali* organisation, there was no Church opposition, even in the 'white' areas of north-eastern Italy. As Willson points out: 'On the question of gender roles, the importance of the family and the dangers of urban lifestyles, Church and regime were in broad agreement.'[46]

Fascist corporatism, and the consequent construction of a 'Corporate State' between 1926 and 1934 was, theoretically, another Fascist policy convergent with Catholic ideals, in this case those of Catholic social doctrine. Indeed, faced by the twin evils of Soviet Communism and capitalism in crisis as a result of the Great Depression, Pius XI strongly privileged the Catholic tradition of corporatism in his encyclical *Quadragesimo Anno* of 1931.[47] Some Italian

Catholic intellectuals, such as Fr Angelo Brucculeri of *La Civiltà Cattolica* and the group of social scientists gathered around such future Christian Democratic politicians as Amintore Fanfani and Paolo Emilio Taviani based at Milan's Catholic University, supported Fascist corporatism.[48] Taviani eventually repented of his support for Fascist corporatism and passed over to the anti-Fascist resistance in 1943. But Pius himself was guarded, even mildly critical in his comments on Fascist corporatism, which was yet another contributory cause of the breakdown in relations with the regime in the summer of 1931.[49]

What effect, if any, did Fascism have upon grass-roots Italian Catholicism? Very little, in all probability. Would the average small peasant proprietor or tenant farmer necessarily have felt any gratitude to Fascism for defending his land against the Socialist (and perhaps even Miglioli's Catholic) peasant leagues with their dreams of collectivisation when he might also have remembered Fascist squadrist violence against his own kind? As Vickie de Grazia has pointed out, Fascism's *dopolavoro* organisation, which provided subsidised leisure-time activities and facilities for various categories of employees, was much more effective in the cities than the countryside and small towns, among state or large-scale private employees than agricultural workers of any description, so that form of Fascist 'socialisation' of the Italian masses barely touched the majority of Italian Catholics.[50] According to Ernesto Brunetta, in the 'white' heartlands:

> the Church, particularly after the signing of the Concordat, participated, sang praises and waved pennants, just like everywhere else in Italy. But here they always held back a little, they were never entirely wholehearted. This was something which the Fascist functionaries, whose job it was to keep an eye on the clergy's behaviour, often failed to understand. It is true that the Church participated, but cautiously, following its own agenda, with an outlook on life, which, from the start, undermined the relationship.[51]

The reports of the police and prefects, particularly in the early 1930s, confirm this judgement. [52]

Vatican diplomacy and Italian foreign policy, 1929–38

Church–state relations at home, and the role of Catholicism in Italian society under Fascism, were also affected by the relationship between Italy and the Holy See as players on the international scene. Though the 1929 Treaty declared that the Holy See 'remains and will remain outside the temporal rivalries between other States and outside the international congresses set up with that object . . .',[53] it is clear that Mussolini intended to harness the influence of Vatican diplomacy in the service of Fascist foreign policy from the beginning.[54] In fact, Mussolini's disappointment with the refusal of the Vatican to support his anti-British aims in the Middle and Near East, and in his ongoing struggle with Yugoslavia, not to mention Fascism's attempts to 'Italianise' the German, Slovenian and Croatian speaking minorities in the north-eastern territories acquired by Italy in 1919, partly explains the bitterness of the 1931 crisis.[55]

Later in the 1930s, the Vatican and Italy had more clearly defined common enemies on the international horizon. Both, for example, had reasons to support Austrian independence against the threat of a resurgent Nazi Germany bent on *Anschluss* between 1933 and 1937, and both regarded the troubled politics of the Second Spanish Republic between 1931 and 1936 with alarm, especially the growing electoral influence of the variegated Marxist and anarchist left in that country. Though the Vatican tried to maintain a neutral stance towards the two sides in the Spanish Civil War that broke out in July 1936, its essential interests in the face of violent republican anti-clericalism were similar to those of Franco and Mussolini. Italian Catholics, including the diocesan press, not surprisingly, took the Nationalist side against the 'red' republic and its anti-clerical violence.[56] Along with the invasion of Ethiopia, Spain was another foreign policy issue on which the Italian Catholic world was at one with official Fascist policy: Spain was an anti-Bolshevik crusade for Italian bishops and clergy.[57]

From the outset, the Italian invasion of Ethiopia in October 1936 drew a strong patriotic response from the average Italian Catholic, somewhat in contrast with Pius XI's own rather ambivalent public statements during the conflict, and the League of Nations economic sanctions in December 1935 and later the capture of Addis Abeba in May 1936 truly united Italian Catholic opinion around the Duce.[58] The successful Ethiopian war of 1935–36, like the previous failed campaigns against Ethiopia in 1888 and 1896, evoked powerful patriotic emotions among Italian Catholics, most especially the bishops.[59] But there were still some doubters, even among the clergy, such as the one who advised women wishing to contribute their wedding rings to the collecting of gold to fight sanctions: 'Why are you giving your gold to the Motherland for another war which will kill you? You are mad. Buy a one-lira ring and hand that in.'[60]

The negative attitude of the western powers, Britain and France, to Italy's invasion of Ethiopia and especially the imposition of sanctions pushed Mussolini into a more favourable stance towards Nazi Germany, particularly following the help given by Hitler to circumvent sanctions. The intervention of both dictators on the side of Franco in the Spanish Civil War helped encourage this rapprochement, and by the autumn of 1936, Mussolini was proclaiming the existence of a 'Rome-Berlin Axis' around which, henceforth, European politics would orbit. This was an unforeseen and alarming development for the pope. Angered by Hitler's repeated violations of the *Reichskonkordat* which had been concluded between the Holy See and the new Nazi regime in July 1933 and the growing evidence of the racial and even neo-pagan character of German National Socialism, Pius XI condemned various aspects of the Nazi regime in his encyclical *Mit Brennender Sorge* of July 1937.[61] Following Mussolini's tough stand against Hitler after the assassination of Austrian Chancellor Dollfuss in the summer of 1934, the pope's best hope had been that Mussolini would lead a 'third force' of Catholic European states to counterbalance *both* the Soviet Union *and* Nazi Germany. That hope was dashed by Mussolini's acquiescence in *Anschluss* in March 1938. Henceforth, Pius XI and Vatican diplomacy turned increasingly towards Britain, France and the United States.[62]

What impact did this major and growing policy divergence at the top have upon Italian Catholicism in the provinces? The development of the Axis alliance, which culminated in the Italo-German Pact of Steel in May 1939, had important domestic consequences for Italy. Effectively speaking, there was a 'second wave' of Fascist totalitarianism from about 1937 onwards. This is the period of the 'reform of custom', the substitution of the formal 'you' – 'Lei' – by 'Voi' and the replacement of the traditional handshake greeting by the Fascist salute; this period also saw the introduction of the so-called *passo romano*, a thinly disguised version of the Prussian goose-step, into the Italian armed forces and the attempt to eradicate foreign linguistic influences, such as replacing 'bar' with the extraordinarily clumsy and cumbersome construct, 'qui-si-beve', literally, 'here one drinks'.[63]

Other significant developments were the increasing attempts to 'sacralise politics' in Fascist Italy from the beginning of the 1930s onwards.[64] Arguably all of the major European inter-war dictatorships tended towards a sacralisation of politics, including Stalin's Communist regime with its embalming of Lenin's corpse, the erection of his mausoleum along the Kremlin Wall and the development of 'pilgrimages' of the 'faithful' from all over the Soviet Union to view its founder. Under Italian Fascism, sacralisation took the form of carefully orchestrated 'oceanic gatherings' of the Fascist faithful to hear Mussolini in the public squares of Italy, replete with rituals, chanting and litanies. Fascism also increasingly borrowed from the vocabulary of Catholicism, using credos and decalogues, litanies and liturgies in the language of cults of the State and eventually of Mussolini himself.[65] If the Fascists thought that their efforts were filling an emotional/spiritual void left in the Italian people by secularisation, they were wrong. Catholicism, in its many forms, was still a strong, vibrant religion lived at the grass roots of Italian society.[66] And Pius

XI criticised the Fascist tendency to what he described as 'statolatry' in his encyclical *Non Abbiamo Bisogno*, during the crisis between the Church and the regime in July 1931, and in private he condemned the adulation that was increasingly lavished upon Mussolini himself.[67] The pope need not have worried because the cult of the Duce had weak roots in Italian society by comparison with the continuing popular loyalty towards the monarchy and the timeless charisma of the papacy itself.

Italian Catholics and the Racial Laws of 1938

Catholics were probably just as irritated as other Italians by these attempts to subvert the established niceties of Italian societies, but a much more serious policy change came with the introduction of the Racial Laws in 1938. We have very clear evidence of Pius XI's hostility towards Mussolini's introduction of the Racial Laws, and not just on the grounds that they violated that part of the Concordat that reserved to the Church the right to decide who could and could not marry, i.e. by forbidding marriages of Catholics and non-Aryans. Pius XI rejected the laws on grounds of principle, and also because he believed that they constituted another example of the baleful influence exercised in Italy by Nazi Germany, thanks to the Axis relationship.[68] His most public riposte to them was his famous comment, 'Spiritually we are all Jews', but the introduction of the Racial Laws prompted a much more considered, substantial and serious response, in his commissioning of the encyclical *Humani Generis Unitas* from American Jesuit John Lafarge as a formal, public condemnation on the part of the papacy of Nazi racial theory in general and racial anti-Semitism in particular.[69] But the 'hidden' encyclical only reached the pope when he was on his deathbed, and his successor decided, rather diplomatically, not to publish it. Thus was missed an important opportunity to isolate Nazi anti-Semitism before it moved onto its more murderous stage.

Overall, however, Italian Catholic reactions to the Racial Laws were much more complex and ambiguous than those of the pope. In January 1939 at Bologna, Padre Gemelli, rector of the Catholic University, spoke of the Jews as 'the deicide people', tragically unable to belong to Italy 'because of their blood and because of their religion'.[70] On the other hand, *La Civiltà Cattolica*, which had for decades waged a ferocious campaign of abuse against the Jews, was swift to distance itself from the introduction of what it perceived to be Nordic racism into Italy, and the official Vatican organ *L'Osservatore Romano* limited itself to deploring the unscientific nature of biological racism, while re-stating the right of societies to adopt segregation legislation to protect themselves against the Jews.[71] It is difficult to ascertain the state of grass-roots Catholic opinion, but it seems to have been as tepid and unenthusiastic about the Racial Laws as Italian opinion generally, and Binchy claims that, just as some leading princes of the Church, such as Schuster and the archbishop of Bologna, condemned racialism, so the lower clergy resisted the Racial Laws.[72] It seems likely that had Mussolini proceeded from the 1938 Racial Laws to measures of eugenic policy, such as sterilisation and euthanasia, as adopted by the Nazis, or even the compulsory pre-nuptial health checks for both sexes, which were being considered by the health authorities in the late 1930s, then there would have been sustained opposition from both the pope and the Italian Church generally.[73]

'A marriage of convenience'

According to Renzo de Felice, the relationship between church and state in Fascist Italy was a 'marriage of convenience', one in which neither side was wholly committed, ideologically and psychologically, to the other.[74] The wariness, distance at a top level, despite the fulsome praise lavished by the one upon the other *in public*, was also mirrored very faithfully at the level of ordinary life. Brunetta's point about the Church in the 'white provinces' never being wholeheartedly committed to Fascism could be applied elsewhere in Italy.[75] Some historians have talked about Catholic attitudes towards the regime constituting a kind of *afascismo*,[76] rather than anything as positive as anti-Fascism, though, as has been seen, pockets of the latter did exist and manifest themselves, especially in the early 1930s. Scoppola has talked about Italian Catholicism as 'an island of separateness' or 'otherness' in Fascist Italy.[77] Certainly, elements of the Catholic sub-culture were in some sense 'separate' from or 'other' than Fascism. Like other groups and institutions, the monarchy and the armed forces, for example, the Church could afford to be largely autonomous of the regime, so long, that is, as it burned the necessary grain of incense on the altar of the cult of the Duce, and under the Church's very ample wings many Catholics who were less than committed to Fascism were able to shelter, including people such as Alcide De Gasperi.

Bosworth, in his adumbration of the concept of 'everyday totalitarianism', has made the very valid point that ordinary Italians often managed to get away with the most minimal form of lip service to the new order, often succeeded in resisting or challenging its demands without too serious consequences, and sometimes even exploited the regime for their own ends through corrupt perversion of its policies.[78] Arguably, Italians, especially southern Italians, had always done this with whatever regime was in power, so we should hardly be surprised if this happened under Fascism. Catholic Italy, especially in the countryside and small towns of the northern and central parts of the peninsula, lived in parallel with official 'Fascist Italy', bowing the knee when absolutely necessary and even joining in enthusiastically at times of national rejoicing as after the capture of the Ethiopian capital, Addis Abeba, in May 1936. But there were frictions – especially over the activities of Catholic Action and its youth organisations and/or the failure of some Catholic parents to send their children to join the Balilla, the official Fascist youth organisation.[79] The period of real tension was between 1929 and 1931 when the exact balance of power between the Church and Fascism had not yet been settled, and there was, in consequence, considerable public conflict between the Vatican and the regime that inevitably had an impact on the complex realities of Italian civil society, and at a time when Italian society was itself unsettled by the disturbing economic effects of the Great Depression.[80]

Catholic Italy and the outbreak of the Second World War

The election of Cardinal Eugenio Pacelli as Pius XII to succeed Pius XI in March 1939 was almost a foregone conclusion, Pacelli having been Pius XI's designated 'dauphin' for some years, precisely because of his vast diplomatic experience and especially his knowledge of Germany.[81] Pius XII, from the very beginning of his reign, which almost exactly coincided with Hitler's occupation of Prague in violation of the September 1938 Munich Agreement, set out to preserve peace. In conjunction with the other 'great neutral', President Franklin D. Roosevelt, who had specifically appointed a 'Personal Representative' to the pope in 1939, Pius was to work tirelessly to prevent the outbreak of war in 1939.[82]

This peace commitment on the part of the Vatican was one element in the situation that presented itself to Mussolini at the end of August 1939 after Hitler had invaded Poland. Mussolini had other reasons for not joining his German ally at this point, but the state of Italian public opinion was a crucial factor. The Vatican was not the only element of the Italian 'establishment' to oppose war: the monarchy and, indeed, sections of the armed forces closest to it were also opposed. As the diary of Galeazzo Ciano, Mussolini's son-in-law and foreign minister, demonstrates, the Duce's patience with both papacy and monarchy was beginning to wear thin by 1939, and he promised to 'settle accounts' with both after a successful war. Giovanni Miccoli cites clear evidence of 'a gradual prevalence inside the [Fascist] party of an openly anti-Catholic and anti-traditionalist line, inaugurated by the violent speech of Mussolini on 3 January 1942 to the PNF Directory', as the war continued.[83]

Wider Italian Catholic opinion was also pacifist at this point, which was hardly surprising given the fact that the Catholic press, from *L'Osservatore Romano* downwards, had been criticising not only German National Socialism but German as opposed to Italian culture generally over the years since 1936 when the Axis had been developing.[84] In any case, it was a trifle 'unnatural', to say the least, to expect Italians – who had long seen 'i Tedeschi' (the Germans), rather than strictly speaking 'gli Austriaci' (the Austrians), as the historical national enemy, a feeling reinforced by the German army's presence on the front line, Venezia Julia, from 1916 onwards – to accept Nazi Germany as the new ally. Unlike the Intervention Crisis of 1915, in 1940 Italian Catholics were not in a position to openly proclaim their hostility towards a war on the side of Nazi Germany. As Giorgio Rumi has explained, 'Catholics, bishops, priests and lay people, gave their outward obedience to the State because there was no alternative.'[85] Certainly, there is no evidence that 'Catholic Italy' was any more enthusiastic about the prospect of war on the side of the Germans in June 1940, when Mussolini declared war on both Britain and France, than it had been in September 1939.

But Catholics, like other Italians, did their duty as required, and would have felt as strongly as anyone else about the expansion of the empire and ultimate victory. On the other hand, as Davide Rodogno has suggested, the morale of the average Italian private soldier was sustained not by party propaganda but by the ministrations of the Catholic chaplains, and this is confirmed by the widespread diffusion in the Italian armed forces of the practice of reciting the 'La Preghiera del Soldato' ('The Soldier's Prayer').[86] It is worth quoting his comments here in some detail:

> Mussolini relied on the military chaplains to help sustain the soldiers' morale. This demonstrates very clearly the failure of the Fascist totalitarian project. The Fascist *uomo nuovo* [new man] would never have seen the light of day had his spiritual guide been the Catholic priest instead of the party.[87]

All this suggests that the Church's role in Italy during the Second World War was rather more extensive and official than in the First World War and that, in broader terms, Mussolini's Fascist, totalitarian state was underpinned by Catholic patriotism. And as Malgeri argues, as the authority of the regime declined, so the prestige of the clergy, especially the rural clergy, increased.[88]

As the war progressed, as Italian military defeat followed defeat, in Egypt, Greece, Ethiopia (lost to the British in 1941) and North Africa, not to mention the terrible Italian losses at Stalingrad on the Eastern Front in 1942–43, and as the Allied bombing offensive against the Italian peninsula revealed the inadequacy of air raid precautions and support for the civilian population generally, Italians of all faiths and none became disaffected from the regime.[89] When Mussolini was overthrown by a conspiracy between dissident Fascists and the king in July 1943, the Holy See stood in pole position as a major intermediary between Italy and the (Western) Allies; indeed, there is evidence that Ciano (dismissed as foreign minister in February 1943) and various elements in the Vatican had put out peace feelers to the Allies before the collapse of the regime.[90]

Invasion, German occupation and resistance

After the German occupation of the Italian peninsula, following the Allied invasion in July 1943, the Church took up a strictly diplomatic, legalistic attitude to the situation. On the one hand, it continued to maintain diplomatic relations with the king's government in the south, as the legal, continuing government of the Italian State; on the other, it refused to recognise Mussolini's restored Fascist regime, the Italian Social Republic based in the north, though bishops and priests everywhere in Italy were obviously willing to treat with whichever authority – royal government, Mussolini's restored Fascist regime, German or Allied occupiers – they found themselves under, sometimes all of them at once. The Church's attitude towards the Armed Resistance that sprang up in the hills and mountains of Axis-controlled northern and central Italy from September 1943 onwards was rather different. The Vatican, and many bishops on the ground, were extremely suspicious of the Resistance, even where there was significant Catholic participation in it. Two factors determined this position. The first was the fear of German reprisals on the civilian population, which, it has to be said, became increasingly fierce as the Resistance became more widespread and effective, and one needs only cite the examples of the atrocities at Marzabotto in Emilia-Romagna and the Fosse Ardeatine in Rome as examples of this. The second was the fear of the massive influence of the Italian Left, in particular the Italian Communist Party, over the Resistance: by mid-1944, it has been calculated that two-thirds of the partisan formations fighting the Germans and the Fascists were led by the Communists, or their close allies, the Socialists.[91]

There was significant active Catholic involvement in the Resistance, though it was not numerically very large. Despite reprisals, *passive* participation by Catholics in the Resistance was, however, very widespread, involving Catholic peasants and parochial clergy sheltering escaped Allied prisoners of war, Jews and partisans, and providing food, other material assistance and information about the Fascist and German forces to the partisans.[92] The hiding of Jews and anti-Fascist leaders took place on an especially large scale in Rome (under German occupation from September 1943 to June 1944), where religious houses and the Holy See's many extra-territorial possessions, and even the Vatican itself, were employed for this purpose.[93] Inevitably, Catholic participation in the Resistance was greatest in northern Italy, in the white provinces of Venetia, Julian Venetia (Friuli), where the Germans were in direct administrative control, Lombardy, southern Piedmont and even parts of Emilia-Romagna. Frequently it was Catholic Action cadres and groups that furnished the Catholic contingent, such as the Fiamme Verdi Tito Speri brigade in Brescia and the Osoppo Brigades in Friuli created from elements of the Movimento Laureato. Piero Malvestiti of the Movimento Guelfo D'Azione played a key role in the Milan-based council of the Resistance, the Comitato di Liberazione Nazionale di Alt'Italia (CLN).[94] There is even evidence that the Vatican's financial manager, Bernardino Nogara, had close links with the CLN in German-occupied Rome and may have acted as the Vatican's unofficial representative to it.[95]

Catholic participation in the Armed Resistance was crucial to the post-war political situation in Italy. It helped wash away the 'sin' of collaboration between the Church and Fascism, gave a patriotic character to the re-emerging Catholic political forces, and guaranteed those forces, the Christian Democrats, representation on the central Comitato di Liberazione Nazionale, the overall governing body of the Resistance movement. Italian Catholics had thus paid their passage and earned a secure place for their leaders, with De Gasperi at their head, in the first Resistance Unity government formed by Bonomi after the liberation of Rome, in June 1944.

Chapter 7

THE AGE OF CATHOLIC 'TRIUMPHALISM'(1945−58)

Italy and the papacy at the end of the Second World War

THE HISTORY OF ITALY IN THE IMMEDIATE post-war years, until at least 1958, is incomprehensible without a clear grasp of the dominant influence of the papacy over the peninsula in this period, a situation that led Richard Webster to describe the country as 'The Papal State of the Twentieth Century'.[1] Writing in 1950, Frederico Chabod likened the position of the papacy in the Italian peninsula after the end of the Second World War to that which it had enjoyed after the fall of the Roman Empire.[2] Certainly, after the collapse of Fascism in July 1943, the papacy stood in a powerful position in relation to the Italian State, which, following the armistice of 8 September, had virtually ceased to exist as an international entity. Though recognised as a 'co-belligerent' with the Allies, it lacked effective and credible armed forces until after war's end, it had limited diplomatic relations, and it would not be admitted to the United Nations; in consequence it would not effectively re-enter the international community until after the signing of the peace treaty in 1947.[3] Within the Italian peninsula, the authority and jurisdiction of the royal government was confined to those territories fully behind the front line, and though they obviously increased as the Allies steadily advanced north against the German forces, even that authority was contested in some areas by very independent, and often explicitly anti-royalist, temporary Resistance administrations.

By comparison, the papacy, whose international stature had been enormously strengthened by the development of a 'special relationship' with the Roosevelt administration (see Chapter 6), was in a strong position. The efforts of Vatican diplomacy to persuade the Allies to spare the Eternal City the horrors of aerial bombardment and, when they failed, Pius XII's visits to the bombed areas of Rome during the summer of 1943, while the hapless Mussolini was paying court to Hitler elsewhere, greatly enhanced 'the personality cult' surrounding the pope himself. In consequence, in the late 1940s the citizens of Rome, or at least their council representatives, would erect plaques to celebrate the pope's status as *Defensor Civitas*, in gratitude for his efforts to protect his native city.[4] The reputation of Pius XII rode high in the post-war period, and did not become seriously challenged until the early 1960s when the first doubts were raised about his role during the Holocaust.

In fact, papal diplomacy had emerged as a key player in shaping the post-Fascist future of Italy sometime before the end of the war. As early as the winter of 1942–43, there is evidence of attempts by anti-Mussolini elements in the regime to use the Vatican as a conduit to the Allies in the hope of negotiating a separate peace.[5] Ciano's appointment as ambassador to the Vatican in February 1943, following his dismissal as Italian foreign minister in Mussolini's last cabinet reshuffle, also seems to have been designed to strengthen those efforts.[6] Both before and immediately after Mussolini's fall, American diplomacy was anxious to sound out the Vatican on the prospects for the *dopo-fascismo* (post-Fascist period). In their turn, the two under-secretaries of state, Tardini and Montini, were anxious to convey to Washington their concerns about the dangers of a Communist takeover, given the Communists' preponderant political influence in the Armed Resistance.[7]

Following the abolition of the monarchy by popular referendum in June 1946, and given the effective absence of the organised anti-Fascist parties and trade unions during the *ventennio,* the Roman Catholic Church with its network of 24,000 parishes throughout the peninsula was now the major surviving *national* Italian institution. It is thus not surprising that Catholicism, in various institutional forms, played a powerful, central role in the post-war reconstruction of Italy, social, economic, political and international. The modern papacy reached the apogee of its power in the reign of Pius; indeed, Alberto Spinosa has described Pius XII as 'l'ultimo papa', the last real pope.[8] Given the particular dominance that Pius XII exercised over the universal Church, the fact that 110 out of the 320 Italian dioceses were immediately subject to the Holy See, rather than forming a part of an ecclesiastical province, and the absence of an Italian Bishops' Conference until 1956, the Italian episcopal hierarchy lacked an independent voice for most of the period under discussion. This meant that, in effect, the papacy *was* the Church in Italy.

The personality and objectives of Pius XII

The first Roman pope for two centuries, Papa Pacelli was deeply conscious of his Roman and Italian obligations. He sought to continue the policies of his predecessor, Pius XI, that is, to seek the 'Christian restoration of Italian society',[9] but more immediate, pressing problems were Italy's economic reconstruction and her political settlement. Above all, the Vatican's concern was the Communist peril that was effectively born out of the Resistance experience and loomed large in parts of northern and central Italy in the years following the end of the war. Despite the Allies' insistence that the partisans lay down their weapons, many Communist groups were still well armed, with the result that 1945 and 1946 were scarred by the unlawful settling of scores against Fascist opponents, as well as anti-Fascist ones, including the murder of several priests in the so-called *triangolo della morte* ('the triangle of death').[10] This left areas of northern and central Italy, especially Emilia-Romagna, disturbed and under strong local Communist influence. The Resistance had been at one and the same time a war of national liberation, a civil war and a class war. Many Communist and Socialist partisans seriously believed that the Resistance movement could and would have a revolutionary outcome, that they would be able to sweep away not only the residues of Fascism but also the capitalist bourgeois state, an expectation encouraged by the success of Tito in Yugoslavia and the continuing Communist struggle in the Greek civil war.[11] When the Communist leader, Palmiro Togliatti, returned to Italy in 1944, he sought to dispel this illusion by explaining to his comrades Stalin's decision that since Italy fell into the Western sphere of influence according to the terms of the Yalta agreement, there could be no revolution there. From this point onwards, Togliatti pursued an essentially parliamentary road to socialism, committed to working with the other 'popular', 'progressive' forces – the Socialists and the Christian Democrats – in a government of Resistance Unity.[12] Nevertheless, some Communists never abandoned their revolutionary dreams, any more than they handed over all their arms to the Allied forces in May 1945: many simply buried them in their backyards, and kept alive their hopes of a real proletarian revolution in Italy. Given the undercurrent of industrial unrest, agrarian agitation and political violence (including neo-Fascist squadrism) between 1946 and 1947, many Italians, therefore, quite naturally feared a Communist insurrection and some Catholic Action leaders, especially those with partisan experience, created their own armed units just in case.[13] The protest strikes and uprisings that followed the attempt on Togliatti's life in July 1948 demonstrated the continuing strength of revolutionary feeling inside the PCI (Partito Communista Italiano).[14]

As well as the revolutionary aspirations of the Communists, there was more generalised desire for radical reform of Italy's institutions, which had grown up during the experience of anti-Fascism and the Resistance. The elections for the Constituent Assembly in June 1946 demonstrated the strength of the radical, reforming and revolutionary forces when 20 per cent of the vote went to the still-Marxist Socialist Party, 19 per cent to the Communists themselves and 25 per cent to mainly reformist and secularist elements of the centre and centre left.[15] And in the 'institutional' referendum that accompanied the elections, 54 per cent voted to abolish the monarchy, despite the papacy's support for an institution that it believed to be central to the maintenance of conservative continuity in Italy. The only clear bright light in this otherwise very volatile and uncertain situation as far as the papacy was concerned was that the 'Catholic' party, now renamed the Christian Democrats, was the largest party in the Constituent Assembly with over 35 per cent of the popular vote. In these circumstances, the Vatican regarded the struggle against revolutionary influences and the safeguarding of the Fascist legacy in the ecclesiastical arena, notably the Lateran Pacts of 1929, as its top priorities, and in particular, it bent all its efforts to persuading the Constituent Assembly engaged in drawing up Italy's new Republican Constitution to enshrine the Pacts in that document, as an insurance policy against a later, possibly leftward, shift in Italian politics.

The rebirth of political Catholicism, 1943–48

Faced by the formidable threat of the combined Marxist left in Italy, Pius XII leaned towards a Catholic/liberal-conservative dominated, semi-authoritarian state as a long-term replacement for Fascism, with possibly a ban on the Communist Party.[16] His preference for a resurrection of the clerico-moderate alliances of the Giolittian era – which had patently failed in the more polarised political situation of the post-First World War period, with the Catholic party playing a subordinate role in a 'grand coalition' presided over by a liberal-conservative politician from the pre-Fascist era, such as V.E. Orlando or Ivanoe Bonomi – demonstrates that, like his predecessor, Pius ultimately had little faith in parliamentary democracy and in the ability of a Catholic party and Catholic politicians to make it work successfully. Even the successful affirmation of the Christian Democrats in the 1946 elections, which was well in excess of any electoral result achieved by their precursors in the Partito Popolare between 1919 and 1924, did not convince him of their ability to give Italy strong, stable government. It would take the combined efforts of two men, Mgr Giambattista Montini, Vatican under-secretary of state, and Alcide De Gasperi, leader of the Catholic party, to change his mind and persuade him to accept the role of the Christian Democrats as the Church-sponsored party in Italian politics.[17] The Vatican was no monolith; on the contrary there were several competing centres of influence there, especially after the death of the secretary of state, Cardinal Maglione, in 1944 and the failure of Pius XII to replace him. Fr Messineo of the influential Jesuit journal *La Civiltà Cattolica* and Mgr Ottaviani, the half-blind and wholly reactionary secretary of the powerful Holy Office, preferred an 'Iberian' future for Italian politics, in other words an authoritarian, semi-dictatorial regime with solid Catholic support, on the model of Franco's Spain or Salazar's Portugal.[18] Cardinal Siri of Genoa, who later became the first president of the Italian Bishops' Conference, and thus was to exercise a powerful influence over the Italian Church for a couple of decades, also preferred this solution.[19]

At its rebirth along with the other major anti-Fascist parties after the fall of the regime in 1943, Italian political Catholicism exhibited strong signs of pluralistic tendencies. Though the core of the reborn Catholic party gathered around Alcide De Gasperi, the historic leader of political Catholicism, and the nucleus of other former Popolare leaders, such as Stefano Jacini and Giambattista Migliori in Milan, Giuseppe Spataro, Mario Cingolani and Mario Scelba in Rome, other new groups with divergent ideological positions had appeared on the scene. The emerging cadres formed by Montini in FUCI and Movimento Laureato were not so divergent in their ideas from old-style *popolarismo,* though their guiding principles, as enshrined in the Code of Camaldoli, differed in some significant respects from De Gasperi's programme for the Christian Democrats published in 1944, which became the founding charter of the new party.[20] The ideas of *ex-guelfisti* such as Piero Malvestiti and other Catholics who took part in the Resistance tended towards a more consciously 'third way' between capitalism and communism (though without any corporatist overtones) and were later to be incorporated into the Republican Constitution.[21]

A more advanced position was represented by another Catholic activist in the Resistance, Enrico Mattei. Together with the leaders of the re-emerging Catholic trade union movement, Gronchi and Grandi, he gave the most explicit commitment to the need for the State to intervene in the economy in the interest of social justice. The position of Giorgio La Pira, university professor and mayor of Florence, was even more radically different. Inspired by the belief in the need for a profound religious and moral transformation of society as the true basis for social justice, La Pira was committed to a Catholic integralist view of politics that required the active and dominant participation of the Church.[22] But the most radical of all Catholic political groupings to emerge in the aftermath of Fascism were the Christian Socialists of Livorno and the Christian left or Catholic Communists of Rome. Influenced by their contacts with the mainstream Marxist left, they advocated a workers' revolution as a social expression of the Gospel. Neither movement secured a mass base for its activities, and the members of the Rome group were excommunicated by Pius XII in 1949.[23] Ironically, when faced with the difficulties of Italy's immediate post-war economic situation, its dependence on American capital and the Christian Democrats' lack of a competent economic elite, all the various social theories of the Catholic party were forced to give way to the laissez-faire policies of an old-fashioned liberal, Luigi Einaudi, who was coopted by De Gasperi to organise Italian economic reconstruction.

The political pluralism latent in this ideological diversity was not to take any significant organisational form immediately after 1945, though it was later to manifest itself in the emergence of factions within the Christian Democratic Party of De Gasperi in 1954. In the short term, the various groupings very quickly coalesced into an essentially compact and united Catholic party, thus providing De Gasperi with the organisational base to bring about the triumph of the Christian Democrats between 1945 and 1948. De Gasperi's clever tactical manoeuvring was also assisted by the confused politics of the CLN, which laid claim to the government of post-Fascist Italy. Another vital factor was the concern of both the Vatican and the USA about the threat from the Italian Communist Party. The Christian Democratic leader's first stroke of luck was to be chosen as a compromise candidate for the premiership when Ferruccio Parri's administration was brought down by the conservatives in December 1945. As the first 'Catholic' prime minister of United Italy and as minister of the interior, the key ministry controlling the provincial governors, or prefects, and the police, De Gasperi was able to exploit the enormous political and ultimately electoral advantage that these two great offices give an Italian politician. His hand was also greatly strengthened by the tactically neutralist role that he insisted that his party should play in the contentious referendum on the monarchy that accompanied the general elections of 1946, with the result that, as has been seen, the Christian Democrats established themselves as the largest of the Italian political parties.

Even after this victory, the Vatican was unwilling to commit itself wholeheartedly to De Gasperi and the Christian Democrats. Only the defenestration of the Socialist and Communist ministers from the government in the spring of 1947, and De Gasperi's success in the same year in inserting a clause into the Constitution that confirmed the Lateran Pacts (against the fierce opposition of the Socialists and other lay parties) convinced the Vatican that the Christian Democrats were the sole reliable instrument for the defence of its interests in Italy.[24]

The Constituent Assembly, Article Seven of the Constitution and the PCI

The major test of the reliability of the Christian Democrats as the long arm of the Vatican in Italian politics came in 1947 during the debates over 'the insertion' of the Lateran Pacts into the emerging Republican Constitution. Alcide De Gasperi and the Catholic party, backed by elements of the far right such as the Monarchists and the Uomo Qualunque Party, proposed to give constitutional sanction to the Pacts by means of an article of the founding charter, which eventually became number seven:

> The State and the Catholic Church are, each in its own order, independent and sovereign. Their relationships are regulated by the Lateran Pacts. Modifications of the pacts, which have been accepted by the two sides, do not require a constitutional amendment.[25]

To this end, the Italian Catholic world, and especially Catholic Action and the Catholic press, were mobilised to sway public opinion and ensure that there were no defections from the ranks of Catholic MPs.[26] The lay parties, especially the Socialists and Communists, argued that the insertion of a special clause into the Constitution was not necessary, that the Pacts stood by themselves and that to 'incorporate' them in any way into the Constitution was an absurdity and a negation of democratic constitutional principles.[27] More seriously, they were concerned, quite rightly, about those clauses of the Pacts that negated some of the basic principles of the Constitution, such as freedom of religion.[28]

In reply, the Catholic press branded the opponents of Article Seven as anti-clerical and anti-religious and *L'Osservatore Romano* and the rest of the Catholic press warned that unless the new democratic regime sanctioned the Pacts, there would be 'a religious war'. De Gasperi, who would at other times seek to limit the direct influence of the Vatican in Italian politics (see below, pp. 119–20), on this occasion totally espoused the Church's point of view, realising that unless the Christian Democrats could deliver on Article Seven in the Constituent Assembly, they would never gain the wholehearted backing of the Vatican. This moral blackmail used by the Catholics paid off. After trying unsuccessfully to persuade the Christian Democrats to accept a compromise, the Communist Party leader Palmiro Togliatti, much to the shock and dismay of many both inside the party and among its allied parties, decided that 'the Republic was worth a mass', that the Party must support Article Seven, in order to avoid saddling the infant republic with a church–state conflict like the one that had been so damaging to the Kingdom of Italy during the first decades of its existence.[29] Togliatti was prescient in his recognition of the powerful role that the Church had now achieved for itself in the post-Fascist era, and against the background of a developing Cold War situation he hoped to prevent the Communist Party from being isolated. Without Communist support, Article Seven would not have been passed, since it required a vote by two-thirds of the Constituent Assembly. Historians and political scientists have used the phrase 'historic compromise' to describe the Communist Party's policies during the crisis-torn years of terrorism in the 1960s and 1970s, but arguably Togliatti's decision to support Article Seven was a historic compromise *ante litteram* of possibly even greater significance. Certainly, support for Article Seven was his first attempt at 'dialogue' with Italian Catholicism, part of a broader strategy of reaching some sort of modus vivendi with the Church while building up Gramscian-style hegemony for the Communist Party in Italian civil society.[30]

Interpretations of the long-term significance of Article Seven have varied: Martin Clark has argued, 'The assumption that Article Seven had somewhat subjected Italy to the Roman Catholic Church is one of the main red herrings of post-war Italian history', whereas the leading jurist, Carlo Calamandrei warned at the time that there had been introduced into the Constitution of Italy 'an irreconcilable contradiction that cannot fail to lead to conflicts between the principle of the religion of the state and the principle of freedom of conscience', and he was quickly proved right.[31]

The 1948 elections and the triumph of Catholicism

Italy was on the 'front line' in two senses during the Cold War. On the one hand, the southern end of Churchill's 'Iron Curtain', Trieste, was on Italy's redrawn frontier with Yugoslavia. The city was still in Italian hands, but only just, and it continued to be disputed with Tito's new Communist regime until 1954. Even more significantly, it could be said that the 'front line' in the Cold War actually passed through Italy itself and that the war was 'fought' on Italian territory because Italy possessed the second largest Communist Party in the West. Allied in a 'popular front' with the still strongly Marxian Italian Socialist Party, it presented a formidable challenge in the crucial 1948 general elections. Pope Pius XII and the Italian Church hierarchy viewed this situation in apocalyptic terms, especially in 1948. Their response was, as the sociologist Gianfranco Poggi has described it, 'one of maximum involvement and maximum commitment' of the Church's resources.[32] The Catholic movement, with its massive presence in most areas of Italian civil society, was summoned to battle, a huge propaganda effort was launched in 1948, and the pulpit was also used as a major instrument of anti-Communist propaganda in the weeks leading up to the poll. It was at this time that the hierarchy coined the slogan 'the political unity of Catholics', which was to be used, unsuccessfully, for the last time in 1994, in order to give support to the Christian Democrats.

Catholic propaganda treated the election as nothing less than a battle between God or Satan, Christ or Antichrist, civilisation or barbarism, liberty or slavery. All of Togliatti's attempts to avoid a confrontation with the Church, of which his agreement to support Article Seven of the Constitution is but one example, were to no avail. Togliatti's assurances of freedom to the Church in its mission were belied by what was happening in eastern and central Europe, where show trials of leading Catholic bishops such as the Hungarian Mindszenty and the Yugoslav Stepinac were accompanied by the arrests of other bishops and priests, and the closure of religious houses and Catholic lay organisations and the confiscation of church schools and landed property.[33] The general elections of 1948 were one of the key milestones in the history of post-war Italy. On the one hand, they confirmed and consolidated the dominant parliamentary position of the Christian Democrats; on the other, they relegated the left – Socialists and Communists – to the opposition benches. And the elections were conducted in a tense, turbulent, almost hysterical atmosphere because to the Church they represented a cosmic struggle between Catholicism and atheistic Communism, Good and Evil.

Against a background of a deepening Cold War situation, the Christian Democrats won the moral and financial support of both the Vatican and the USA in the crucial elections, the first under the new Republican Constitution, held in April 1948.[34] In particular, thanks to a Vatican policy of 'total commitment', the very substantial forces of Catholic Action were thrown into the contest on the side of the Catholic party. Whereas the organisations of the working class sub-culture had to be virtually rebuilt from scratch, Catholic Action had survived the Fascist era intact, and at war's end it was Italy's largest and most effective voluntary organisation, with branches in every one of the peninsula's 24,000 parishes. Though Article 43 of the Concordat (see Chapter 6, p. 92) forbade the involvement of Catholic Action in politics, its president, Luigi Gedda, got round this by creating the 'Civic Committees' as a front organisation for Catholic Action to intervene in the electoral campaign.[35]

There were other reasons for the success of the Christian Democrats in 1948. One was the fact that women voted in elections in Italy for the first time. It has been estimated that over the decades, the percentage of the Christian Democratic electorate who were female was rarely less than 60 per cent.[36] The other reason was the fear of Communism throughout Italian society.

In the shadow of the Prague coup of March 1948, and under a massive propaganda barrage, the Christian Democrats were seen as the ark of salvation by much of Italy's middle classes. The 1948 general elections, therefore, witnessed a kind of 'Giolitti-Gentilone Pact' in reverse, with hundreds of thousands of voters forsaking the Liberal and other right-of-centre parties to put their trust in the Christian Democrats. As Vittorini said of them, '*Vanno alla chiesa, cercando fascismo*' ('They go to church seeking Fascism').[37] The Catholic historian Pietro Scoppola has argued that but for the mobilisation of the Italian Catholic world and the consequent Christian Democratic success in the 1948 elections Italian democracy would have been threatened by both Leninism in the Communist Party *and* the residues of Fascism among the middle classes.[38]

As a result of the Cold War, the 1948 general elections also made it possible for the Christian Democrats to break out of political Catholicism's geographical 'ghetto' in the Catholic heartlands in northern and eastern Italy and expand into southern Italy and the islands, thanks to the support that they received from the traditional local political notables and their networks of clients. The Christian Democrats became a truly national political party in a way that the Partito Popolare had not been; they won 48 per cent of the national vote, and due to a quirk of the Italian system of proportional representation over 50 per cent of the seats in Parliament. In the short space of less than 50 years Italian political Catholicism had made the transition from being an anti-system movement to the dominant party of government, and would remain such until 1994. The Christian Democratic 'regime' thus lasted over twice as long as its Fascist predecessor.

The 'Papal State of the Twentieth Century'?

Webster's description of Italy as 'The Papal State of the Twentieth Century' was chiefly a reference to the hegemonic position that the Christian Democrats attained in government at a local and national level, but it was also a reflection of the wider power that the Church had established for itself in Italian society as a whole. The formal recognition of the Lateran Pacts in a clause of the Republican Constitution of 1948, coupled with the triumph of the Christian Democrats at the 1948 elections, had important consequences for relations between the Catholic Church and the Italian State, and also for the religious minorities. It seemed that in Italy after Fascism the 'Christian restoration of society' was at least assured. It looked as though a kind of theocratic system had been erected (or maybe re-erected) in Italy, justifying Webster's claims. The Italian State now seemed to have truly become the long arm of the Church, enforcing Catholic principles and policies in a variety of fields, for example the banning of censured priests from employment giving them contact with the public, the banning of contraceptive advertising and the de-legalisation of brothels.[39] In broader terms, Calamandrei's prophecy was proved correct. The quasi-constitutional status of the Concordat led to the development of a body of case law clearly in conflict with the constitutional principles of freedom of religion and freedom of conscience. In the 1950s and 1960s, the Italian courts handed down a series of judgments that declared that since the Constitution had implicitly recognised the principle that Catholicism was the sole religion of the State (i.e. in the preamble to the Lateran Treaty), then the protection of the interests of that religion had priority over the rights of religious minorities. Thus as late as 1967, the Corte di Cassazione (Supreme Court) even imposed limits on the freedom of religious discussion, arguing that 'constitutionally speaking, [it is] blasphemous libel to claim that the Catholic Church teaches the opposite of what Jesus wanted and that its dogmas are the inventions of priests.'[40]

The same principle inspired decisions affecting matrimonial law, church property, religious instruction in schools, and the rights of non-Catholic churches. The harassment to which the latter were subjected in the 1950s and 1960s at a local level has been documented by various authors.[41] Here we are faced with an irony: the legal instrument used against the Protestant churches after 1945, the law on the culti ammessi (permitted cults), had not been used in this way by Mussolini, who, as we have seen, conceived it as offering tangible proof to Fascist critics of the Concordat and to Anglo-Saxon admirers of Fascism that he had not abandoned the Risorgimento tradition of religious liberty and that the religious minorities were now under the tutelage and protection of the State (see Chapter 6, p. 96). Other juridical instruments created by the Fascists, such as the article of the Concordat relating to the sacro carattere (sacred character) of the city of Rome and the ban on the public employment of censured priests, were used with equal effect by the Christian Democratic successors of Fascism. The Church authorities demanded the use of Fascist police laws, which remained on the statute book until the 1970s, to censor books and newspapers that they found offensive.[42] In the case of censured priests, they were turned out of elective offices such as those of assessore (head of a department of the municipal administration) and mayor.[43]

The high point of Catholic triumphalistic power was reached in 1958. In that year, in the Bishop of Prato case, the judgement of a lower court that the bishop had slandered a couple who had contracted a civil marriage by declaring that they were living in sin was overturned by the Court of Appeal on the grounds that the 'spiritual acts' of the clergy were immune from legal proceedings.[44] An analogous case in the same year had an identical outcome.[45]

In 1959, Arturo Jemolo described the climate of confessionalism that had been created in Italy over the years in these words:

> In Italy, there is a strong climate of disapproval and discrimination against those who do not visibly form part of the community of believers, that is those who have only a civil marriage ceremony, who do not accept the sacraments at the moment of death and who insist on a secular funeral. And it has engendered in many atheists a tone of unctuous reverence towards the external manifestations of religion . . . This is a confessional state where not only non-believers but 'il mal pensante'(literally 'bad thinking') and 'il cattivo'(wicked person) are unable to claim equal rights and equal opportunity for advancement.[46]

Obviously, the intensity of the climate of confessionalism varied from place to place in Italy: it was at its worst in the 'Catholic' provinces of the north and east, but less pronounced elsewhere and much diminished in the 'Red Belt'. On the other hand, there is overwhelming evidence of direct Vatican influence upon Italian government policy at the highest level. Indeed, it was the deliberate policy of Alcide De Gasperi to maintain the centrist coalition of the Christian Democrats with the 'lay' parties – Partito Socialista Democratico Italiano (PSDI), Partito Liberale Italiano (PLI) and the Partito Republicano Italiano (PRI) – long after he had achieved an absolute majority in 1948, in order to reduce the effects of ecclesiastical pressure upon his government. But that was not an entirely successful policy. It did nothing to prevent ecclesiastical bodies obtaining fiscal and financial privileges – thus permitting those organisations to engage in frenetic building speculation that helped to disfigure the face of the Eternal City.[47] Nor did it prevent the Church from intervening, directly and repeatedly, in Italian political debates and elections, culminating, in 1949, in its excommunication of all those who voted Communist or were in any way associated in the activities of the Communist Party.

On the other hand, there were occasions when the Christian Democratic leadership willingly utilised the weight of the Vatican's influence for its own purposes, as in 1947 when its weight was used to overpower neutralist elements in the party opposed to Italy joining the North Atlantic Treaty Organization (NATO); yet even here, the ultimate consideration in the pope's mind was whether the decision served the higher purposes of the Holy See itself.[48] The most blatant and serious attempt on the part of the Vatican to interfere in Italian politics came in the 1952 local elections in Rome. Faced with the clear evidence that the Christian Democrats and their centrist allies ran the risk of losing control of the city council to the Left, Pius XII instructed De Gasperi to ally with the neo-Fascist Movimento Sociale Italiano and, ironically, used the former Popolare leader, Don Luigi Sturzo, as the figurehead for this essentially 'clerico-moderate' operation. De Gasperi was only able to elude involvement in what would have been a damaging political manoeuvre for the Christian Democrats by a technicality, and his party retained control of the city.[49] But Pius XII never forgave this act of 'disobedience', and as a punishment he refused to receive De Gasperi in private audience again.

Catholic culture and Catholic Italy under Pius XII

Post-war Italian society and politics are generally seen as being dominated by two ideological 'sub-cultures' – the Marxist and the Catholic. Indeed, Pier Paolo Pasolini, the Communist intellectual and film-maker, once commented, slightly tongue in cheek, that 'Everybody in Italy is a Marxist, just as everybody in Italy is a Catholic.'[50] There is a real element of truth in his assertion, which points up the complex dialectic between the two, which will be elucidated later. In fact, it would be more accurate to say that after 1945 Italy was the home of three or four different sub-cultures, since a much smaller and isolated one, that of the neo-Fascists, had clearly embedded itself sufficiently well in Rome and major cities of the south to sustain the Movimento Sociale Italiano as a parliamentary political force, and a radical/liberal lay but non-Marxist one persisted as a numerically tiny but not entirely negligible cultural and political force.[51] Be that as it may, the dominant sub-cultures in northern and central Italy, and to a somewhat lesser degree in parts of the south, were the Marxist and Catholic ones.

As far as the Marxist sub-culture was concerned, though it had originally been built around the Socialist Party, after the Second World War the Italian Communist Party became its major component. Thanks to Togliatti's Gramscian strategy of tactical alliances with other class groups such as shopkeepers, peasant farmers and even small businessmen, the Communist Party quickly consolidated its presence in Italian civil society in the post-war years, transforming itself from a small, elite party into a mass movement that extended beyond the boundaries of the urban, industrial working class. In coalition with the Socialists, the Communist Party was able to win control not only of some big cities in the north but also of provincial and municipal administrations in a swathe of rural areas in central Italy, the so-called 'Red Belt'.[52] In the late 1940s and 1950s, the Communist Party, like the Christian Democrats, also succeeded in building up a party base in the south and Sicily. In 1967, Sidney Tarrow wrote:

the Italian Communist Party in southern Italy has more than doubled its vote since 1946 [from 10 to 23.7 per cent]. It has mobilised thousands of peasants for a violent assault on the landed estates. It has earned the hatred of such divers bastions of southern Italian society as the Mafia and the Roman Catholic Church.[53]

The 'Red Belt' had been among the pre-Fascist strongholds of the Socialist left (see Chapter 4, p. 65). After the war, Emilia-Romagna in particular became a major battleground between the Left and their political opponents, chiefly the Christian Democrats. Bologna city council was a notable centre of this struggle, and David Kertzer's book *Comrades and Christians* provides an excellent analysis of this experience.[54] The struggles were also carried on in microcosm in the country areas, Giovanni Guareschi's *Don Camillo*, with its eponymous hero, who is parish priest, and his great opponent, Peppone, the local Communist Party leader and mayor, being a not entirely unfaithful fictional representation of them.[55] Liliano Faenza's scientific study of a parish outside Rimini in 1959 suggests that, despite the ecclesiastical denunciations and threats of excommunication, in the countryside people may more easily be able to reconcile Catholic religious practice with Communist voting behaviour.[56] In fact, officially at least, the PCI since its 1946 National Congress had claimed that, 'religious or philosophical convictions should not be an obstacle to joining the Party.'[57] This made particular sense in those areas where, as part of the Gramscian strategy of social hegemony, small peasant farmers and businessmen were being successfully wooed by the Party.

The Catholic sub-culture also embarked upon a hegemonic project in post-war Italy, if only as the natural successor to Fascism, and in pursuit of this project it possessed an ideology almost as coherent as that of its Marxist rivals. At the heart of the Catholic sub-culture during the years of Catholic triumphalism there was a cluster of values that Percy Allum has defined thus:

> frugality, the value of private property, the family and the subordinate status of women, the myth of the land, the acceptance of one's social station and the virtue of obedience, the castigation of sinners and revolutionaries . . . [and] a command to obey the Church as an institution and to regard the ecclesiastical hierarchy as the only true interpreters of God's will.[58]

To these might be added a strong belief in the 'nobility of work'. Of course, none of these values was new to Italian Catholicism, but submission to the will of the hierarchy, and especially to the charismatic authority of the pope, had been reinforced by the Church's experience of combating the Liberal State and cohabiting uneasily with Fascism.

These values fitted nicely with the *geographical* confines of the Catholic sub-culture, which, as has been seen, was rooted in the small towns and rural areas of northern and eastern Italy, and parts of the centre, a patriarchal, largely agrarian society. They were also to be used very effectively in the drive to secure extended bases for the Catholic sub-culture in general and the Christian Democrats in particular.

Where it was strongest, as in the Lombardo-Veneto region, the Catholic sub-culture enjoyed a truly hegemonic influence: at its heart was the Verona, Vicenza, Treviso, Padua 'quadrilateral'.[59] And in general, that influence was often exerted directly by the bishops and parochial clergy. It was they who chose the leaders and other organisers of the various Catholic lay associations and, in their role as '*assistenti ecclesiastici*' (ecclesiastical assistants), guided the work of the organisations, including the banks and other economic organisations. It was also they who usually gave the *imprimatur* to the selection of leaders of the Christian Democrats and even its local councillors and parliamentary candidates.[60] Given the strong influence that many bishops and parish priests enjoyed with the local (usually Christian Democrat-controlled) authorities and local employers at this time, the *raccomandazioni* (references) of the clergy provided their parishioners with powerful advantages in their search for jobs and for the *permessi* (permits) required to carry on a multitude of activities, such as this case from Naples:

> After 1950 . . . at the Allocca and Bell companies you had to pass through the Cardinal, the captain of the Carabinieri etc. We faced up to the blow by not accusing comrades who tried to ship in among the friends of the Cardinal.[61]

In organisational terms, the Catholic sub-culture was a formidable instrument of social and political control. Over 300 bishops and 65,000 clergy in 320 dioceses and 24,000 parishes ministered to a Catholic population getting on for 50 million; in addition, 200,000 male and female religious ran schools, hospitals and charitable initiatives and thus impacted strongly upon Italian society.[62] On this organisational base, the membership of Catholic associational networks comprised roughly 10 per cent of the total population. As well as Catholic Action itself, which was firmly and directly under the control of the hierarchy, and its dependent organisations for youth, women, cultural and recreational activities etc., which counted 3 million members, there were several collateral organisations. Coldiretti, the Catholic small farmers organisation represented 1.5–1.6 million peasant families or 7 million people and exercised enormous economic and political influence at both a local and national level.[63] Associazioni Cattoliche Lavoratori Italiani (ACLI), the workers' branch of Catholic Action, had 1 million members and, like the Communists, provided bars and social clubs. It strongly supported the Christian Democrats and the Confederazione Italian dei Sindacati Liberi (CISL). The CISL, which was strictly speaking not Catholic but 'aconfessional', was a trade union confederation with 2.5 million members and was growing in strength in the 1950s at the expense of the Confederazione Generale Italiana del Lavoro (CGIL). There was also the Consorzio delle Cooperative di Consumo (CCI), a powerful network of various peasant producer and consumer cooperatives that worked hand in hand with Coldiretti.[64] Another close partner of both was the network of Catholic small savings banks, the *casse di risparmio*, firmly tied in with the larger Catholic banks such as the Banco Ambrosiano (Milan) and the Banca Cattolica del Veneto (Veneto), which operated in most of the provinces and small towns of northern and central Italy, and in an increasing number of southern towns as the Christian Democrats established their political influence there.[65] They were also tied in to the banking, insurance, commercial and industrial empire in Italy that Bernardino Nogara had established for the Vatican from the beginning of the 1930s onwards.[66] This economic empire ensured that Catholic political hegemony in the post-war period was underpinned by an extensive Catholic stake in the Italian economy.[67]

Finally, there was a large Catholic press and publishing sector that controlled 1,800 publications with a total circulation of 16 million copies, 'more than half the periodical sales in Italy'.[68] Two periodicals alone – *Famiglia Cristiana*, whose title and content reflected the core values of the Catholic sub-culture, and *Il Messaggero di Sant-Antonio* – had a massive circulation for a country that still had high levels of adult illiteracy; their circulation was only a little behind the best-sellers *Sorrisi e Canzoni* (a sort of Italian *Radio Times)* and *Gente*, a 1950s Italian version of *Hello* magazine.[69] It should also not be forgotten that the Church had gained a powerful place in the overall organisation of Italian culture because of its foothold in the Italian state educational system as a result of the fact that Mussolini had made (Catholic) religious instruction compulsory in primary and secondary schools and that the largest primary school teachers' association was Catholic-dominated.

Then there were the Christian Democrats, who were effectively Italy's Church-sponsored, governing political party. In these circumstances, the structure and composition of the Christian Democrats under De Gasperi (1943–53) was an unusual, not to say unique, one among Italian/European political parties. In reality, the Christian Democrats were essentially a *parliamentary* or caucus party with little or no independent mass base at a local level, the membership and electorate being effectively provided by the Church and the broader Catholic movement. Decision-making at a local level was frequently in the hands of the local Catholic Action branch officers, or as often as not, the parish priest; when, for example, in August 1964, the Christian Democrats of the village of Castano Primo, province of Milan, had to decide who should be their mayoral candidate, the parish priest chose a 25-year-old Catholic Action militant, Angelo Caloia, who would later become the president of the Vatican Bank.[70]

As Allum has perceived, the Christian Democrats' absolute dependence upon the institutional church and the organisations of the Catholic movement to mobilise both the party activists and the voters, marked it out from its precursor, the Partito Popolare, which had in some sense operated independently of the Church. And in the south, until the mid-1950s, the Catholic party essentially operated through the traditional networks of leading local notables and their clientele.[71] Inasmuch as De Gasperi had an understanding with Confindustria, the Italian private sector employers' association, the Christian Democrats enjoyed the financial support of that organisation too.[72]

The continuing Catholic struggle against Communism

As far as the Church was concerned, the struggle with Communism was not over in April 1948. Though, like Gramsci, Togliatti may have learnt the lesson of Fascism that open hostility towards the Church in Italy was suicidal, and have moderated the natural anti-clericalism of Italian Communists accordingly, there was little or nothing he could do to control events outside of Italy. Stalin's 'Godless offensive' in the countries of eastern Europe progressed relentlessly in the late 1940s. After the trial and execution of Mgr Tiso in Slovakia and the trial and imprisonment of Cardinal Stepinac in Yugoslavia, Cardinal Mindszenty, primate of Hungary, was tried and imprisoned in Budapest in 1949 as part and parcel of a systematic persecution of the Church that had followed in the wake of liberation by the Red Army.[73] That was what mattered in the Vatican, and they offered perfect ammunition in the anti-Communist propaganda war.

So the Church continued to fight Communism with the threat of excommunication at every level for decades thereafter, and a number of different weapons were used to mobilise and sustain Catholic lay support in the struggle, particularly in the early period. Just as Italian Communism in this period adopted many of the forms of a secular religion, so Italian Catholicism seemed to assume more and more the characteristics of a mass political movement with a charismatic leader – the pope. Oliver Logan has shown how the papal 'cult of the personality' reached its peak in the reign of Pius XII. He argues that this cult was built around the myth of the 'victim pope' initiated by Pope

Pius IX, who saw himself as the victim of Italian aggression against the Papal States and consequently described himself as the 'prisoner of the Vatican'.[74] It was developed by his successors Leo XIII and Pius X. Even the authoritarian Pius XI exploited the myth of the 'victim pope' when he was in conflict with Mussolini, claiming that Fascist attacks on members of Catholic Action 'wounded his paternal heart', and the same sort of rhetoric was employed by the Vatican newspaper *L'Osservatore Romano* when Pius XII was attacked in the left-wing press.[75] Pius XII was dubbed *Pastor Angelicus* (the Angelic Pastor), and a film of that name, shot in the Vatican during the war, was shown in the 4,000 parochial cinemas in the late 1940s, giving further substance to the papal personality cult. Pius XII was also, fortuitously, a Roman, the first Roman pope for over 200 years. This had made it possible for him to appropriate Mussolini's much-vaunted ideology of *Romanità*, the idea that Rome was the centre of the civilised world, and that by utilising the Roman virtues of order and discipline, Fascism would create a second Roman Empire. Pius XII exploited the idea in a different way, putting the emphasis on the Christian significance of Rome during his attempts to persuade the Allies not to bomb the city. And by visiting the Roman populace when the Allies had gone ahead and bombed the capital in July 1943, he had effectively eclipsed the charisma of the Duce even before the latter was overthrown later that month.

Rome became a leitmotif of much Catholic rhetoric during the Cold War, which was fitting because the city was a major battleground in the struggle in Italy: 'Rome or Moscow' was a typical battle cry. Its character declared 'sacred' by the terms of the Lateran Pacts, Rome could not be allowed to fall into the hands of the 'barbarians'. That Pius XII seriously feared such an eventuality, and the consequent danger of ending up as a defendant in a 'peoples' court', can be adduced from a remark he made to the Irish ambassador. Of the 'show trial' of Mgr Stepinac, he said, 'My place is in Rome and if it be the will of the Divine Master I am ready to be martyred for him in Rome.'[76] Rome, and more specifically St Peter's Square and the monumental Via Della Conciliazione constructed to commemorate the Lateran Pacts, was also the location of massive, carefully choreographed meetings of Catholics with the pope, which were a key feature of the campaign against Communism. In Pius XI's reign, the gatherings in St Peter's Square had already begun to compete with Mussolini's own, 'oceanic' meetings of the Fascist faithful in Piazza Venezia. It can thus be argued that the Church, and in particular Catholic Action, 'borrowed' from the Fascist propaganda repertoire in their efforts to contain the Communist menace, including the use of loudspeakers outside churches to summon the faithful to political meetings. But Italian Catholicism hardly needed Fascist models in its operations at a local, popular level. It was, for example, able to utilise traditional popular devotions, especially to the Sacred Heart and Our Lady. Pilgrimages to Marian shrines – and not only national ones such as the Holy House at Loreto but also regional shrines such as Monte Berico near Vicenza and the Santuario D'Oropa in northern Piedmont – were already important manifestations of Italian Catholic identity and loyalty during the Cold War period.[77] In addition, there was the phenomenon of *Madonna Pellegrina*, that is, a means of whipping up popular fervour by taking the statue of the Madonna in procession around the streets of towns and villages, and on occasion allowing it to 'stay' with a family for a few days to be reverenced by friends and neighbours. The Marian cult reached its height during the Holy Year of 1950, which in itself was utilised to generate Catholic enthusiasm on a massive scale. It was in that year that Papa Pacelli, in the first exercise of infallibility since its definition in 1870, proclaimed that the bodily Assumption of Our Lady into Heaven was now part of Catholic dogma.

And for those unable to participate in the great events in the Eternal City, there was a group of itinerant preachers, in the medieval tradition, ready to bring the Christian, anti-Communist message to the remotest areas. The most famous of them was Jesuit Fr Lombardi, or 'God's Microphone' as he became known.[78] Lombardi's exceptional oratorical skills took him to Italy's major cities and guaranteed him large audiences. Eventually, he became a radio personality as well. Lombardi and his fellows preached unabashed anti-Communist politics, their main themes being: the intrinsic materialism of Communist ideology; its conflict with Catholic social teaching as well as theology; the need for a Christian 'third-way' between Capitalism and Communism; and the importance of the Christian family as against the alleged amorality of Godless atheism.[79]

The Italian Church of Pius XII

From the outside, the Italian Church under Pius XII looked strong and compact, the religious life of the faithful lively and intense. But all was not well. Though levels of weekly attendance at Mass were at an all time high, reaching 90 per cent of the population in the Veneto, elsewhere the figures were much lower.[80] Towards the end of Pius XII's pontificate, the bishops of southern Italy expressed concern about the unhealthy interest of the faithful in what they described as an 'exterior cult', directed towards the sanctuaries of local patron saints and 'miracle-working' images (especially the Madonna).[81] It is significant that the cult of the Italian Franciscan friar with the stigmata, Padre Pio, also reached its peak at this time.[82] The secular clergy, who had increasing, largely electoral, responsibilities, had actually fallen in numbers by a half since 1881 and managed to cope only thanks to the energies of 22,457 religious priests.[83] In a meeting of the newly founded Italian Bishops' Conference at Pompei in 1953, various Italian prelates also expressed worries about the state of the clergy, in particular the increase in the numbers seeking a dispensation from the vows of celibacy.[84] In broader terms, the meeting represents the first serious manifestation on the part of the Italian Church of its concern about the impact of the cultural and social changes that accompanied the economic 'miracle' of the late 1950s and early 1960s, including a growing feeling that the Church needed to undergo a process of fundamental pastoral renewal.[85]

In this perspective, the Vatican of Pius XII had little to offer. Pius and his most influential collaborators still held fast to a highly centralised and hierarchical concept of ecclesiastical authority, as set out in his encyclical of 1943, *Mystici Corporis Christi*, which allowed little space to movements advocating change inside the Church.[86] The 'modernisers' in the Vatican were in a minority, and their influence was further reduced after the 'exile' of Mgr G-B Montini to Milan as its archbishop in 1954. The only area in which there were some signs of change during Pius XII's reign was the liturgical one. The relaxation of the Eucharistic fast, the introduction of evening Mass on the vigil of Sundays and Holy days and the permission for the limited use of the vernacular in the Mass all went some way towards meeting the needs of Catholics faced by rapid economic, cultural and social change.[87] Similarly, the approval by the Holy See of the statutes of the Little Brothers of Jesus, a religious order specifically designed for mission among the urban working classes, was a response to an increasingly difficult pastoral situation.[88] Otherwise, at the end of Pius XII's reign the Italian Church was left in a kind of limbo, some would say a state of creeping crisis, with no clear signs of a way out.

The consolidation and transformation of political Catholicism

In the 'division of labour' between the institutional church and the Catholic party, while the former had responsibility for the mobilisation of the Catholic masses at elections and other times, the latter's task was to manage power at a national level. Though, as we have seen, the Vatican was not averse to intervening in matters of national political importance such as the outcome of the local elections in the capital – and Pius XII is alleged to have pored for hours over the minutiae of Italian election results at both a local and national level – it was the Christian Democratic leadership, and especially De Gasperi, who fixed electoral grand strategy. This was especially true for the 1953 general elections. By the time general elections came round again, though the rigours of the Cold war had not abated, large sections of the landed and middle classes had become alienated from their erstwhile saviours, particularly in the south where the Christian Democrats' land redistribution measure had enraged local elites, who had abandoned the party in large numbers. Anticipating defeat, De Gasperi resorted to the so-called 'swindle law'(thus dubbed by its Communist and Socialist opponents because of its unfortunate resemblance to Mussolini's electoral law of 1923), which awarded two-thirds of the seats to the party or coalition of parties that obtained more than 50 per cent of the votes.[89] The coalition failed to qualify for the two-thirds majority of seats by only 50,000 votes; it failed because the Christian Democrats had, predictably, lost ground to the extreme right, the monarchists and neo-Fascist Movimento Sociale Italiano (MSI), especially in the south, their vote being reduced to 40 per cent.[90] The Christian Democrats were condemned to rule for another ten years with precarious, unviable parliamentary majorities provided by support from the small centre parties. De Gasperi resigned as prime minister, was sidelined as party secretary and died a year later.

In the battle for the succession, Amintore Fanfani, professor of economics at the Catholic University of Milan and a former supporter of Fascist corporatism, sought to take over the mantle of De Gasperi's authority but without enduring success, and the Christian Democrats never again had an undisputed leader. Faced by the threat of further electoral decline, Fanfani sought to create a new model party built around a more autonomous party organisation with an electoral base independent of the Church and Catholic Action and with sources of party funding other than from Confindustria. As Giorgi Galli, a leading authority on the post-war Catholic party has put it, Fanfani no longer wanted the Christian Democrats 'to be the servant but the leader of the [Italian] Catholic world'.[91] Fanfani's project had only limited success in the short term, as far as the party's structure and electoral base were concerned, but the pursuit of funding from public sector companies had more success and initiated the process whereby those companies became incorporated into a system of state clientelism. The creation of a ministry of state holdings in 1956 and the withdrawal of the state companies from Confindustria in 1957 brought the large Italian state sector, which controlled 80 per cent of Italy's banks and 40 per cent of its manufacturing industry, more directly under the control of the politicians. In this way, in the longer term, the Christian Democratic Party was to become more independent of both the Church and organised Italian private capitalism.[92]

The new organisational and electoral strategies of the Christian Democrats were not entirely new to Italian political practice or culture. Like the large state sector itself, which was a legacy of economic policy during the Fascist period, the use of jobs in the state bureaucracy and the state, party organisations and the state economic sector had been pioneered by the Fascists. Fanfani and his Christian Democratic allies followed suit on a larger scale in the 1950s and 1960s, colonising industrial undertakings, banks and local credit institutions with their appointees in order to reward political favours, win electoral support, and guarantee access to new sources of party funding. In consequence, the relationship between the Christian Democrats and their electorate would be increasingly conditioned by personal, clientelistic factors, the clientelistic relationship augmenting, and increasingly superseding, the ideological cement of the Catholic sub-culture.

While this process became common throughout Italy, it was most pronounced in the south. Here, despite the setbacks of 1953, in desperately poor and job-hungry regions the Christian Democrats managed to consolidate the process of binding sections of the electorate to it by exploiting the patronage resources – jobs and contracts – of the land reform agencies, the Southern Development Fund (Cassa per il Mezzogiorno), and the ministries of interior, justice, posts and telegraphs, and public works. From 1953 onwards, and possibly earlier, the Christian Democratic Party in the south began to metamorphose into a largely clientelistic party, and one also increasingly penetrated by organised crime: the Mafia in Sicily, the 'Ndrangheta in Calabria and the Camorra in Naples.[93]

Conclusion

Between 1945 and 1958, Catholicism had its best chance to re-establish its absolute hegemony in Italian society, to carry to completion Pius XI's great project of a 'Christian restoration of Italian society'. Despite the tremendous moral and spiritual authority of the papacy at the end of the Second World War, despite the effectiveness of the Church as a bulwark of anti-Communism to those who feared revolution, and despite the absolutely essential and dominant role that the Christian Democrats established for themselves in Italian parliamentary politics, the project failed. The failure may be attributed to a number of factors. One key factor was the resilience of lay, anti-clerical forces in Italian society and politics, despite clerical pressures, especially after 1953 when the Christian Democrats' loss of an absolute parliamentary majority rendered the lay centre parties more and more essential to the governing of Italy. The presence of the Communist Party (and the Socialists), which consolidated its own sub-cultural ghetto and remained as a challenge to the Catholic sub-culture especially in northern and central Italy, was another important factor. But even more important in the longer term were the massive social and cultural changes generated by both the economic 'miracle' and Anglo-Saxon influences that were already having an impact before Pius XII's death in 1958. Arguably, therefore, like Papa Pacelli's body at his funeral, Catholic 'triumphalism' was already in a state of advanced decay.

Chapter 8

THE NEW SECULARISATION (1958–78)

Introduction

IN THE 20-YEAR PERIOD between the death of Pius XII in 1958 and that of Paul VI in 1978, Italy changed profoundly, becoming a modern, urban and industrialised state akin to other western countries. In consequence it also underwent a process of secularisation. Some of the causes of this latter transformation were essentially economic, the impact of the so-called economic 'miracle' of the 1950s and 1960s, while the cultural 'invasion' of Italy by Anglo-Saxon, largely American, influences played an important role as well. In addition to these 'exogenous' factors, there were processes of change internal to the Church itself, the launching by Pope John XXIII of the Second Vatican Council and his broader policy of *aggiornamento* (literally, 'updating') of the Catholic Church. The Council had both positive and negative effects. In the short term it brought about liturgical and pastoral renewal, but in the longer term it created dissent and division in the Italian Church. Overall, the consequence of the changes would be to undermine religious belief, diminish the practice of the faith, subvert the bases of the Catholic sub-culture and weaken the influence of the Church in Italian politics and civil society in the reigns of John and of his successor, Paul VI (1963–78).

The impact of John XXIII

The election of Cardinal Angelo Giuseppe Roncalli, patriarch of Venice, as Pope John XXIII in the 1958 conclave was to have a profound impact on the Roman Catholic Church throughout the world over the next decade, but nowhere more so than in Italy. On the one hand, like the last patriarch of Venice to be elected pope, Giuseppe Sarto, Roncalli was the very epitome of Catholic Italy. A 'son of the soil' – his parents were small peasants in Sotto il Monte (Bergamo province) – Roncalli went through first diocesan and then Roman seminary education, and served his bishop, Radini-Tedeschi, as secretary, the classic journey of those ultimately destined for high ecclesiastical office.[1] On the other hand, he had had a more diverse, nay eclectic, career than most modern popes, first of all serving in the Italian armed forces as a chaplain (medical orderly) in the First World War. In 1921, his career took a different turn when he was recalled to Rome and ended up in the missionary dicastery of the Roman Curia, Propaganda Fide, eventually being sent as apostolic delegate to Bulgaria, later Greece, and then Turkey.[2] The Balkans in the later years of the Second World War were a tragic, turbulent cauldron, and Roncalli was involved in efforts to save Jews of that region from the clutches of the Nazis.[3] His international experience as a Vatican diplomat was broadened and consolidated when he was sent to Paris in 1945 as *nuncio* to resolve several vexed questions between the Vatican and Charles De Gaulle's new resistance government, including the fate of 32 bishops who had been over loyal to the collaborationist Vichy regime, and to sort out the French 'work priest' movement that was causing so much concern in the Vatican.[4] But given that the Venice diocese now included two major industrial towns, Mestre and Marghera, his return to Italy in 1954 as head of that diocese meant that he was brought back to the complex and difficult reality of the Italian pastoral situation in the early years of the economic 'miracle' before being elected pope.[5]

Ecclesiologically, but perhaps not, in the final analysis, theologically, Papa Roncalli was a conservative – his Rome diocesan synod of 1959 was managed in exemplary top-down fashion with the primary focus being on the restatement and re-enforcement of clerical discipline, such as the wearing of the cassock in public.[6] Yet the Second Vatican Council was to have radical, not to say revolutionary, effects on the whole Catholic Church, including the Church in Italy, in ways that John XXIII certainly had not intended. John XXIII's 'opening to the East', including his attempts to mediate during the Cuban Missile Crisis of 1962, revolutionised Vatican diplomatic policy, laying the foundations of Mgr (later Cardinal) Agostino Casaroli's *Ostpolitik* in the succeeding pontificate.[7] It also impacted on Italian politics as Christian Democratic politicians sought an 'opening to the left' in order to find a way out of their parliamentary difficulties. Given the dramatic, radical impact of Pope John's pontificate, that of his successor, Paul VI, was essentially, and inevitably, a coda in which the consequences of John's 'revolution worked themselves out'.[8] On the other hand, Mgr Montini had been the 'ghost' at the 1958 conclave, absent because he had been banished to Milan, and never awarded the red hat that always went with that archiepiscopal title. So for many, Roncalli was simply 'keeping the seat warm' for his friend, who was the great white hope of reformists in the Sacred College. In this sense, many of Papa Roncalli's policies and initiatives were those of Montini also.

The economic 'miracle' and social/cultural change in post-war Italy

As a background to the reign of John XXIII and the experience of the Second Vatican Council, it has to be understood that the economic, cultural and social changes that led to a new wave of secularisation in post-war Italy were already under way before Roncalli's election in 1958. By the mid-1950s, the results of Italy's post-war economic reconstruction and recovery, which, like that of other European countries, was massively underpinned by America's Marshall Aid programme, had created a situation in which Italian industrial production figures surpassed those of the pre-war period, and a sustained boom was in train, the 'miracle', which persisted into the early 1960s.[9] In the 1950s, Italian gross national product (GNP) increased by 6 per cent per annum and between 1956 and 1963, Italian industrial production doubled, a feat exceeded only by Germany and possibly Japan.[10] Italy's spectacular growth in this period was the result of a multiplicity of factors,[11] but, ironically, it was particularly assisted by the underdeveloped nature of the economy of much of the peninsula. High levels of agrarian unemployment and underemployment in most rural areas, but especially the south, provided a virtually unlimited reservoir of cheap labour to fuel the expansion of manufacturing and other industries.[12] This meant that as well as some migration abroad, mainly to Australia and the countries of north-western Europe, huge waves of internal migration took place, from countryside to town, especially in the north, and from south to north: according to Ginsborg, 'more than 900,000 Italians changed their places of residence from the South to the North' in the period of the economic 'miracle'.[13]

In total, it has been estimated that 5 million people changed their place of residence between 1945 and 1971 and whereas in 1951 only a third of the Italian population had lived in urban areas with more than 100,000 inhabitants, by 1981 over half did so.[14] Over the years, this movement massively disrupted traditional, patriarchal, rural Italian society, the bedrock of Italian Catholicism, and fragmented what had hitherto been a fairly stable class 'system'. Hundreds of thousands of those formerly employed (or unemployed) in agriculture, including small tenant/owner farmers and sharecroppers, found themselves in unskilled and semi-skilled jobs in nearby towns or became part of the volatile, floating masses of lumpenproletariat living in alien surroundings, in the *barrache* or *coree* (flimsy, ramshackle housing named after scenes from the Korean War) of the large northern Italian cities and in Bari, Naples and Palermo. This almighty upheaval also resulted in serious social problems in the big cities – lack of decent housing, schools and welfare facilities, especially for immigrants – which would lead to major political protests in the 1960s and 1970s.

One of the consequences of all this was that the institutional Church also faced problems, and on a scale unprecedented even in comparison with those that it had faced during the period of the *prima industrializzazione*. On the one hand, it had to provide for the literally hundreds of thousands of new inhabitants of major cities such as Milan, Turin, Genoa, and also Rome and Florence, smaller cities in the north such as Bergamo, Brescia and Padua (and the new Mestre-Marghera industrial-port complex on the mainland opposite Venice), not to mention southern cities such as Naples, Palermo and Bari. But as well as having to provide for the 'un-churched', largely rural, immigrants into towns and cities, it also had to confront the problems posed by the depopulation of the villages and small towns the immigrants abandoned, especially in the foothills of the Alps, and in those of the Apennines all the way down the Italian peninsula, where often only the very young and very old were left behind.[15]

The response of the ecclesiastical authorities

The scale of the problems facing the ecclesiastical authorities can be gauged from two examples, Milan and Rome. In 1955, Mgr G.B. Montini took possession of his archdiocese, which was one of the largest in Italy, with 1,000 churches, 2,500 priests and 3,500,000 souls.[16] The city of Milan, not counting the satellite industrial towns in its hinterland, all in the archdiocese, grew from 1.274 million people in 1958 to 1.68 million in 1963.[17] Consequently, Archbishop Montini struggled to build churches to meet the needs of ever-expanding numbers of faithful in the diocese: 41 were built in Milan city and the number increased by 10 per cent in the diocese as a whole: Hebblethwaite claims that '3 or 4 more [new churches had to be built] each year because of the influx of immigrants'; by the time he left the archdiocese, he had opened 34 churches, and construction was proceeding on a further 91.[18] In 1957, Montini launched a massive mission to bring back the 'lost souls' of Milan to Christ and he even seriously considered a radical restructuring of the organisation of the diocese for pastoral purposes.

By the end of the 1950s, Rome was another metropolitan see showing the effects of the economic and social transformations that were taking place in

Italy. Even Pius XII, not known for any great concern for what was, after all, his own diocese, expressed his alarm about the spiritual state of the city in his last address to Lenten preachers in February 1958: 'So it can be said that Rome has its shadow areas, its islands in need of evangelisation, and that it is missionary territory.'[19] In the 19 years since Pacelli's election to the papal throne, the population of the Italian capital had increased from 770,000 to 2 million inhabitants, from 62 to 190 parishes with a total of nearly 600 priests, secular and religious (not counting the hundreds working in the Roman Curia), and yet the city was still growing as it developed an industrial periphery in its outer suburbs.[20]

At least in the 1950s and 1960s, unlike 70 years previously, the Church, especially in Rome, had enormous material resources at its disposal to remedy the problems. And in Pacelli's successor the city had an indefatigably pastoral bishop. John XXIII was not content to leave the problems to the pope's cardinal vicar, Micara, or his deputy, Traglia: he summoned a diocesan synod, the first for centuries, and even began to visit the parishes of the city, something that no pope had done, *force majeure*, between 1870 and 1929, and that neither of his two predecessors had done, though they would have been able to.[21]

'Americanisation'

As bishops and parochial clergy grappled with the pastoral consequences of Italy's latest domestic process of modernisation, an arguably more insidious cultural form of modernisation was impacting on Italy from outside, 'Americanisation', which would only compound their problems. The limited and spasmodic American influences brought by returning emigrants since the beginning of the century, and then more intensively by the American occupation armies between 1943 and 1945, were now superseded by the much more pervasive and enduring cultural influences that came in the wake of the establishment of American economic and political hegemony in post-war Europe with a particular impact in Italy. As Ginsborg describes it: 'De Gasperi had chosen America; even more importantly, America had chosen Italy . . . Catholicism, Americanism, anti-Communism; together they made an unlikely but formidable base for a ruling ideology.'[22]

What 'Americanism' meant in material terms was the flooding into Italy of key elements of contemporary American culture such as Coca-Cola and Pepsi, Disney, 'boogie-woogie' and rock music, and new, casual fashions in dress, sexual mores and social behaviour generally. In the 1950s, the principal medium of influence was film – according to Dunnage, from the 1930s through into the 1960s, Hollywood films dominated the Italian market, and their celebrities were the key role models in Italian magazines.[23] Books and magazines were another, though less important, vector of American culture given the high levels of illiteracy in Italy, especially in the south, even if levels of literacy and educational attainment improved substantially in the 1940s and 1950s. In the 1960s, television took over as the primary medium transmitting American culture and its values to Italian audiences. What was perhaps most impressive about the change in lifestyles was the fact that spending on all forms of entertainment nearly doubled in Italy during the 1950s, suggesting that Italians in all walks of life, and in both town and country, were forsaking the simple, inexpensive pleasures of family, parish and village/neighbourhood community.[24]

The section of society most strongly and immediately affected by this cultural invasion was the young, and insofar as the biggest influences on the music and fashion scene for young people in the 1960s were actually *British*, i.e. the Beatles and the Rolling Stones and Carnaby Street, it might be more accurate to say that what we are really talking about are Anglo-Saxon cultural influences.[25] The Church was, of course, seriously alarmed about the impact of foreign cultural influences on youth, but however repressive it tried to be, even in the medium term it could not win. One particular aspect of the fashion revolution of the 1960s bears this out. Jeans, especially Levi jeans, ruled the world of youth fashion in the 1960s, nowhere more so than among Italians, who rather slavishly insisted on calling them 'blujeans'. As one might have expected, the enterprising and energetic Italian fashion industry created several of its own brands, most notably 'Rifle', 'Super rifle' and 'Carrero', but only it could have come up with the brand name, 'Jesus Jeans'. The advertising for this product, 'which coupled the erotic image of the behind of a girl in cut-down jeans with the caption "whoever loves me should follow me"', seemed to epitomise a blasphemous revolt of youth against the Church and all it held dear.[26]

The Church's response to these phenomena was predictable: American consumerism/hedonist values were anathema, and anathematised they were on a regular basis: in sermons, pastoral letters and other messages to the faithful, cosmetics, beauty contests, 'immoral dress' and modern dances were all denounced, particularly dances, just as they had been under Benedict XV and Pius XI.[27] Ultimately, what was feared and deplored was the breakdown of the unity of the family under the strains of a new youth culture and a lifestyle lived increasingly outside the home. As far as films were concerned, the Church still possessed a network of parochial cinemas and two film production companies with which it might hopefully insulate the rural faithful from the worst evils of Hollywood and, more importantly, it was able to lean on Christian Democratic ministers to employ the still effective machinery of censorship inherited from Fascism to vet imports from America, which ex-FUCI leader and junior minister Giulio Andreotti did willingly, so that some of the worst excesses of American culture were barred to Italians. Television was even more easily controllable since it was, from its inception, a state monopoly, though here, too, consumerism inevitably reared its ugly head. Christian Democratic control of RAI (Radio Audizioni Italiana), the state radio and television corporation, ensured that this was 'slavishly Christian democrat in politics and piously Catholic in cultural values'.[28] As Augusto D'Angelo has pointed out, the Christian Democrat-appointed management of RAI 'tried to use a typical instrument of an industrial, mass society to promote . . . a culture whose roots lay in the models of a rural society'.[29] Of course, as the economic 'miracle' progressed, the reality of Italian society corresponded less and less to these models.

Ironically, the Communist sub-culture had even more problems with the influence of the new media since it had much less control over them than the Church. Ginsborg recounts the story of the reaction of local Communists when the Christian Democratic boss in a Tuscan village introduced a television set into the local bar: some comrades denounced it as 'Priest's garbage'.[30] The little world of both Don Camillo and Don Peppone in Guareschi's novels was turned upside down by the economic, social and, consequently, cultural changes of the 1950s and 1960s, but it would be true to say that, of the two sub-cultures, the Catholic adapted better to the social/cultural transformations of Italy in this period, however uneasily and unwillingly. This is borne out by Stephen Gundle's excellent analysis of two popular, mass circulation, magazines of this period, the Catholic *Famiglia Cristiana* (literally 'Christian Family') and the Communist *Vie Nuove* (literally 'New Ways').[31]

The situation facing Italian Catholicism in the decades after the war was a complex and difficult reality: the Church was in fact fighting a war on *two* fronts: against Communism and against another, perhaps more insidious, enemy, the cultural influences emanating from the USA. Christopher Duggan hits the nail on the head when he characterises the dilemma of the Church in the 1950s and 1960s when confronted by the flood of Anglo-Saxon values thus:

> If it sympathised in many ways with the collectivist values of Communism and also shared something of the austere communist view of morality, it could not brook its atheism or hostility to the family: and while the Church endorsed the anti-Communism of the western powers, it could not accept the unbridled materialism and individualism at the heart of free-market capitalism, nor the hedonism and sexual permissiveness that seemed to go with it.[32]

The Italian Communist Party was as hostile and suspicious towards the cultural imports from America as the hierarchy of the Catholic Church. Conversely, it was actually rather less hostile to the family and its values than Duggan suggests, and shared many other values with Catholicism, including the attitude towards work. Indeed, even at the height of the Cold War, a strange convergence between Italian Catholicism and Communism, which would always be repudiated by both sides, was beginning to emerge and would manifest itself very strongly in the 1970s and 1980s.

The opening to the left

The crisis of 'centrism', that is, the increasing difficulties that the Christian Democrats and their coalition allies encountered in maintaining an effective parliamentary majority, which became apparent in the early 1950s (see Chapter 7, p. 130), had worsened by the end of Pius XII's reign. Though the centre coalition's percentage of the vote went up by nearly three points in the 1958 elections in comparison with those of 1953, and its parliamentary majority rose from 18 to 40, it was too precarious given the policy differences between the constituent parties of the coalition, not to mention the deep-seated faction fighting inside the Christian Democrats itself. Consequently, it became impossible to confront the very serious social and economic disequilibria produced by the 'miracle' and carry out those structural reforms of the state administration and that upgrading of the provision of state services, especially in education, health, housing and public transport, that economic modernisation had rendered such an urgent necessity, thus adding to the difficulties faced by an increasingly beleaguered centre-right administration in the late 1950s and early 1960s.

On the other hand, the left, and especially the Communist Party, was growing in electoral strength at both a local and national level. Between 1953 and 1958, the Communist/Socialist combined share of the parliamentary vote had increased from 34.4 per cent to 36.7 per cent, the PSI being the major beneficiary of this development.[33] There was, in consequence, a strongly felt need on the part of the leadership of the Christian Democrats to broaden the electoral/parliamentary base of the governing coalition, to split the 'united left' of the PSI and the PCI and isolate the latter.[34] And within the Socialist Party itself, there was a growing impatience with, not to say resentment against, the dominant role exercised by the Communists in their relationship with the Socialists. Some of the latter, under the leadership of Pietro Nenni, made it increasingly clear that, after more than 70 years of opposition, they were not disinclined to enter into a governmental coalition, and to this end made the key gestures needed to escape the 'anti-system' corner into which they had boxed themselves, most notably by publicly accepting the necessity of NATO and the European Economic Community (EEC).

But this 'opening to the left' was blocked by conservative elements among the Christian Democrats, by the US administration, and above all by the intransigent hostility of the ecclesiastical hierarchy. Under the leadership of Pius XII the Vatican refused to countenance any compromise with the still Marxist-orientated PSI. Relief only came with the death of Pius XII and the election of John XXIII in 1958.[35] Papa Roncalli's new course in Vatican international policy, the first steps towards an 'opening to the East' (see p. 132 above), paralleled the Christian Democrats' attempts at an 'opening to the left' in Italian domestic politics. Even more important was John XXIII's determination to disengage the Italian Church from his predecessor's policy of total involvement in Italian politics. Though obstructed by conservative elements in both the Vatican (the 'pentagon' of Cardinals Ottaviani, Pizzardo, Canali, Rossi and Mimmi) and by the incumbents of major Italian archiepiscopal sees, such as Siri of Genoa and Ruffino of Palermo, John managed to establish at least *the principle* that Italian Catholic lay politicians had the right and even the duty to make fundamental changes of direction by themselves. In his famous 'Wider Tiber' speech to Prime Minister Fanfani on 11 April 1961, he declared:

> The special situation of the Catholic Church and the Italian State – two organisms which differ in structure, character, level and aims – presupposes a certain respect (*riserbo*) in the relationship which, based on courtesy and respect, makes the occasion on which their representatives do meet from time to time all the more agreeable.[36]

This was about as far as he could go in making it clear that Italian churchmen had to hold back from dictating to Italian politicians, even Christian Democratic politicians. But the promulgation of *Pacem in Terris* in 1963, inasmuch as it declared that Catholic political cooperation with parties of a Marxist inclination was licit (see above, p. 129) provided the final green light for a new parliamentary working relationship between the Christian Democrats and Socialists, one that in an under-the-counter way was already in existence.[37]

In the long term, the experience of a full blooded centre-left political experiment, with Socialist ministers in government, was in many ways not a very positive one. The Socialist Party actually split over participation in government, and few of the deep structural reforms proposed by the Socialists were actually realised.[38] But the centre-left coalition system had extended the life of Christian Democratic political hegemony. Under a succession of prime ministers who were mostly veterans of FUCI, starting with Aldo Moro, and with the apparent blessing of his former mentor, Montini, now Pope Paul VI, the Christian Democrats succeeded in splitting the left and reducing the Socialist Party to the status of a usually dependable governmental ally. In the short term, the launch of the experiment in 1963 was overshadowed by electoral disaster for both Christian Democrats and Socialists and dramatic success for the Communists: the Christian Democratic vote fell from 42.3 per cent to 38.35 per cent and the Communist Party's share of the votes increased by 1 million.[39]

Some Italian conservatives blamed the Christian Democrats' 'opening to the left', but much of the responsibility was laid directly at John XXIII's door for having 'gone soft' on Communism and, in particular, for having welcomed Alexis Adzhubei, editor of *Izvestia* and Khrushchev's son-in-law, into the Vatican in February 1963. One Milan evening newspaper even changed the title of *Pacem in Terris* to *Falcem in Terris*: *falce* means 'sickle', as in the hammer and sickle.[40] Yet the irony of all this is that though Italians were now voting increasingly for the Communist Party, John XXIII was acclaimed as much by the Italian population as 'Good Pope John', or 'the Peasant Pope' as by people in the rest of the world, and even that arch-conservative, Cardinal Siri, was forced to admit that there were pictures of John in the homes of most of the people in his see city, Genoa, including those of the workers.[41]

The impact of the Second Vatican Council

The Second Vatican Council of the 2,500 bishops of the Roman Catholic Church was held in Rome in a series of sessions between October 1962 and December 1965. On the whole, with some notable exceptions such as Cardinal Montini of Milan, the Italian espicopate was neither very enthusiastic about the Council nor well prepared for it.[42] If they saw anything positive about it, then this lay in their expectation that it would provide a forum to reiterate past condemnations of Communism, and as far as doctrinal issues were concerned, perhaps the most that they expected was a further statement about the role of Mary in salvation history. Some Italian Council fathers had concerns about the ultimate effects of its deliberations and decisions in Italy, and they were not proved wrong, because the Council was to have a powerful impact on the Italian Church, creating turbulence and dissent on an unprecedented scale. Of course, this experience was common to the Church in other parts of the world.

The Council had both positive and negative effects on the Italian Church, but initially it seemed to offer solutions to some aspects of the malaise that had afflicted it towards the end of Pius XII's reign, in particular in the liturgical and pastoral fields. The first was the new emphasis on the role of the laity in the Church in the decree *Lumen Gentium*, where Church is described as the

'People of God' and where the laity are attributed a direct role in the mission of the Church and 'not simply participation in the mission of the hierarchy', as members of Catholic Action had hitherto been described.[43] This new place for the laity was given visual form by liturgical changes. These changes sanctioned the hitherto unofficial use of the 'dialogue Mass'(the congregation saying the responses normally made by the altar server), permitted the general use of the vernacular rather than Latin, and allowed Mass with the celebrant facing the people, that is, a return to early Christian practice whereby the celebrant (now called 'the president') faced the people across the altar table rather than standing with his back to them, a symbolic breaking down of the barriers between ordained ministers and lay people.[44] This last change was undoubtedly a spiritual plus, despite the fact that the consequent re-ordering of churches was frequently an architectural disaster. The updating of the catechism, a book of religious instruction essentially desired for a largely illiterate laity, and the new emphasis upon the common study of the Bible, were also benefits.[45] In all of these ways there was brought about a real liturgical and pastoral renewal involving the laity, a development institutionalised by the establishment of a Pastoral Council in each parish. In view of the crisis among the clergy that would explode in the 1960s and 1970s, it was timely because even the re-introduction of married deacons and a certain growth of the religious orders and congregations would not make up for the loss of priests who wished to marry.[46]

The Council fathers also upheld the importance of the individual conscience as against the absolute authority of the teachings of the Church. This, and the emphasis on the role of the laity, would produce a crisis of authority in the Italian Church. By the end of the 1960s, such had been the weakening of internal discipline that a number of groups of both clergy and laity were in dispute with their bishops. The most clamorous cases were the occupation of Parma Cathedral in September 1968 and the parish of Isolotto, in a working class suburb of Florence, where the parishioners had sent a letter of support to the Parma occupation: the parish priest was eventually dismissed by the archbishop of Florence, Cardinal Florit, for his part in the affair.[47] In fact, there developed in the Italian Church a wide array of groups in conflict with the hierarchy — i cattolici del dissenso — of variegated hues, including from the early 1970s feminists and homosexuals, usually, but not always, organised in communità di base ('base or grass roots communities') outside parochial structures.[48] Though the communità di base movement brought some acknowledged benefits to the Church, many were explicitly and formally condemned by Paul VI in his encyclical Evangelii Nuntiandi of 1975 for 'radically contesting (the authority of) this church'.[49] The major issues for Catholic dissenters were liturgical changes (which were usually not radical enough for dissenters who indulged in their own experiments), the proclamation by clergy and laity alike of the need to take the Church's social teaching on justice and peace at its face value, and the rejection of the institutional, 'juridical' church, with the need to dismantle the legalism, privileges, wealth and power structures of the Church in order to return to 'apostolic purity'.

This dissent was clearly not solely the product of the Second Vatican Council but, like the student movements of 1967–68 in Italy (see below), a result of foreign ideological influences as well. The first influences of nascent 'liberation theology' reached Europe after the Medellín congress of Latin American bishops in 1967. These blended with a more relaxed attitude towards Marxist categories of thought and action that had been created by Pope John John's 'opening to the East', his removing of the ban on a Christian Democratic 'opening to the left' (i.e. parliamentary cooperation with the PSI), and, above all, the thrust of his encyclical *Pacem in Terris*, which made a clear distinction 'between a false philosophy of the nature, origin and purpose of men and the world, and economic, social, cultural, and political undertakings, even when such undertakings draw their origin and inspiration from that philosophy'.[50]

Catholic lay challenges to the institutional church also manifested themselves in the 1967–68 student rebellion; indeed, they could be said to have been at the heart of them inasmuch as the first major eruption of student revolt took place in the autumn of 1967 in the social sciences faculty of the University of Trento, which had been founded by the left wing of the local Christian Democratic Party precisely in order to provide the Church with loyal, obedient but well-educated intellectual cadres who 'would analyse and direct the complex processes of transformation that were then under way in Italy'.[51] Even more startling was the fact that the rebellion quickly spread to the very Catholic University of the Sacred Heart in Milan, the flagship of Italian Catholic higher education efforts in Italy. In both the Trento and Catholic University situations it is clear that the broader, more radical Marxist ideological influences at work in the wider student movement – from Third World guerrilla groups, Marcusian libertarian Marxism and perhaps even the Maoism of the Cultural Revolution – were also important.[52]

If there was a massive rise, not to say explosion, of dissenting Catholic movements in the 1960s, then it is also true that there was a massive decline, nay collapse, of Catholic lay associationalism of the traditional type. Membership of Azione Cattolica Italiana, and especially of its youth organisations, dropped dramatically – overall, from a starting figure of 2.6 million, membership actually halved between 1966 and 1970, and had halved again by 1978.[53] What was much more alarming for the Church was that many of the youth who defected joined the Communist Party or, worse, entered the ranks of the extra-parliamentary groups to the left of the Communists such as Lotta

Continua, Avanguardia Operaia and the Partito Democratico dell'Unita Proletaria (PDUP): 'there were so many Catholics in it that one of the in-jokes was that the PDUP was the second largest Catholic party in Italy'.[54] A few ex-Catholic militants, such as Renato Curcio and Margherita Cagol, actually ended up inside terrorist groups such as the Red Brigades.[55]

Perhaps the most serious blow for the Church was the 'defection' of a whole wing of the Italian Catholic movement, ACLI, the association of Catholic workers, which had played such a key role in combating Communism during the Cold War. ACLI increasingly moved away from the position of its parent body, Catholic Action, and from under the authority of the ecclesiastical hierarchy. Led by Livio Labor, it established an autonomous role for itself by the end of the 1960s, adopting a 'class choice', rather than inter-class, position, and it effectively went over to Socialism. At its congress in June–July 1969 it officially ended its special relationship with the Christian Democrats of which it had hitherto been one of the strongest supporters, and left its members free to vote for whichever party they chose.[56] Three years later, in the 1972 general elections, Labor was to launch the first serious experiment in Catholic political pluralism since the war by offering an alternative list of left-wing political candidates under the name of the Movimento Politico dei Lavoratori (Political Movement of the Workers); the candidates won a paltry 0.4 per cent of the vote.[57] The Cristiani per il Socialismo (Christians for Socialism) movement, which sought to conciliate Marxism and Catholicism, had even less success in the longer term, though it encouraged some Catholics to stand as independent candidates in the PCI list in the 1976 election, with some success and to the outrage of many bishops.[58]

Faced with waves of dissent and disobedience in the 1960s and 1970s, the Italian Church of Papa Montini would find some eventual consolation in two lay movements of a more obedient and non-dissenting kind, the Focolarini and Comunione e Liberazione. Ironically, the former had nearly been suppressed by the Italian Bishops' Conference (CEI – Conferenza Episcopale Italiana) in 1960.[59] The latter was actually an older movement founded by Don Giussani in the 1950s, but it only got its name in 1968.[60] These two movements offered a haven for Catholic adults and young people respectively who were more accepting of ecclesiastical authority, and they would therefore provide an important 'reserve' for Pope John Paul II in his battles with liberally inclined Catholics in the 1980s and 1990s.

The 'Catholic–Communist dialogue' in the 1970s

The 1970s was undoubtedly one of the most crisis-ridden decades in the history of modern Italy. It was characterised by the disruptive, and sometimes violent, grass roots activities of social and political movements: *auto-riduzione* (non-payment or reduced payment for goods and services by, usually, young customers); squatters; *comitati di quartiere* (neighbourhood committees); the wildcat strikes of the Cobas (Comitati di Base – grass roots union groups) and terrorism of both left and right. And all this was against the background of the economic effects of the Yom Kippur War of 1973, such as rising unemployment and inflation, as well as the ineffectiveness of the centre-left ruling coalition. Consequently, the Christian Democrats and their allies in government were the chief targets of protest. But so were both the Church and the Communist Party in their different ways. The dissent and protest that the Church faced has been seen. That faced by the Communist Party came largely from outside, from the extra-parliamentary left, all of which criticised what they saw as the party's abandonment of 'the revolutionary path'.[61] In the 1976 general elections their parliamentary representatives, Democrazia Proletaria (Proletarian Democracy) won 1.5 per cent of the vote and six seats; another new protest party, Radicals, with a definite libertarian, feminist appeal, won a further 1.1 per cent and four seats. When the fact that the Communist Party reached its electoral high point in 1976, with 34.4 per cent of the votes, is taken into consideration it is clear that had the nearly 900,000 votes that went to these groups gone to the Communist Party, it would have come very close to the Christian Democrats' electoral showing of 38.7 per cent.[62]

The 1976 elections also show that, in the exercise of their newly found freedom of conscience, many Catholic voters had in general terms drifted to the left. There was a wide intermediary ground between the two great institutions of Italian civil society – the Church and the Communist Party. There was a growing feeling among some Catholics and Communists alike that they had more in common than divided them. Ginsborg says in his analysis of the ideological basis of Communist Party leader Enrico Berlinguer's 'historic compromise', an offer of political cooperation with the Christian Democrats:

> He presented it as a grand strategy in which Catholics and Communists would find a shared moral and ethical code on which to base the social and political salvation of Italy. The Catholic emphasis on solidarity would combine with the Communist practice of collective action to produce a new political order.[63]

Berlinguer, whose marriage to a devout Catholic was a sort of 'historic compromise' in miniature, and who was 'Catholic Communist' like Franco Rodano, might believe that there was a dialogue, or at least the possibility of one, and the auguries looked good from the mid-1960s onwards, but in reality there was never a dialogue at an *institutional* level. The Church might no longer be thundering out repetitions of the 1949 excommunication, but Paul VI, and later John Paul II, would reiterate that the philosophical chasm between Catholicism and Marxism remained. When the 'historic compromise' finally came to pass it would be a transient and largely unsuccessful phenomenon (see below, pp. 151–2).

The 'dechristianisation' of Italy?

While it is undeniably true that the economic, social and cultural changes of the 1950s and 1960s had a massive impact on Catholic belief and practice, not to mention political behaviour, in Italy, there is little consensus about the exact nature of that impact. The assumption has always been that these changes profoundly affected religious belief and religious practice in an essentially negative way, i.e. in the direction of 'secularisation'. The first methodological issue that needs to be resolved before changing patterns of religious belief and practice can be measured is what the basic criteria of those beliefs and practices are. The yardsticks generally used by sociologists of religion to measure Catholic religious adherence are observance of the 'dominical' and 'pascal' precepts. The dominical precept is the requirement – for all Catholics at that time, on pain of mortal sin – to attend Mass on all Sundays and other holy days of obligation (greater feasts).[64] The pascal precept requires that every Catholic receives communion at least once a year, normally at Easter or soon after.[65] Given the penalty of mortal sin, the dominical precept must surely be the absolute bottom line of regular religious observance; it seems likely that those discharging their Sunday obligations would also be taking communion once a year anyway.

Not surprisingly, the numerous polls of religious practice taken since the Second World War have tended to use the dominical precept. Thus the Doxa polling organisation's report published in 1962 used the latter as the basis of its various surveys of religious observance made over the preceding seven-year period and came up with the results shown in the table.

Attendance at Sunday Mass in Italy according to the size of the Comune*

Answer	Less than 10,000	10–50,000	More than 50,000
Yes	60%	53%	43%
No	40%	47%	57%

* municipal district
Source: cited in S.S. Aquaviva, *The Decline of the Sacred in Industrial Society*, Oxford: Oxford University Press, 1979, p. 79.

The survey confirms what could have been surmised about the differences between urban and rural religiosity, that the falling away from the Church was greatest in the big cities. It also predictably distinguished between men and women with the result that whereas 61 per cent of women had been to Mass the previous Sunday, only 39 per cent of men had: on the other hand, it suggested that there was virtually no difference in patterns of Mass attendance between different social groups defined as 'upper and upper-middle', 'middle and lower middle' and 'lower' class, whatever those terms mean.[66] As far as generational change is concerned, in 1989 Leonardi and Wertman argued that it 'has been a major factor in secularisation; in the 1950s and 1960s, as many among the young as among the old attended church weekly; since then, considerably fewer of the young than the old do so'.[67] Another survey, cited by Clark, claimed that Mass attendance had fallen from 69 per cent of adults in 1956 to 53 per cent in 1961, to 48 per cent in 1968 and to 35 per cent in 1972.[68] So, over the 1956–68 period there was clearly a very sharp and significant fall in traditional religious observance in Italy.

Aquaviva makes the point that in Italy there was in this period a 'collapse of the so-called "devotions" . . . these represent in turn the decay of the sense of the sacred'.[69] A similar 'collapse' is observable in most parts of the Catholic world after the Second Vatican Council, and thanks to its stress on the centrality of Eucharistic worship and its requirements for the re-ordering of Catholic churches to symbolise that centrality, most new Catholic churches built thereafter were largely devoid of the devotional 'trappings' – statues of the Sacred Heart of Jesus, for example.[70] That 'collapse' was probably not as swift or as clear-cut as he suggests. There had always been a gap between 'official religion' and 'popular religion' in Italy, and the evidence suggests that popular devotions to the Sacred Hearts of Jesus and Mary persisted strongly among the older faithful, along with the recital of the rosary. On the other hand, liturgical 'dissidents' were not numerous: as Melloni explains, 'those nostalgic for Latin were a small, vociferous though inoffensive minority'.[71] The changes that were most probably felt most acutely were not so much the innovations of the Second Vatican Council as those experienced by the many southern immigrants who attended church in the towns and cities of northern Italy from the late 1950s onwards. For both them and the local clergy, it must have seemed as if they were living through a veritable 'culture clash', between the warm, 'sentimental' religion of the southerners and the 'cold', rather more intellectual, liturgical preferences of the northern clergy.

What are equally, if not more, significant are the changes in religious identity. Whereas hitherto to be a Catholic had meant to be 'in good standing' with the institutional church, i.e. the clergy – hence the necessity of regular

Mass attendance, participation in Catholic organisations of one form or another and adhering to the moral guidelines issued by the hierarchy – from the 1960s onwards more and more Italians when questioned in surveys would say that they believed in God, that they called themselves Catholics, but that they saw no incompatibility between this and infrequent attendance at Mass and an almost complete failure to adhere to Catholic moral teaching on such issues as contraception, divorce (as witnessed in the referendum on the subject in 1974) and abortion (see Chapter 9, pp. 153–5). Indeed, as in other parts of the Catholic world, so in Italy, Paul VI's attempt to hold the line against 'artificial contraception' in his encyclical *Humanae Vitae* of 1968 probably led to the apostasy of many thousands of the faithful.[72]

In the years of the 'miracle' there was arguably a deeper problem at work that undermined the religious beliefs and observances of many Catholics in Italy: the essential superficiality of their faith. This was hinted at by two very perceptive members of the parochial clergy at the time, Don Lorenzo Milani, parish priest of S. Donato, Barbiana, in the Tuscan diocese of Pistoia, and Don Giulio Bevilacqua, friend of Mgr Montini, a parish priest in the diocese of Brescia.[73] The failure of religious education in schools and catechism classes at church to inculcate a clear, structured Catholic belief system into their peasant parishioners meant that religious observance was essentially a formalistic manifestation of local collective identity, epitomised by the 'sort of folkloric ritual with which the majority of the adults in the rural environment solemnise the annual feasts as rites of passage'.[74]

According to Liliano Faenza, in a study of sharecroppers near Rimini in the early 1950s, 'the religious beliefs of the masses are the absolute negation of any intimate experience of the divine'; half of Italians were 'indifferent believers' who may have attended church but ignored her teachings and a further 20 per cent, according to him, were simply superstitious, believing in the power of the evil eye, or the powers of local saints, or witches – a view confirmed by many observers of southern ritualism.[75] On the other hand, the indifference or hostility to religion that was to be found in those cities, towns and villages that formed part of the Marxist sub-culture had not substantially increased, even if it was perhaps now more open and evident, as is illustrated by this description of the reception afforded to Mgr Montini in some sections of his diocese of Milan:

> Montini's efforts to reach out to the workers sometimes caused mirth. He became a familiar sight in the city, approaching workers with a sad smile and outstretched hand, despite their hoots and jeers. In the end they usually accepted *la main tendue*.[76]

He responded to this situation in much the same way as his late nineteenth century and early twentieth predecessors in the see of Saint Ambrose had done, by establishing a sort of 'worker-priest' organisation, the Missionaries of the World of Work, precisely at the time when the life was being throttled out of the actual worker priest movement in France by the Vatican. He also created a new journal *Relazioni Sociali* around a nucleus of ex-FUCI students to publicise the pastoral problems of the industrial milieu among Catholic activists.[77]

The transformation of the Christian Democrats: from Catholic party to 'party of the state'

The electoral situation did not get any better for the Christian Democrats as the 1960s progressed into the 1970s; on the contrary, it never returned even to the low point (40 per cent) of 1953, hovering around 38 per cent until it plummeted in 1983.[78] Support for the Catholic party was shrinking due to the effects of secularisation and the Second Vatican Council. Another factor was the impulse towards Catholic political pluralism that had been most dramatically manifested in the emergence of the Movimento Politico dei Lavoratori (MPL) but was actually more widespread and dangerous. There was a tendency for increasing numbers of Catholics to ignore the instructions of the ecclesiastical hierarchy and vote instead for left-wing parties such as the Socialists or Communists or even the smaller 'lay' parties' of the centre. The near-monopoly of the Catholic electorate by the Christian Democrats had been finally broken.

The failure of the reformist project of the centre-left may also be attributed to a deliberate choice on the part of the Christian Democrats, who were afraid that the effects of reform would upset the precarious balance of social forces on which its electorate was built (as in the south in the late 1940s and early 1950s). Whatever the explanation, there can be no doubt that the trend towards state clientelism accentuated from the 1960s onwards, as the Christian Democrats strengthened their links with the 'state bourgeoisie' composed of finance speculation and parasitic elements, all feeding on the patronage resources provided by control of the governmental apparatus, be it at a national, regional or local level, and the vast state economic sector. And while tactical/strategic manoeuvring at the parliamentary level was a key factor in the survival of the Christian Democrats in the 1960s and 1970s as the dominant party in the ruling coalition, fundamental to it also was the fact that in this period it continued the policy initiated by Fanfani in the mid-1950s of colonising the vast patronage resources at its disposal in state and para-statal, provincial and municipal institutions for electoral and parliamentary purposes. In consequence, the relationship between the Christian Democrats and their electorate in the 1960s and 1970s became increasingly conditioned by personal, clientelistic factors, the clientelistic relationship augmenting, and increasingly superseding, the ideological cement of the Catholic sub-culture. In this way, the Christian Democrats became, like the Fascists before them, a kind of 'party of the state' or 'regime'.[79]

In particular, the Christian Democrats began to exploit the massive state sector inherited from Fascism for electoral purposes. As a result of the operations of the Istituto per la Ricostruzione Industriale (IRI – the industrial reconstruction institute established during the Great Depression to bail out 'lame duck' industries and banks), according to Ricossa, 'after 1936, the Italian State owned a proportionately larger part of industry than was the case in any other European state with the exception of the Soviet Union'.[80] Though Enrico Mattei had been given the task of dismantling this massive state sector, beginning with Agenzia Generale Italian di Petrolio (AGIP), the state petrol distribution firm, by capitalising on the discovery of natural gas in the Po Valley, he added a whole new dimension to that holding – Ente Nazionele Idrocarburi (ENI – the national hydrocarbon agency). This he used in restructuring and modernising Italy's economic system, with greatly beneficial effects during the economic 'miracle'.[81] Thus, after the Second World War, the Italian State had a controlling interest in economic activities ranging from transport (railways, airlines and some coach lines) to engineering, chemical and energy-producing industries. In addition, the state controlled, directly or indirectly, the lion's share (roughly 80 per cent) of Italy's banking and credit sector. Mattei was the first Christian Democratic politician to use systematically the funds of a state-controlled industry to influence internal party struggles between factions.[82]

In fact, the Fascists had already pioneered the use of jobs in the state bureaucracy (and in that sense were simply imitating their Liberal-conservative predecessors), the party, the corporations, and possibly in the state economic sector too, for the purpose of 'manufacturing consensus'.[83] The Christian Democrats followed suit on a larger scale, colonising industrial undertakings, banks and other credit institutions, municipal utility agencies and even the media with their appointees to reward political favours, win electoral support and guarantee access to new sources of party funding.

The re-rooting of the Catholic party in Italian civil society, north and south, in this period, on a largely clientelistic basis took place without raising serious concerns on the part of the ecclesiastical hierarchy. The 'corruption' implicit in these relationships raised no eyebrows; rather they were accepted as a necessity if 'our people' were to be kept in power and the 'enemy' kept out. Because of the Communist threat, as the leading Catholic politician

Aldo Moro once famously said, the Christian Democrats were 'condemned to govern'. Moreover, these clientelistic relationships were seen by many as part of a long-standing, traditional Italian political practice; arguably they had been the very essence of Italian political culture since Roman times. As a means of providing and sustaining employment in areas of poverty and deprivation, i.e. mainly the south, they were, indeed, seen as wholly legitimate and consistent with the Catholic social doctrine of 'social solidarity', reiterated by John XXIII and Paul VI in such encyclicals as *Mater et Magistra* (1961), *Pacem in Terris* (1963), *Popolorum Progressio* (1967) and *Octogesima Adveniens*. As the means of clientelistic 'exchange' – i.e. the price paid for the vote – were extended to the distribution of pensions and other social security benefits, as well as mortgages and bank loans, *lo stato assistenziale* (difficult to translate but 'the assistance state', more or less) seemed to be just a peculiarly Italian form of the 'welfarism' practised elsewhere in Europe and North America.[84]

The divorce referendum and the tragic end of Paul VI's reign

The chickens of secularisation came home to roost in a spectacular way in the referendum on the Divorce Law in 1974. Decline in the influence of the Church and new ideas of women's liberation had a powerful impact on Italian attitudes to the role of women, family structure and sexual behaviour. The decline of Catholic women's organisations and the advent of the Socialists to power in 1963 meant the possibility of change in one important aspect of family structures – divorce. Pressure from within the Socialist Party, aided by support within the lay centre parties and more hesitant support from the Communists, always fearful of provoking a row with the Church, provided a fillip to those advocating reforms such as divorce and the revision of family law.[85] In 1970, they succeeded in persuading Parliament to pass the Fortuna-Baslini divorce law, one which, it has to be said, was very mild and restrictive.[86] It was followed in 1975 by a new law on the family that removed many of the iniquitous provisions of the Fascist Code of law – in particular, prosecution of women for adultery without a similar provision against men and the moral, legal and financial subordination of the wife to the husband – and made them jointly responsible for making decisions about their children.[87]

Despite five separate assertions by the Constitutional Court after 1970 that the Divorce Law was constitutional, the Church would not accept the situation lying down. The response of the Christian Democratic majority around Fanfani was to promote a referendum to repeal the Divorce Law as a means of rallying 'Catholic' Italy to the Church, and more importantly to the party, and to defeat the left, especially the Communists. The referendum failed miserably. It actually divided Catholics: CISL refused to take a stand on the matter, ACLI and the Christians for Socialism upheld the principle of the non-interference of the Church in state matters, and a not insignificant number of Catholic intellectuals participated in a campaign called 'I Cattolici per il "No"' (no to repeal, that is).[88] The Vatican even tried to use strong-arm tactics to silence Catholic dissenters.[89] But Fanfani had backed the wrong horse because nearly 60 per cent voted against repeal of the Divorce Law, many of them women.

Paul VI was especially upset by the defeat in the divorce referendum, tending to see it as the 'end of Catholic Italy'. This was an unduly pessimistic view. What it did signify was the beginning of the end of the Church's hold on the thinking of the Italian people in terms of sexual behaviour, marriage and family relationships. In broader terms, Catholic religious practice had seriously declined, as the figures on p. 145 demonstrate, and the response of the Italian Bishops' Conference was to declare Italy 'mission territory', a rather embarrassing thing to have to do in a country that was supposed to be the panting heart of Catholicism but, then, it was only Rome on a larger scale. In order to bring back some unity and purpose to the Italian Church, a national convention of Italian Catholics was organised in Rome in October 1976 under the watchwords 'Evangelisation and Human Promotion'. 'Unity' was seriously impaired by the fact that some leading Italian prelates, including Cardinal Albino Luciani, the future Pope John Paul I, *deliberately* stayed away.[90] Nevertheless, on the whole it was representative of the many different currents among Italian Catholics and succeeded not only in permitting some serious dialogue between them but also in drawing up a pastoral plan to meet the Church's mission 'crisis' for the coming years.[91]

In the meantime, the 'opening to the left' moved towards its logical conclusion, a 'historic compromise' between the Christian Democrats and the Communists at a parliamentary level. The centre-left, being unable to carry out the necessary structural reform of Italy's government and bureaucracy, was faced by serious and widespread social unrest, and now terrorism, principally of the left but also of the neo-Fascist right, had raised its ugly head. An 'opening to the Communists', who already cooperated with the governing coalition in under-the-counter parliamentary deals, was deemed necessary to resolve these problems. For their part, the Communists led by Enrico Berlinguer were fearful of a repeat of the CIA-backed military coup against Chile's President Allende being tried in Italy. In any case, like the Socialists before them, the Communists had broken free from Soviet control, condemned the 1968 invasion of Czechoslovakia and espoused 'Euro-Communism', which would permit acceptance of NATO. Between 1976 and 1979, the Communists cooperated with a series of Christian Democratic *monocolore* (single party) governments by abstaining from votes of confidence but voting for agreed policies, especially relating to terrorism.[92] In the spring of 1978, it seemed that Aldo Moro, the chairman of the Christian Democrats, had succeeded in carrying out a remarkable political operation to translate the 'historic compromise' into actual Communist participation at ministerial level. But Moro, Papa Montini's close friend, was kidnapped and murdered by Red Brigades terrorists, precisely in order to obstruct that operation, hence the fact that his corpse was left in the boot of a car exactly halfway between the headquarters of the Christian Democrats and those of the Communists in the centre of Rome. For Paul VI, this was the end. Himself suffering from cancer, he had to endure the agonies of seeing all his efforts to rescue Moro rebuffed, including his famous 'Letter to the Red Brigades', not only by the terrorists but also by the Christian Democrats who, for reasons that still remain a partial mystery, were not prepared to bargain with his captors.[93] So Paul's reign ended in pain, disillusionment and despair.

Chapter 9

ITALY IN THE AGE OF RELIGIOUS PLURALISM (1978 TO THE PRESENT DAY)

Introduction

THIS CHAPTER COULD HAVE STARTED in at least three different years: in 1984, when a new concordat, replacing that of 1929, was signed between Italy and the Holy See, thus inaugurating a quite new and different concordatory regime; in 1981, when Catholic attempts to reverse the introduction of abortion into Italy were resoundingly defeated; or in 1978, when Paul VI, the last Italian pope, died.

The year 1978 makes more sense because it also marked other important watersheds in the history of both the Church and the Italian State. Italian democracy survived the Red Brigades' 'blow at the heart of the state'. Despite widespread fears that Moro's murder marked the triumph of Red Brigades terrorism, and consequently the end of the 'first (Italian) republic', the efforts of the terrorists ultimately failed; the 'historic compromise' enacted in the form of Communist parliamentary abstention from voting against the new government's reform programme ('no no-confidence') ensured that the Communists, and the trade union movement that it controlled, the CGIL, closed ranks with the Christian Democrats and other democratic forces in defence of the republic, supporting legislative and other measures that would eventually defeat terrorism from all sides.[1]

The year 1978 was also important for another reason: following Paul VI's death and the one-month pontificate of John Paul I, Cardinal Albino Luciani, patriarch of Venice, who died suddenly and unexpectedly in October, the first non-Italian for 525 years was elected to the papal throne, Karol Wojtyla, cardinal archbishop of Cracow in Poland. The election of a non-Italian pope inevitably posed all sorts of questions about the future role of the Church in Italian society, and its relationship with the Italian State.[2] Though Papa Wojtyla spoke Italian well enough, as he demonstrated in his first speech in St Peter's Square following his election, and probably had some knowledge of the problems of the Italian Church, it could not be expected that he would be able to follow them, and even less the complexities of Italian politics, with the same interest and knowledge. But throughout his pontificate, John Paul II was to demonstrate a real concern for Italian political matters that affected the life of the Church in the peninsula and a willingness to speak out openly in the defence of Catholic interests, as during the abortion referendum of 1981. Employing a succession of leading Italian cardinal archbishops, Siri of Genoa and Poletti and Ruini, cardinal vicars of Rome, as president of CEI, the Vatican maintained a tight control over the Italian Church.[3] John Paul would play a pivotal role in ensuring the conclusion of negotiations for a new concordat in 1984.

The 1984 Concordat and its consequences

Attempts to abolish or re-negotiate the 1929 Concordat had a long 'pre-history'. The first attempt was prompted by the banning of the performance in Rome, in 1965, of Hochuth's play, *The Deputy*, which was critical of Pius XII's response to the Holocaust.[4] Parliamentary motions were raised in subsequent years and in 1968 the Italian government appointed the first commission to study revision of the 1929 Concordat, led by the greatest academic authority on church–state relations, Carlo Arturo Jemolo. The presence of the Socialists in government, as a result of the embedding of the centre-left coalition formula by the end of the 1970s, helped build up parliamentary pressure for change. Pressure had also been building up in Parliament for a revision of the Vatican's tax exemption on the profits from its investments, and Italy's financial relations were further strained in the late 1970s and early 1980s by the operations of the Vatican Bank, the Istituto per le Opere di Religione (IOR). Things came to a head after the Sindona and Banco Ambrosiano banking scandals, which eventually led to judicial action against the IOR's president, archbishop Paul Marcinkus.[5] On the sidelines, the newly emerged Partito Radicale led by Marco Pannella, representing a whole array of libertarian and anti-clerical forces, conducted a vociferous campaign for repeal rather than revision; many of the *dissenso cattolico* and, most spectacularly, a group of Catholic intellectuals led by the historian Pietro Scoppola supported the cause.[6] On the other hand, the passage of the Divorce Law, another result of the Socialist presence, led to the Vatican withdrawing from negotiations about a new concordat on the grounds that the Law was in breach of the 1929 Concordat. Serious negotiations resumed in 1976, but despite the broader parliamentary consensus for revision of the Concordat generated by the existence between 1976 and 1979 of what was already a government of the 'historic compromise' to which the PCI gave 'external support'(i.e. support in secret parliamentary votes or abstention, but held no ministerial office), the negotiations became mired in the Byzantine politics of the centre-left coalition and the tortuous backdoor negotiations between Papa Montini's Secretariat of State and his *prediletti* (friends and favourites) among the Christian Democrats, Colombo, Moro and Rumor.[7] In all, thanks to these complications, no less than five drafts were gone through before agreement was reached.

A breakthrough came in 1981. The abortion referendum of 1981, in which 67 per cent of those voting supported retention of Italy's abortion law, clearly confirmed the message of the 1974 divorce referendum, that Italian society had become more secularised, thereby strengthening the hand of the reformers. Another important factor was the weakness of the Christian Democrats, the most serious dimension of which was factionalism, the bitter disputes between the various factions inside the party. According to Clark: 'It [the Christian Democratic Party] was just a loose alliance of squabbling factions with no acknowledged leader.'[8] As a result, the first non-Christian Democratic prime minister since December 1945, the republican Giovanni Spadolini, was appointed. When the Christian Democrats did badly in the 1983 elections, he was followed by another non-Christian Democrat, the aggressive Socialist leader, Bettino Craxi; between them, Spadolini and Craxi held the prime ministership for most of the period 1981–87. The argument goes that just as in the 1920s the Partito Popolare was not strong enough to negotiate a solution to the 'Roman Question' and the Vatican did a deal with (the ex-Socialist) Benito Mussolini instead, so, in the 1980s, the Christian Democrats were equally unsuccessful (or unwilling?) and so the Vatican did a deal with a Socialist prime minister, Bettino Craxi.

Craxi's success in 1984, when his predecessors had failed, was not solely due to his energy and determination. There had not only been a major change of personnel at the head of Italian government, i.e. from a Christian Democratic prime minister to a Socialist one (and to a Socialist president of the republic, Sandro Pertini); there had been an equally radical change in the Vatican. Papa Montini, with his incestuous relations with the Christian Democratic leadership, had been replaced by a Polish pope who seems to have felt that what was on offer was a good deal by the standards of his country and that the Italian Bishops' Conference should accept it.[9] In addition, the French cardinal Jean Villot had been replaced as Vatican secretary of state by the Italian, Agostino

Casaroli, whose experience of *Ostpolitik* probably inclined him to the same conclusion as his master's.

The most striking feature of the arrangements established by the new Concordat signed on 18 February 1984 by Craxi and Andreotti (the foreign minister) for Italy and Casaroli for the Vatican was the omission of the formula that Roman Catholicism is 'sole religion of the State'.[10] For the first time in the modern history of the Italian State, the Church had been 'dis-established', with state 'vetting' of episcopal and other major ecclesiastical appointments abolished, though some legal and financial ties remained between them, nevertheless. Church property became fully taxable, which had been a bone of contention between Italy and the Vatican in the 1960s and 1970s (see p. 153), and the Vatican Bank came under Italian legal regulation.[11] Also significant was the abolition of the concept of 'the sacred character' of Rome, something that had become increasingly meaningless since the 1970s. It was replaced by a much blander statement: 'The Italian Republic recognises the particular importance that Rome, as episcopal see of the Pontiff, has for the Catholic community'.[12] Another obnoxious feature of the 1929 Concordat, the clause effectively forbidding the employment of 'censored' priests, was removed, and, indeed, dioceses were actually encouraged to allot funds for them.[13] Thus were the most serious offences against religious liberty, as contained in the former concordatory system, at last eliminated.

The Church took over the administration of the ecclesiastical endowment funds (Fondo per il Culto etc.) formerly administered by the state, and income from these funds was supplemented by some once-and-for-all subsidies by the state, by covenanted offerings of the faithful and a system modelled on the German 'church tax', though different because it is not compulsory. Italians can elect to have 0.8 per cent of the income tax they pay assigned to the benefit of the Catholic Church or, alternatively, to other religious communities or specified charities. As de Franciscis notes: 'For centuries Italians had never had to make a commitment to their Catholic faith, and even less, a financial commitment.'[14] So the Italian Church would now become more like the Church in other countries, increasingly dependent upon the offerings of the faithful for its financial survival. A public opinion poll soon after the signing of the Concordat indicating that 59 per cent of Italians accepted the new system of financing was a good augury for the future.[15] In fact, a Ministry of Finance report of 1989 showed that well over 15 million out of 27 million Italian taxpayers had chosen to exercise their to right to assign eight-thousandths of their income tax (or taxes) to religious or charitable purposes, and of these 11,300,000 taxpayers, 41 per cent had opted to give it to the Catholic Church.[16] The 1984 Concordat provided parents with the right to opt *into* religious instruction in state schools rather than opt *out*, as had been the case under the 1929 system, but it took two years to negotiate a mutually acceptable set of arrangements to implement this. A survey made in 1987 banished the fears of bishops and religious instruction teachers that these arrangements would lead to mass desertion of religious instruction classes: overall, 94 per cent of Italian primary and secondary school pupils enrolled for religious instruction in July 1986.[17]

So did the new Concordat really change that much in the relationship between church and state in Italy? In some ways it did, but the institutional church still maintains a visual omnipresence in public buildings – courts, schools and offices – thanks to the hanging of the crucifix, which has only been recently contested by non-Catholics (see below, p. 169) and which symbolises the Church's continuing strong influence in state institutions as well. For example, the Church still appoints chaplains to hospitals, prisons, the police and the armed forces and plays a role in some state or semi-state ceremonies, such as the funerals of the victims of major natural disasters or organised crime and of Italian servicemen killed abroad. It could thus be argued that this is not very dissimilar from the position of the *established* churches of England and Scotland in Britain, in a country with, admittedly, much lower weekly church attendance rates (5–10 per cent) than in Italy.

But the fact that the 1984 Concordat retains part of the wording of Article Seven of the Republican Constitution suggests that, even towards the end of the twentieth century, the Roman Catholic Church still claimed to be on an equal footing with a sovereign nation state:

> The Italian Republic and the Holy See reaffirm that the State and the Catholic Church, each in its own order, are independent and sovereign, and pledge to fully respect such principle in their relations, and to mutually cooperate for the promotion of mankind and the welfare of the Nation.[18]

The minority religions

Perhaps the most significant change brought about largely by the new Concordat has been in the status of the minority religions in Italy. Arguably one of the short-term consequences of the Church's defeat in the 1974 divorce referendum was the willingness of the Italian government to repeal Mussolini's *culti ammessi* laws, which were declared unconstitutional by the Constitutional Court in 1977.[19] Following this, the Italian government negotiated 'mini-concordats' with other faiths, most notably the Jews and the Waldensians (the latter merged with the Methodists in 1981 to form a church of 30,000 members), which guaranteed their rights and property before Italian law. That for the Waldensians was ready in 1978, but not promulgated until after the new Concordat of August 1984.[20] In 1993, other religions were allowed access to the 'Otto per mille' (0.008) provision.[21] But there are virtually no resemblances between these 'mini-concordats' and the 1984 Concordat with the Catholic Church. The other religions have no special rights or subsidies and no matrimonial jurisdiction. A series of further 'mini-concordats' was negotiated: with the Seventh Day Adventists in 1986, with the Assemblies of God (Pentecostalists) in 1987 and with the Baptists in 1993.[22] As far as the Jewish communities are concerned, the status of the *Communità israelitiche* as entities in public law was recognised, and arrangements about kosher food, the observance of the Sabbath etc. were made for Jews in the armed forces and in hospitals.[23]

Clientelism, corruption and crime: the decline and collapse of the Christian Democratic regime in the 1980s and early 1990s

In the spring of 1994 the Christian Democratic regime collapsed, with all of the component parties of the coalition disappearing, though some only temporarily and others ultimately managing to recycle themselves. But the bottom line was that the political hegemony of the Catholic party had come to an end. While, as will be seen, the immediate causes of the collapse were the impact of the *Tangentopoli* or 'Bribesville' scandals and well-publicised trials of the previous 24 months, the Christian Democrats had been in serious electoral decline for nearly two decades. The party's vote in elections for the Chamber of Deputies went from 38.8 per cent in 1976 to 34.3 per cent in 1979, and there then followed a sudden drop to less than 33 per cent in 1983: four years later it recovered temporarily to 34.3 per cent, only to reach an all-time low of 29.75 per cent in 1992.[24] There can be no doubt that this decline was as much a long-term consequence of the process of secularisation from the mid-1950s onwards, and the liberating impact of the Second Vatican Council on Catholic political choices, as contingent political circumstances.

It can be argued that the Christian Democrats had started digging their own grave by presiding over the economic 'miracle' of the late 1950s and early 1960s, with its concomitant processes of social change, migration and urbanisation, all leading to a decline in allegiance to the Church. The rigid sense that it was a Catholic's duty to vote Christian Democrat waned, and Catholics felt able to make an electoral choice more freely. Thus the party increasingly had to find other means to prop up its vote. In consequence, in the 1970s and 1980s, the Christian Democrats, like the other parties in the centre-left coalition, PRI, PSDI, PLI and Socialists, sought to exploit more and more heavily the 'exchange vote', in other words, multifarious forms of clientelism. An important form of clientelism that increasingly gained ground in the 1980s was the *lottizzazione* of jobs in the public sector, that is their allocation strictly on the basis of party allegiance or sympathy: if one did not actually belong to a political party one was expected to be a part of its 'area', so that when RAI's various TV channels were parcelled out among the major parties, an announcer, presenter, scriptwriter, journalist, technician or administrator was working for RAI 1 was expected to belong to the 'Christian democratic area', since the Christian Democrats controlled that channel. They, and to a lesser extent the other coalition parties came also increasingly to rely upon the assistance of organised crime, especially in the south, and most especially in Sicily. Indeed, the shift in the balance of support for the Christian Democrats from north to south demonstrates this very clearly.

This trend reached its peak in the 1992 general elections when the Christian Democrats received only 25 per cent of the vote in the centre–north, compared to nearly 39 per cent of the vote in the south.[25] So they were becoming more and more of a *southern* party, and a further confirmation of this was the fact that in the late 1980s a southerner, Ciriaco De Mita, was elected secretary of the party, and later served as the last Christian Democratic prime minister.

The Italian electorate from the beginning of the 1980s sought to punish the Christian Democrats, and to a lesser extent the Communists, and it did so by various forms of 'protest voting'. The Greens steadily increased their share of the vote between 1983 and 1992, as did the Partito Radicale, the party of libertarianism, anti-clericalism and protest, par excellence.[26] Many Italian voters simply refused to vote at all, or if they did, spoiled their ballot papers. By 1992, these amounted to 14 per cent and 8 per cent of the electorate respectively, extraordinary figures in a country that traditionally had very high voter turnout, thanks to voting having originally been compulsory.[27] But the most important form that the protest vote took, especially in the northern regions of Lombardy, Piedmont and the Veneto, was support for a new political force, the various northern leagues. This movement was protesting against what it saw as 'partyocracy'(rule by the parties and not the electorate), clientelism, corruption and the links between organised crime and the political class. It should be noted that similar patterns of voter dissatisfaction with the ruling political elites, especially centre-left coalitions of Christian Democratic and Socialist/Social Democratic parties was to be found elsewhere in Europe in the 1980s and 1990s – especially in Austria, Belgium and the Netherlands.[28]

The leagues were hostile to the Rome government, which they accused of heavily taxing the industrious, productive north in order to subsidise the lazy, parasitic south. They complained about the new and disturbing phenomenon of immigration of *extra-communitari* (people from outside the European Community) and high levels of crime and taxation. The most telling quotation from the propaganda of the leagues was a claim that whereas Lombardy region possessed only 16.5 per cent of Italy's population, it was paying 23 per cent of the country's taxes.[29] The leagues chiefly drew support from small business people, professionals, small farmers – many people who had hitherto voted either Christian Democrats or Socialist, and their rise was swift. In 1983 the Liga Veneta won only 4.3 per cent of the votes in the Veneto, and in 1987 the Lega Lombarda won only 3 per cent of the vote in its region.[30] But on the eve of the 1992 general elections, the Lega Nord, a merger of the separate leagues, was in a very strong position with a charismatic leader, Umberto Bossi, a strong local organisation and a clear programme – the clearing up of political and administrative corruption, devolution of power over the economy and taxation, education and social welfare from the central government in Rome to three autonomous republics of the north, the centre and the south. As a result, it gained an extraordinary 8.7 per cent of the national vote in those elections, with 25.5 per cent of the vote in the Veneto and 23.6 per cent in Lombardy, both formerly the heartlands of the Catholic party.[31] In the 'deep south', Sicily, anger at Christian Democratic involvement with the Mafia led to the success of the *La Rete* organisation led by the former Christian Democratic mayor of Palermo Leoluca Orlando. It won nearly 2 per cent of the votes for the Chamber in 1992.[32]

Precisely at the point when the Christian Democratic regime was heading towards its fall, the constituent parties were at the height of their apparent success, with vast suites of offices, fleets of cars and lavish spending on party conferences, entertaining, literature and magazines. Party officials were getting individually fat on the proceeds of corruption: one notorious Christian Democratic Party official managed to accumulate 14 Swiss bank accounts and $100 million in cash as a result of, as he said when he appeared in court, 'forty years of personal savings'.[33]

In the case of the Christian Democrats, the party's decline was not merely an electoral phenomenon. It also involved a failure to renew the ranks of the younger membership and leadership. Catholic young people with ideals were simply not coming forward to join the party in the way that they had in the past. They were disillusioned with the party because of its association with clientelism and corruption and became involved in other political parties or voluntary activities instead. Ironically, the party membership figures looked healthy. The operative word is *looked*. In reality, thousands of people on the books were paper members, and many were quite simply dead. It paid the various factions to inflate the membership figures; it helped them in their battles with other factions in votes during party congresses. Leaving aside the phenomenon of the dead, a similar pattern can be observed in other ruling parties in Europe at this time, in particular in the British Conservative Party prior to its catastrophic defeat in the 1997 general elections.

The secularisation and the shrinking of Catholic sub-culture, with knock-on effects for the electoral fortunes of the Christian Democrats, were paralleled by the decline in those of the Communists. There was a shrinking of the working class sub-culture of central Italy, especially the 'Red Belt'. Indeed, the Communists suffered as much from the decline of class and ideological allegiances as the Christian Democrats in the 1980s, in particular a loss of membership: by 1985 Communist Party membership was down from a high point of 2.5 million in 1976 to 1.6 million.[34] A further blow came with the collapse of Communism in eastern Europe and the Soviet Union. Communism was discredited, and with it the Communist Party. Though the party tried to escape this by renaming itself the Partito dei Democratici di Sinistra (PDS – Party of the Democratic Left) in 1989, it got the worst of both worlds: on the one hand, this 're-branding' of its image failed to win it votes, while on the other, it led to a split, with the formation of the group Rifondazione Communista, which took away a sizeable proportion of the party's members and voters.

But the collapse of Communism did not help the Christian Democrats and their allies. With the Communist bogeyman virtually banished once and for all, for many voters there was really no longer any reason to hold their noses and vote Christian Democrat. So one of the biggest props to the regime had been pulled away. Similarly, the USA was now much less concerned about the danger of Communism in Italy, and therefore rather less committed to propping up the Christian Democrats and their allies. And Italy's very minimalist involvement in the Gulf War of 1990–91 also cooled American attitudes towards Italy.

The Church in the crisis of the Italian Republic, 1992–96

In the four years between the spring of 1992 and that of 1996, Italy went through a series of political crises almost without parallel in her modern history, crises that deeply involved Italian political Catholicism and affected the institutional church. By the time that general elections were due in the spring of 1992, the Italian political system was facing a serious crisis of *legitimacy*, and this problem most particularly affected the Christian Democrats and their coalition allies. Large sections of the Italian electorate challenged their right to rule and in particular the methods that they used to stay in power. The clearest evidence of this had come only a few months before, in a referendum that had been held in the summer of 1991 when 95.6 per cent of those voting in a referendum did so to modify the personal preference voting (PPV) system.[35] This was the system whereby voters, after having cast their ballot for the party of their choice, then cast another vote or votes for preferred candidates on that party's list. This was really quite crucial to the 'exchange vote system': through PPV the voter was able to reward the politician who had granted him or her some personal, material favour. The almost unanimous rejection of that system by the electorate, which took place against the declared wishes of most of the political class, was accordingly a slap in the face for the politicians. So, in the elections of 1992 a number of chickens finally came home to roost.

The shock of the outcome of the elections was, in the short term, reasonably well absorbed by the Italian political system: the parties of the Christian Democratic regime were, at this juncture, down, but not yet out. Parliamentary government, Italian style, continued. But very quickly the system was engulfed by a growing number of corruption scandals and trials, and the added ingredient of spectacular Mafia murders. Such things had been far from unusual in the post-war history of Italy, but when Mario Chiesa, a Socialist Party official, was arrested on charges of taking bribes (*tangenti*) from suppliers and contractors in February 1992, this led the Milan public prosecution service to a vast network of bribery and corruption within his party, and, inevitably, in other parties, including the Christian Democrats.[36] By the end of the year, the *Tangentopoli* ('Bribesville') prosecutions involved a third of all those elected to Parliament and implicated a thousand people, including four former prime ministers, Bettino Craxi (PSI), Arnaldo Forlani, Giulio Andreotti and Ciriaco de Mita (all Christian Democrats), and many other politicians, businessmen and civil servants.[37]

The determination of the public prosecutors to pursue their campaign against corruption into the heart of the Christian Democratic regime was the product of the fact that the political situation had been changed by the results of the 1992 general elections, which severely weakened both the Christian Democrats and the Socialists. The prosecutors felt that whereas in the past their efforts had often been blocked or 'deviated' by covert political activity, the top politicians had less ability to do this now. They were not proved entirely correct because, to the outrage and stupefaction of most Italians, Parliament refused to lift the legal immunity of the biggest cheese of them all, Craxi, who promptly fled to the safety of Tunisia. The Mafia murders in 1992 of a leading a leading Sicilian Christian Democratic politician, Salvatore Lima (in March) and two public prosecutors, Giovanni Falcone (in May) and Paolo Borsellino (in July), in Palermo also generated a wave of anger among their colleagues at the cover-ups by politicians with links to organised crime.[38]

Consequently, for the Christian Democrats, the nadir of their fortunes was reached on 28 March 1993 when Giulio Andreotti was informed by the public prosecutor that he was under investigation for the crime of association with the Mafia. 'Beelzebub', as the left-wing La Repubblica described him, was the very personification of political Catholicism in post-war Italy. A devout Catholic and former president of FUCI, and therefore another favourite of G.B. Montini, he was also intimate with several popes.[39] He had served his political apprenticeship with Alcide De Gasperi as parliamentary under-secretary in the prime minister's office from 1946 to 1950, and thereafter he was scarcely out of office either as defence or foreign minister, and he went on to serve as prime minister seven times. Many people simply wouldn't believe that such a man could have been an accomplice to murder, as the Mafia supergrasses alleged, though his party faction's links with the Sicilian Mafia had been journalistic speculation for decades.

The attitude of the Church to Tangentopoli

As the Tangentopoli affair unfolded, the Italian Church, and especially the Vatican, naturally expressed more and more concern. In early 1992, even before the worst revelations of corruption had been made, CEI expressed its unequivocal condemnation of the misdemeanours of politicians, businessmen and others involved in corruption.[40] But as the numbers of politicians accused of wrongdoing mounted, it changed its tune, and in December 1993 it warned of the risks inherent in a generalised desire for justice – 'recriminations, contempt for the accused and demands for revenge' – and these themes were increasingly taken up by official Catholic organs, such as L'Osservatore Romano, La Civiltà Cattolica and L'Avvenire. The real turning point came in January 1994 when John Paul II openly criticised the work of the public prosecutors: it did not go unnoticed that this came 24 hours after allegations were made during an ongoing corruption trial in Milan that the Vatican Bank had 'laundered' a bribe of 80 million lire.[41]

All this reflected the ambivalent attitudes of the clergy to corrupt practices more widely: as Ginsborg points out, 'there was clear, if controversial evidence that while some of the highest organs of the Church urged respect for legality and the duties of democratic citizenship, the body of the clergy were much more tepid'.[42] A fairly unscientific survey of confessors' advice carried out by a journalist posing as a Christian Democratic party functionary who had accepted bribes produced a fairly depressing though hardly surprising set of results. The overwhelming majority of responses to the moral dilemma regarding corrupt practices that the 'penitent' posed to confessors in the confessional boxes of the cathedrals or society churches of Rome, Milan and some other major centres were dismissive of the moral gravity of accepting bribes on behalf of the party. Some confessors did so on the basis that 'everybody's doing it', others that in no circumstances should the penitent feel obliged to turn himself in to the police, and that sexual sins were much more serious than 'social' sin, i.e. corruption.[43] Another interesting revelation that came out of this survey of ecclesiastical opinion was the belief that not declaring all one's taxable income was barely a sin at all, given the demands of the taxman and the inadequacies of state services.[44] This fits with the point made by Gino Bedani that the manual of moral theology in use in Italian seminaries in the 1960s and 1970s specifically dealing with the dilemmas of the taxpayer was incredibly lax in its attitude to those who failed to declare in full. He quotes from it:

> Religious morality, which confers a higher dignity on the laws of civil society, cannot, on the other hand, and must not, distort the common moral sensibility, and do harm to the true sense of social justice through excessive severity in the letter of the law. Therefore, in tax declarations one must not demand the mechanical execution of bureaucratic prescriptions, leaving out of account the real conditions of life.[45]

This extraordinary statement clearly implies that: a) civil law is relative, and inferior to religious law; b) citizens are not under an absolute obligation to obey civil laws; c) perceptions of social justice in relation to the circumstances of the individual are more important than the common good; and d) there is no immorality in telling lies and making false legal declarations. It would help explain the ambivalence of some Italians towards their civic obligations, and thus it can be argued that Church teaching seriously undermined respect for, and the moral legitimacy of, the Italian State under the republic, an issue that will be explored further in the concluding chapter. The statement is emblematic of a broader Italian Catholic attitude that the demands of social justice, or social 'solidarity', justify clientelism and corruption. Thus, in a TV interview in the 1980s, the Christian Democratic secretary and prime minister, Ciriaco De Mita, justified recourse to hundreds of thousands of fraudulent invalidity pensions by arguing that this was essentially a southern form of redundancy payment and unemployment benefit.[46] Clearly, the end justifies the means, the demands of social solidarity, social justice, justifying the use of illegal practices that also, of course, served the clientelistic interests of the Christian Democratic and other parties operating in the south.

The Italian Church had, therefore, at least an indirect moral responsibility for *Tangentopoli*, even if its leaders would never have admitted it. For decades it had turned a blind eye to the corrupt practices of Christian Democratic politicians. On the principle of the *minor male*, the lesser of two evils, clientelism, as has been said before, was seen as a necessary form of social solidarity and a way of defending Catholic political hegemony. Church leaders had even turned a blind eye to the Mafia and other forms of organised crime. Had members of the Sicilian hierarchy really been unaware of the links between the island's Christian Democratic leaders – such as Salvatore Lima – and the Mafia, or for that matter between Lima and Andreotti and the other big shots in Rome?

The Re-foundation of the Christian Democratic Party and the failure of the Partito Popolare Italiano

In the midst of this turmoil, and against the background of a collapsing Christian Democratic share of the vote at local and regional elections throughout 1993, a serious attempt was made to reform and re-found the Catholic party with the backing of the Church. Mario Segni said of the Christian Democratic Party in October 1993 that it was a 'rotten apple with a healthy core': he was probably wrong – some parts of 'the core' were rotten too – but he at least was one of the 'healthy' parts of the apple. It was he who had tried single-handedly to reform those parts of the electoral system that he felt acted as mechanisms facilitating and encouraging clientelism and corruption. It was he who had promoted the referendum on PPV in 1991, and in April 1993 he promoted another referendum, which largely abolished the proportional representation electoral system and introduced a three-quarters element of the 'first past the post', simple majority system for elections to the Senate. Again, it was idealistic, and courageous, former Christian Democrats who had helped launch Leoluca Orlando's *La Rete* anti-Mafia protest movement in Sicily.

In October 1993, Mino Martinazzoli, a 'clean' northern Christian Democrat notable, was elected the party secretary with Rosa Russo Jervolino, a scion of a Partito Popolare–Christian Democratic dynasty and a politician from Naples who was remarkably uncontaminated by the clientelism and links with local organised crime, the Camorra, which had characterised the Christian Democrats there for decades. Martinazzoli and Jervolino struggled to rebuild the party's credibility by purging its ranks of those on trial, under arrest or under suspicion, including De Mita, who was denied a party candidature in the forthcoming elections. The fact that another 'clean' Christian Democrat, Oscar Luigi Scalfaro, was now president of the republic seemed to bode well for the success of the operation to re-launch the Catholic party and ensure that it was able to maintain or resume its accustomed political role.

Thus, as 1994 dawned and a date was set for new general elections, the future seemed reasonably bright for the Christian Democrats. In fact, the re-launch proved to be a failure, not to say a debacle. The Christian Democratic Party was formally dissolved and re-constituted on 18 January as the Partito Popolare Italiano (PPI), an attempt, by harking back to its pre-Fascist predecessor, to recall the ideals of Italian political Catholicism, but it did not work. Mario Segni, one of the most credible figures on the Catholic political scene, resigned from the party in order to try his luck with what was effectively a one-man party (the Patto Segni) in the forthcoming elections. And despite a strong admonition to preserve 'the political unity of Catholics' (i.e. 'vote PPI'), issued by Cardinal Ruini and the CEI and publicly reiterated by Pope John Paul II, quite the reverse happened.[47] There was a veritable diaspora of former Christian Democratic politicians to all points of the political spectrum, and consequently many former Christian Democratic voters followed suit in the elections.

Effectively speaking, what happened at the beginning of 1994 was that under the pressure of crisis, and above all the imperative of political survival and the concomitant fear of extinction, all the deep ideological conflicts, policy differences and factional tensions that had existed inside the Christian Democrats for decades finally exploded. Left-wing Catholics led by Ermanno Guerrieri and Pierre Carniti formed a party of the Cristiani sociali (Christian Social Party), and linked themselves to the PDS in a progressive alliance for the elections. Elements of the former Christian Democratic centre-right around Mastella, Casini, D'Onofrio and Fumagalli-Ombretta formed the Centro Cristiano Democratico (CCD – Christian Democratic Centre), and allied themselves for electoral purposes with the new-born Forza Italia! party of media tycoon Silvio Berlusconi. And on the far right, those Christian Democratic notables with entrenched positions in the webs of Roman and southern clientelism, such as Publio Fiori and Gustavo Sella, passed under the umbrella of Gianfranco Fini's Alleanza Nazionale, a fortuitously re-branded version of the former neo-Fascist MSI.

The consequences in the March 1994 general elections were predictable: the PPI's intransigent decision to fight an independent campaign in the centre under the new mixed proportional representation–first past the post system condemned it to the status of a small, minority parliamentary force with only just over 11 per cent of the vote. Sassoon explains the failure of the PPI very succinctly:

> It was inevitable that the PPI would fare so abysmally, partly because the electoral system penalised parties unable to form an alliance, partly because the corruption scandals could not fail to damage

the electoral prospects of the successor party to the Christian Democrats, partly because, without political power, the PPI was less attractive to conservative voters wishing to keep the left out of power.[48]

The result was that the 'Catholic vote' followed the ex-Christian Democratic politicians. Former Christian Democratic supporters voted in large numbers for CCD–Forza Italia!, fewer perhaps for the Lega Nord, and large numbers in the Christian Democrats' former clientelistic strongholds in Rome and places south threw in their lot with the Alleanza Nazionale, making it the third largest party and a party of government when Berlusconi formed his first centre-right cabinet of CCD–Forza Italia!–Lega Nord–Alleanza Nazionale in May 1994.

But Italy's political turmoil was not ended by Berlusconi's first government in 1994. On the contrary, Italy was in for a further two years of political instability. The first Berlusconi government was riven by tensions and divisions, especially between Bossi's Lega Nord and the Alleanza Nazionale, an entirely predictable conflict given the anti-Rome and anti-southern prejudices of the leagues. As a result, the government collapsed in December 1996 when Bossi withdrew his support. In the aftermath, the gravity of the political impasse became apparent as Italy was ruled from January 1995 until March 1996 by a government of 'technicians' led by the banker Lamberto Dini, rather than politicians, albeit sustained by the 'external' support of the politicians of some parties in Parliament, effectively a repeat of the Ciampi government of 1993–94.[49]

The mixture of majoritarian and proportional representation electoral arrangements had not brought the stable, government/opposition, bi-polar party system Anglo-Saxon style that many had naively hoped and imagined that it would. Nor had it reduced the number of political parties: there were now at least 15 whereas before the 1994 elections there had been only ten. The most striking thing about the 1994 to 1996 situation was the consequent fluidity and instability of some of the parties, which would continue into the late 2000s. And the most fluid and unstable of all parties was the PPI. It was the continuing debate over the PPI's future electoral alliances, whether to go with the PDS and other parties of the centre-left or with Berlusconi's centre-right, that precipitated a split in the party in March 1995, when Rocco Buttiglione led a break-away group with the title of the Cristiani Democratici Uniti (CDU), which was more inclined towards an alliance with Berlusconi's Forza Italia! An unseemly public battle over the assets of the PPI, including its headquarters (eventually divided up between the two groups), the 'Libertas' logo and the newspaper *Il Popolo*, had to be settled in the courts. The CDU won a number of seats in the 1996 general elections and subsequently worked closely with the CCD, and there was much talk of reconstructing the old Christian Democratic Party around them, perhaps even of re-unification with PPI, but this did not happen. However, following the fall of the Prodi government in 1998, the CDU was effectively absorbed into the new Unione Democratica per la Repubblica €UDR) (Democratic Union of the Republic), formed by the maverick ex-president of the republic, Francesco Cossiga. The CCD also split up, with one of its leading lights, Clemente Mastella, joining the UDR along with several disgruntled personalities from Forza Italia!, including Carlo Scognamiglio (ex-president of the Senate) and Tiziana Parenti. Thus, in spite of holding only 5 per cent of the seats in the Chamber of Deputies, the UDR occupied a leading position and so was able to play a crucial role in the formation of the new centre-left government of Massimo D'Alema in October 1998. In consequence, the UDR obtained three cabinet posts.

In all of these extraordinary convulsions among the Catholic political class, the CEI, led by Cardinal Ruini, vicar of Rome, had played an important part. Ruini was slow to accept the weaknesses of the PPI but eventually repented of his support of the party.[50] But whereas Cardinal Martini, archbishop of Milan, and Piero Dossetti, now a priest, were quick to denounce 'the dark', i.e. the emergence of Berlusconi and Forza Italia!, Ruini's sympathies seemed to move increasingly in precisely that direction, and he rejected an alliance between the PPI and the PDS.[51] Articles that appeared in *L'Osservatore Romano* and *L'Avvenire* in the autumn of 1994 demonstrate that the Vatican and the Italian Church had effectively espoused a new version of the clerico-moderate alliances of old, supporting Buttiglione's movement towards the right.[52]

When general elections came round again in 2001, they prompted further convulsions on the part of the Partito Popolare. Their leaders, Bianco, Bindi, De Mita, Mancino and Marini, threw in their lot with Rutelli's La Margherita ('The Daisy') grouping of centre-left MPs. Others drew closer to the UDC. In the 2001 elections, the UDC got 3.2 per cent of the vote. Given their constant changes of name and tactical alliance, it is amazing that 'Catholic' politicians have managed to hang on to any support from the confused electorate.

The emergence of religious pluralism in Italy in the 1980s: new religious minorities

Nowadays, Italy's largest religious minorities are neither Jewish nor Waldensian–Methodist. 'Imported' Protestant denominations – such as the Seventh-Day Adventists, the Mormons, the Pentecostalists and Jehovah's

Witnesses, with roughly 350,000 adherents between them, of which the Witnesses have the largest part (150,000) — and the Buddhists (in part due to the widespread success of Bertolucci's film, *The Little Buddha* in 1993) and New Age and other cults are fast growing forces in Italy's religious 'market'.[53] Giammanco attributes the phenomenal growth of the Protestant denominations, especially those originating from America, to the social and cultural upheavals of the 1960s onwards:

> [these denominations] have made inroads in the most displaced and powerless segments of the population . . . the recently urbanised, traditionally Catholic southern *lumpenproletariat* who had been uprooted from peasant life. They no longer found the Church's message meaningful, but their situation made them receptive to a new kind of religious message.[54]

In addition, there has been a growth of witchcraft, paganism and Satanism.

However, Italy's largest — and newest — religious minority group is undoubtedly the Muslim community. In the 1980s, Italy, after over 100 years of being a country of *emigration*, became for the first time a country of *immigration*, thanks to the economic prosperity that it had achieved and to its geographical proximity to areas of economic migration, especially North Africa. Thus in the 1970s, 1980s and 1990s there were successive waves of migration from Morocco, Algeria, Tunisia and Egypt, from Italy's former colonies in East Africa — Eritrea, Ethiopia and Somalia — and to a lesser extent from the Indian sub-continent. Because many are still unregistered or illegal immigrants, it is difficult to estimate the exact size of the Muslim community, but it probably lies between 300,000 and 400,000 souls: the largest Muslim community is in Rome, where there is now a major mosque and a thriving Islamic cultural centre, with other major centres in Milan, Catania and Palermo.[55] The community is making itself felt in a variety of fields of human endeavour. In 2003 a very vocal leader of the Muslim community, Adel Smith, protested against the presence of a Christian symbol, the crucifix, in public buildings, especially the school in which his daughter was taught. He lost the case eventually. As James Walston states, 'Previously, the only calls for the removal of crosses from public spaces came from secularists and were equally unsuccessful.'[56] In the wake of 9/11 and other terror bombings by Islamic militants, but also as a result of the growing visibility of Muslims in some of Italy's big cities, there has been a backlash against them.[57] In common with Catholic bishops in other European countries, Cardinal Biffi, formerly archbishop of Bologna, has expressed alarm about what he perceives to be the threat posed by the growing numbers of Muslims to the Christian character of Italian society, and in this he is supported by local politicians of some centre-right parties, most notably the Lega Nord and Alleanza Nazionale. For the first time since the late 1930s, strong prejudices are beginning to emerge against a religious/racial minority in Italian society. But religious intolerance can occasionally be a two-way street: recently, Muslims in Italy who have converted to Christianity have had to have their identities protected for fear of reprisals.[58]

Church, state and society in the third millennium

Clearly, Italy has changed enormously as far as religious allegiances are concerned: not only is Catholicism no longer 'the sole religion of the State' as it was in the 1860s: at least formally speaking, Italy is not even 'a Catholic country' in the way that it was then, as the preceding pages have shown. Instead, it is now, at the beginning of the third millennium, a country of a new, and uneasy, religious pluralism. Not only are there growing numbers of people claiming allegiance to non-Catholic and non-Christian religions, there are more agnostics and atheists, or people who profess no religion at all, than there were roughly 150 years ago. On the other hand, the majority of Italians still claim to be Catholics, but show little sign of conforming to the officially accepted beliefs and practices of Catholicism. Only half admit to following teaching of the Church.[59]

As Francesco Alberoni has put it, 'They believe in God, but they don't go to visit him at home'.[60] On the one hand, between 15 and 20 per cent go to weekly mass, which has to be regarded as the normal requirement of a practising Catholic, and this figure has remained stable for over two decades. On the other hand, the numbers who direct that a portion of their taxes should go to the Church, the numbers who marry in church, who have their children baptised and whose funerals take place in church are overwhelming evidence of a continuing *cultural* attachment to Catholicism. Among Italy's major institutions, confidence in the Church is highest at 63 per cent.[61] Some, of course, would say that this does not mean much since Italians have such minimal confidence in public institutions anyway.

Yet this 'Catholicism' is lived by Italians in much the same way as by hundreds of millions of others in western Europe, in 'Catholic' and Protestant countries alike. Artificial contraception and family planning are almost universal in Italy, there are high levels of co-habitation, high levels of illegitimate births, low levels of church marriages, which fell from 7.7 to 5.7 per cent of population as a whole, increasing numbers of civil marriages, separations and divorces (though as far as the latter is concerned, the number is still low by British or Scandinavian standards) and an increase in the numbers of abortions, with the result that in 1986 Italian population growth reached zero.[62] So Italy exhibits all the signs of a free and easy, hedonistic and materialistic society, in line with other countries. Pope John Paul II particularly stigmatised Emilia-Romagna as 'Sodom and Gomorrah' in an outburst in the early 1990s.

Yet there is, undeniably, still a 'Catholic Italy' centred around a fairly large remnant of faithful Catholics. Despite the depredations of secularisation, the Catholic Church remains a major force in Italian society and politics today: at between 15 and 20 per cent, Italy's rate of regular Sunday Mass attendance is easily among the highest in Europe. Adherence to and the practice of the faith firmly transcends class. Italian Catholicism is emphatically not a middle-class phenomenon. Admittedly, there are several geographical 'black-spots', notably the former so-called 'Red Belt' of central Italy – Emilia-Romagna, Tuscany and Umbria – and the big cities, as one might expect, where civil marriages, for example, are higher than anywhere else in Italy. Indeed, Italian Catholicism remains a *national* religion in geographical terms, even if it is no longer officially the religion of the state: during the last three decades there has also been a significant revitalisation of the Church in the south, where popular, traditional Catholicism is still strong. Moreover, leading bishops in the south, including Cardinal Giordano of Naples, have given public warnings about the need to preserve welfare provision for the poorest and most vulnerable groups.[63] The Italian Bishops' Conference has repeatedly warned against organised crime, economic decline and the resulting disintegration of southern urban society, and the heroism of anti-Mafia priests has resulted in two of their number being murdered.[64] In May 1993 during a visit to Sicily, John Paul II made a public denunciation of the Mafia, calling upon its members to repent of their crimes: 'In the name of this resurrected Christ . . . I call upon those responsible: convert – for one day the judgement of God will come.'[65]

Some of the key elements of the old Catholic sub-culture remain. The *institutional structure* of the Italian Church, the dioceses and parishes, remains largely intact, despite the decline in the numbers of the ageing parochial clergy, and its capacity to mobilise Catholic opinion is undiminished, as its role in John Paul II's intransigent campaigns against the Iraq War in 2003 demonstrate.[66] If traditional Catholic associationalism (Catholic Action etc.) is somewhat in decline, support for such movements as the Focolarini, the 'Catholic Charismatics'(Neo-Catechumenate), Comunione e Liberazione, the Sant'Egidio community, Opus Dei, and voluntary organisations generally demonstrates the continuing idealism and commitment of Catholic young people.[67] While Sant'Egidio has played a powerful role as an auxiliary of papal diplomacy, and has thus helped to resolve some serious inter-state conflicts in

Africa, the most influential 'inspired' movement at work in the Italian Church is undoubtedly Comunione e Liberazione, which enjoyed a privileged access to Pope John Paul II. It is particularly strong among secondary school and university students, with highly successful rallies at Rimini in the summer and on Catholic World Youth Days. An integralist and conservative organisation, Comunione e Liberazione has tended to be intolerant of even its Catholic critics, describing them as 'neo-pelagians' or 'crypto-protestants'. The influence of Comunione e Liberazione in Italy cannot be underestimated: it has two well-read journals, *Il Sabato* and *Trenta giorni*, with Giulio Andreotti the editor of the latter for many years; its Compagnie delle Opere run manufacturing and service industries and social welfare organisations valued at two billion pounds worldwide; and its political arm, the Movimento Popolare, exerted much influence on, first, the Christian Democrats and then the CDU. One of its leaders, Roberto Formigoni, is president of the Lombardy region.[68]

There is also still an extensive network of Catholic newspapers, periodicals and publishing houses, which testifies to the intellectual vitality of Italian Catholicism. *Famiglia Cristiana*, with a steady readership of close to 1,000 million, is still the largest weekly magazine in Italy, followed by *Il Messaggero di Sant'Antonio* with 900,000 readers.[69] With its reassuring mixture of popular piety, feature articles, recipes, an 'agony aunt' column, fashion and music reviews and lots of glossy advertising, *Famiglia Cristiana* still exerts a powerful influence on the Catholic laity, even if its attempts to achieve real editorial independence have been frustrated in recent years. It is these publications that still penetrate to the Catholic faithful in town and country, whereas daily newspapers such as *L'Eco di Bergamo*, *Il Cittadino di Lodi* (both diocesan controlled) and *L'Avvenire* (owned by the Italian Bishops' Conference) barely survive with small circulations. As well as diocesan and parochial weekly/monthly bulletins, which, though small-scale, seem to flourish, there is a variety of more intellectually 'heavyweight' publications that demonstrate the diversity and complexity of the Italian Catholic world.[70] In addition, there is an independent Catholic news agency, Adista, based in Rome, which publishes news of Catholic 'dissent' of all kinds round the world, news that the Vatican would often prefer was not broadcast. There are over one hundred avowedly 'Catholic' publishing houses in Italy, large and small, some of which bear comparison with major Italian publishers such as Einaudi, Laterza, Mondadori and Rizzoli. Given the massive decline in 'intellectual' journals of the left, particularly Marxist left, in recent years, arguably Catholic publishing is the most successful ideologically 'committed' publishing in Italy. Italian Catholic groups also control radio eight stations and one television station, Telepace, as well as having access to the national radio and television network, RAI, and a presence on the internet.

Significantly, despite secularisation, the Catholic Church also remains a substantial provider of health, welfare and educational facilities, and it is in the forefront of action to meet the twin evils of drug abuse and HIV/AIDS and to meet the needs of Italy's rapidly growing immigrant populations.[71] Taking all of these factors into account, it is clear that the Catholic Church remains a major cultural, social, economic and, in a somewhat different form, political influence in Italy at the beginning of the third millennium.

The Church and Italian politics in the new millennium

Indeed, one could argue that, despite the demise of the powerful Church-sponsored party and 'the political unity of Catholics', the influence of the Church/Catholicism upon Italian politics has never been so strong. There may no longer be a 'Mamma DC', as some used to call the Christian Democratic Party, but Catholics are present and influential in every 'pole' and in virtually every individual political party or movement, big and small, of which these electoral alliances are made up. Even some of the racist 'Nazi-skins' pay lip service to the traditional role of religion in society.[72] Most obviously, there are still some, albeit relatively small but nevertheless influential, political parties of an avowedly Catholic inspiration operating in Italian politics at the time of writing (2007). In the centre-left Ulivo grouping that won the 2006 general elections, the La Margherita formation still has a hard core of ex-Christian Democrats/Partito Popolare politicians and the DCN+PSI fraction in the same grouping won .75 per cent of the vote and five seats in the Chamber of Deputies. In the centre-right electoral alliance, the Casa delle Liberta of Berlusconi, UC-CD won 6.7 per cent of the vote and 39 seats, while the 'unattached' Partito Popolare-UDEUR faction won 2 per cent and ten seats.[73] Two ex-Christian Democratic politicians, two dissident Catholics and one so-called 'Catto-Communista'(Livia Turco) now hold major cabinet posts in Romano Prodi's new government of 25, just as ex-Christian Democrats held major posts in Berlusconi's government from 2001 to 2006.[74] And, of course, the presence of a contingent of ex-Christian Democratic politicians such as Publio Fiori helps sustain Alleanza Nazionale support among ex-Christian Democratic voters, particularly pensioners, in Lazio and other southern regions. Even the Lega Nord, with which the Church has been most frequently at loggerheads on such matters as immigration, subsidies to the south and the preservation of Italian unity,[75] has a strong following among Catholics and has even produced the most remarkable of all Catholic politicians, Irene Pivetti. This devout, traditionalist/Tridentine Catholic was elected president of the Chamber of Deputies in May 1994 following the victory of the Polo della Libertà (including the Lega Nord) at the tender age of only 31.

But perhaps the strongest evidence of the enduring capacity of Catholics to play a key role in Italian politics is none other than Romano Prodi who, though he had been more of the 'area DC' than the Christian democratic party itself, has had a remarkable political career over the last ten or twelve years. A university professor of economics (a classic profession of Christian Democratic politicians), a technocrat who was briefly a minister in the 1996 Dini government, Prodi headed the Industrial Reconstruction Institute where he initiated the privatisation of Italy's large and unproductive public sector.[76] In 1995–96 he set off in his 'battle bus' on a one-man quest (the 'journey to the one hundred cities') to provide Italy with political salvation. In 1996 he led the Ulivo electoral alliance to victory and was subsequently prime minister until 1998 when he was appointed President of the European Community. He then returned to Italy to lead the Ulivo back to victory and became prime minister for a second time in June 2006. Ironically, though he is such a classically Italian Catholic figure that he is usually depicted as a priest (or a pope) by political cartoonists, he has never been entirely accepted by the Vatican and by the former president of CEI, Cardinal Ruini, because of his electoral and coalition alliances with the remnants of Italian Communism to the left of the PDS – Rifondazione Communista and the Partito Communista.

In the absence of a major governing party that is exclusively or even largely Catholic in its inspiration and leadership, in the last ten years the Church, and more precisely the Italian Bishops' Conference, has emerged as a major player in Italian politics in its own right and has entered into a direct dialogue with the electorate and the political class on some key issues: immigration, the financing of Catholic schools, the Iraq War, bioethics and the European Parliament's 1996 motion on same-sex unions. The CEI, backed up by the Catholic charity, Caritas, and by ACLI, was the strongest opponent of the 2003 Bossi-Fini law on immigration, one of the few major areas of Berlusconi government policy on which the leaders of the leagues and Alleanza Nazionale were able to agree upon. In consequence, Bossi and his colleagues fought back fiercely, sparing no one, not even the bishops and the pope himself from their criticisms.[77] On the question of war, the Iraq War, the Italian Church, from the pope downwards, opposed it all the way and gave Berlusconi's government a hard time when it announced general support for the Bush-Blair initiative.[78]

The Church also waged a long campaign to get state financial support for Catholic schools, an issue that at other times in the post-war history of Italy had threatened the collapse of governmental coalitions.[79] This time, however, a joint commission agreed on a compromise solution whereby parents would be able to use 'school vouchers' to purchase a private education for their children. Probably the most difficult ethical and emotional issue confronting governments has been in the area of bioethics and most particularly the question of treatments for infertility, *fecondazione assistita,* and stem-cell research. Whereas easily the largest percentage (45 per cent) of people polled on this issue believed that artificial insemination was morally acceptable, politicians of both the centre-left and centre-right parties have been unwilling to defy the Church's teaching on this subject and legislate accordingly, and a referendum on this subject in June 2005 was effectively sabotaged by the Church's campaign for abstention.[80]

During the course of his pontificate, John Paul II repeatedly condemned both homosexuality and the legalisation of same-sex unions allegedly as part of his 'defence of the family', and it has to be said that the Church in Italy has been remarkably successful in dissuading even centre-left politicians from supporting gay rights: in 2000, La Margherita politician Rutelli, whose roots lie in the libertarian, secularist and anti-clerical Partito Radicale, as mayor of Rome was dissuaded from giving the official support of the city to the Gay Pride March that had been planned for Holy Year. (Given the attention that the centre-right devotes to the defence of the family it is ironical that a number of their leading figures live in decidedly irregular relationships from the Catholic point of view.) More recently, there have been regular denunciations of the proposed legislation by the president of the Italian Bishops' Conference and individual bishops and priests, and a massive popular mobilisation was organised in support of a 'Family Day'. Given the fragility of Romano Prodi's government, which won the 2006 general elections by literally a few thousand votes and contains a number of devout Catholics, it is very likely that the Church will succeed in blocking parliamentary approval of the legislation.

So we are faced with a paradox. After decades of 'secularisation', Italian Catholicism remains a powerful political force. As the eminent Italian political scientist, Ilvio Diamanti, put it:

> The Church is actually increasing its political weight . . . to the point that it is able to produce greater results by comparison with when the 'party of Catholics' governed and Catholics constituted the majority of society. It has a greater capacity to impose its issues and its agenda exactly when . . . [it] has abandoned direct links with parties, when Catholics are in a minority in society and among the electorate . . . The moral influence of the Church, therefore, seems to be greater among politicians than Catholics themselves.[81]

Certainly, both political groupings, the centre-left and Polo of centre-right, are actually very deferential towards Church/Catholic opinion as the above examples show.

This phenomenon is to be explained by a number of factors. Perhaps Italians are actually more conservative on some of these issues, especially homosexuality and artificial insemination, than they have been willing to admit to pollsters. Politicians are still very insecure in the Second Republic, under the new electoral system. Silvio Berlusconi felt so insecure that he changed the electoral system back to PR just before the 2006 elections and was even willing to stretch out the hand of friendship to blatantly racist groups such as Forza Nuova in his anxiety to get re-elected, hence his unwillingness to offend Catholic sensibilities. And he may not be wrong. The row over the crucifix in schools seems to suggest an underlying Catholic cultural identity of the Italian people. Maybe the Church's influence is still the 'default' characteristic of the nature of Italian society and politics today. Despite a long secular, even anti-clerical tradition in Italy, as Ezio Mauro has described it, there is the lack of a 'laic culture, conscious and confident of itself and its values, and capable of giving substance to them in politics and legislation'.[82]

Chapter 10

CONCLUSION

Catholicism in modern Italy

O NE OF THE ESSENTIAL CHARACTERISTICS of Italian Catholicism throughout the modern period has been the dichotomy between 'official' religious practice, i.e. that endorsed and propagated by the Church, and popular piety, and it remains so. Despite all the efforts on the part of the Italian clergy to establish a uniform, post-Tridentine and later a post-Second Vatican Council form of religious observance, with a special focus on the Eucharist as the centre of Catholic communal worship, popular devotions have continued to co-exist alongside the 'official' ones. Throughout the 1940s and 1950s, for example, and despite the strong disapproval of the Church, many people in Italy, and in other Catholic countries too, insisted on a devotion to Padre Pio, the friar of San Giovanni Rotondo in Apulia who claimed to possess the stigmata (that is the external, bodily signs of the crucifixion of Christ). The Vatican even inhibited Padre Pio from appearing in public, but the cult continued to grow and quickly became one of the most widespread and popular in the Catholic Church; now Padre Pio is under consideration for beatification.[1] There are still sightings of 'weeping', even 'bleeding', statues of the Madonna, and the cult surrounding the liquefaction of the blood of San Gennaro in Naples is still going strong, as are the *romeaggi* and other celebrations of local shrines. Italian city churches and streets are still testimony to the enduring power of local cults in another way, that is, prayers to the Madonna and local saints for favours, whose success is recorded by the presentation of votive artefacts at their statues. These phenomena are largely, but by no means entirely, southern Italian ones. But regional diversity is not the only criterion here; generational differences are also important. The older generation of Italian

Catholics remain much more attached to the cult of the Sacred Heart and the recitation of the rosary than the younger faithful: one only has to sit at the back of an Italian church in the early evening to confirm this. There has also been resistance among some Italian Catholics, as elsewhere, to a kind of 'protestantisation' of Catholic Eucharistic worship, the apparent removal of 'mystery' by making the priest face the people across what appears to be a 'table' rather than an altar and the replacement of Latin with the vernacular in the celebration of Mass. There are now thousands of Italian Catholics who belong to organisations that are liturgically and doctrinally traditionalist (and often politically right wing). There are even supporters of Mgr Marcel Lefebvre, the deceased French archbishop who denounced the Second Vatican Council as 'the work of the Devil' and consequently led his followers into schism.[2] That said, 'Papal' Italy has seen schisms before, but they have been marginal and transient phenomena.

On the other hand, another characteristic of Italian Catholicism in the modern era has been the use of devotions, including popular devotions, for political ends by the institutional church. The cults of the Sacred Hearts of both Jesus and Mary were classic devotional forms used in the nineteenth and early twentieth century Ultramontane battles to whip up popular support against liberalism, secularism and anti-clericalism. They were also used in that way in the Cold War years, but in that period extra-liturgical Eucharistic devotions, such as Exposition of the Blessed Sacrament, had a political purpose as well: they served as a means of sustaining and reinforcing Catholic identity against Communism in many Catholic countries. Eucharistic congresses, both national and regional, while ostensibly organised as a means of reinforcing the message of the centrality of the Eucharist in Catholic worship and religious practice, have also served as massive manifestations of Catholic identity in the face of the 'enemy'.

Marian devotions were also crucial in the post-1945 Catholic 'culture war' against Communism, especially in Italy. The *Madonna Pellegrina* phenomenon referred to in Chapter 6 is an obvious example of this, but the culmination was undoubtedly 1950 and the proclamation of the dogma of the Assumption. That Holy Year celebration had all the classic hallmarks of successful Catholic *political* mobilisation: mass pilgrimage, an emphasis on a doctrine that absolutely characterised Catholic religious belief and practice (and also sharply divided it from Protestant Christians) and the focus around the cult of the pope – Pius XII. Pilgrimages to Rome, especially during the Holy Years of 1900, 1925, 1933–34 (an extraordinary one to commemorate the 2,000 years said to have elapsed since Christ's crucifixion), had already been used as a means of countering the attempts at cultural hegemony on the part of the liberals and Fascists by Leo XIII and Pius XI respectively. And John Paul II used the enormously successful Holy Year in 2000 in an attempt to hold the line on Catholic moral teaching (see Chapter 9, p. 175).

Throughout the modern period, the popular understanding of what it means to be a Catholic, the forms of 'believing' and 'belonging' to the Church, have frequently changed. There have always been those whose understanding and acceptance of Catholic doctrine were limited and whose attendance at Mass was irregular, whereas there were also those who adhered to at least the dominical, if not the pascal, precepts. Liliano Faenza and others have demonstrated that a real understanding of Catholic beliefs was fairly minimal among many peasants in central Italy (Chapter 8, p. 147), and this must have been true of other parts of Italy, especially the Mezzogiorno. The differences between the forms of 'believing' and 'belonging' that emerged in the 1960s and 1990s, and are widespread in today's Italy, are not necessarily profoundly different from those of 50 or 100 years ago. The beliefs of the majority of Italians as far as faith and morals are concerned are somewhat out of line with the official teaching of the Church, and the majority now go to church on a very irregular basis, mostly for baptisms, weddings and funerals, or for the confirmations/first communions of their or their relatives' children, as well as at the time of the greater feasts, such as Christmas and Easter. Yet they still believe themselves to be 'Catholic'.

Obedience to the political directives of the ecclesiastical hierarchy was for long an essential part of being a Catholic in Italy in the modern period, yet there was always the phenomenon of those who, while believing, and observing necessary religious practice such as attending Sunday Mass, did not belong *politically* to the Catholic community. One can cite the examples of Catholic Liberals during the Risorgimento, or the Conciliatorists afterwards, such as Stefano Jacini, who accepted a place in the Senate in the 1870s[3] and thus did *not* follow the official Catholic policy of abstentionism. At a rather different social level, there were others, such as the women of Cene, who rejected the Church's admonitions against joining Socialist trade unions (Chapter 4, p. 58), or those 'faithful' who ignored the Church's incessant preaching against having anything to do with the Communist Party (or the Socialists for that matter), and the solemn 'bell, book and candling' for any involvement with the PCI in 1949. There is ample evidence that even after these thundering denunciations, many Italians managed to reconcile their consciences and remain practising Catholics, while voting Communist (or Socialist). Faenza cites peasants in Emilia-Romagna who ignored the 1949 excommunication and claims that there were rarely sudden losses of faith, except where the local parish priest engaged in incessant 'preaching against Communism'.[4] Almost all Catholics with Communist inclinations continued to marry in church and receive the last sacraments.[5] As late as 1972, a staggering 67 per cent of those who voted for the PCI claimed to be practising Catholics.[6] Many could be described as 'belly Communists', voting Communist because of the benefits in improved public services, especially housing and schools, that accrued from living in areas where PCI/PSI coalitions ruled local government.

Was this the origin of that strange phantom-like phenomenon of Italian society and politics, 'Cattocommunism'? The tendency of some Italians to suffer split allegiances, to be both believing and practising Catholics and Communists at the same time never amounted to a movement, and may have been largely a journalistic construct. But at the elite level, the Catholics who entered the PCI-sponsored Sinistra Independente (Independent Left) list of candidates in the 1968 general elections, such as Raniero La Valle, Ettore Masina and Adriano Ossicini, looked horribly real to Italy's bishops at the time and outraged their sense of the political loyalty that Catholics owed.[7] Again, despite the manoeuvres of Cardinal Ruini in the late 1990s and early years of the twenty-first century, there has been a tendency for some Catholic politicians from the PPI to get closer and closer together, not only with those of the variegated, 'lay' left such as Rutelli, in the Margherita formation, but also with the exponents of the ex-Communist Democratici di Sinistra (DS) in the centre-left Ulivo electoral alliance of 1996 and 2001, and the Unione electoral alliance of 2006. Now they are getting together even more closely in the new Partito Democratico,[8] though that still leaves a lot of fellow Catholic politicians sitting in the centre or the centre-right. Talking of the PPI-CDU split in 1996, Sandro Magister has written, 'For some time now, the political unity of Catholics had ceased to exist. In fact, it never had existed – not even when the DC [Christian Democratic Party] was far and away the leading Italian party.'[9] The history of Catholicism in modern Italy would seem to bear him out.

Catholicism in Italian society

Much of Italian Catholicism's success in meeting and surviving the challenges posed by the different ideological rivals it has faced over the last nearly 150 years is undoubtedly due to its deep embeddedness in Italian civil society. The ruling class of the Liberal State between 1861 and 1922, and especially during the decades following unification, spectacularly failed to put down roots in Italian society, most importantly rural society, in an Italy that remained predominantly rural and agrarian until after the Second World War. Liberalism in its various forms never became anything more than the ideology and politics of sections of the urban middle classes and the rural notability. Because of this, and because of the failure to establish an effective, universal and secular school system on the lines of that created by the Third French Republic, the

Liberal State was unable to contest successfully the cultural domination of the Church among the rural masses. In particular, the frenzied attempts by Crispi and others to establish some sort of national 'civic religion' to compete with Catholicism failed to move the majority of the population. By entering into clerico-moderate alliances with Catholics at a local level, in part to defend the teaching of the catechism, sections of the Liberal political class were tacitly admitting that failure.

For much the same reasons Fascism also failed in its project to 'nationalise' and 'fascistise' the masses, to create a new 'Fascist man' (and woman) and sink the roots of its totalitarian state deep into Italian society. Like liberalism, Fascism was not very successful in embedding itself in Italian society, except in parts of Rome and some southern Italian cities. As for rural society, it succeeded in only a few small, isolated areas. One example was the province of Latina, at the heart of Mussolini's biggest land reclamation project, the *bonifica* of the Pontine Marshes south of Rome: thanks to the gratitude of the landless peasants whom Mussolini brought there, a Fascist 'culture' was passed down through the generations. Thus Latina remains one the major centres of support for the former neo-Fascist Alleanza Nazionale, and also for more extreme fringe groups of the Italian right, such as Forza Nuova and Azione Sociale. Fascism's failure to achieve serious penetration of Italian society is borne out by the experience of the Opera Nazionale Balilla (national youth organisation)[10] and the Opera Nazionale Dopolavoro (national 'after work' recreational organisation)[11] and even the Fascist Party itself. The Partito Nazionale Fascista (PNF) increasingly became an organisation of opportunists and hangers-on, and at the level of local politics became essentially a vehicle for political clientelistm – much like the Christian Democratic Party from the 1950s onwards.

It should be said at this point that the 'Fascist Revolution' as such did not pose as serious challenge to Italian Catholicism as the other processes of change that occurred in the history of modern Italy. Despite A.J. Gregor's claim that the Italian Fascist regime was a 'developmental dictatorship',[12] there is little sign that Fascism constituted a serious process of 'modernisation' in the economic or social spheres, even allowing for the fact that some of its cultural roots lay in Futurism, the 'modernist' movement par excellence of pre-1915 Italy. Its protection of the interests of the least modern economic forces, such as the southern landowners, and its more general policy of privileging rural over urban society, proves this conclusively. A 'developmental dictatorship' would, first and foremost, have had to carry out either massive land redistribution or collectivisation, which would, of course, have seriously damaged the interests of the landowning classes on whose political support Fascism was dependent. In fact, its policy of 'ruralisation' was precisely one

of the features of Fascism that commended it to the Church and made possible
an (admittedly uneasy) 'marriage of convenience' between the Church and
the regime for most of the Fascist *ventennio*. Equally, Fascism's tendency
towards what Emilio Gentile calls the 'sacralisation of politics', attempting
to create a new 'civic religion', no more constituted a serious danger to the
integrity of Italian Catholicism, for the reasons that have been set out in
Chapter 6, than liberalism's previous attempt to found one. As Richard
Bosworth has remarked:

> If the regime preached a fervent gospel, it is not clear that its
> principles and beliefs were able, or were consistently intended,
> to wipe Italian minds free of other attitudes and concepts. While
> the Vatican stood, neither numinousness nor liturgy was a Fascist
> monopoly in the streets of Rome.[13]

But the post-Second World War Italian Communist Party presented a real
threat to Italian Catholicism precisely because it *did* succeed in penetrating
Italian civil society and putting down roots, and not just in industrial society
in the great cities but in rural agrarian society in the north, the centre and
even the south. As Kertzer has pointed out, the difference in the conflict
between Catholics and the '*borghese laica*' [secular bourgeoisie] during the
Risorgimento and after, and the conflict between the Church and Communism
after 1945 was that the first battle was not fought out in 'the world of the
masses', whereas the second one was. Consequently the PCI posed a serious
threat of 'replacing the Church in the role of influential institution among the
masses.'[14] The essentially Gramscian strategy of the post-1945 PCI of seeking
to establish cultural hegemony in Italian civil society as a prelude to political
power by drawing into its various collateral organisations, and even the party
itself, non-proletarian elements such as shopkeepers, small businessmen etc.,
as well as agricultural workers and small peasant farmers meant that in the
'Red Belt' and other areas it became a serious cultural rival to the Church.
Its thick network of local party *sezioni* (branches) with their multifarious
activities began to rival the system of Catholic parishes and, above all, the
annual 'Festa de *L'Unità*', the late summer-autumn celebrations at national,
regional and local levels, centring around the party newspaper *L'Unità*, provided
attractive alternatives to church festivals and celebrations. It might even be
said that Italian Communism became a sort of alternative, 'political church':
certainly the adherence of many of its supporters in the decades after the
Second World War and beyond was characterised more by 'faith' than by
clear intellectual choice. As some cynics described it, the PCI became 'Santa
Madre Partito Communista'(Holy Mother Communist Party).

Just as for that other 'religion', Italian Catholicism, so for the Communist Party things became difficult during the economic 'miracle' of the 1950s and early 1960s. The PCI was not equipped to deal with the consequences of successful capitalism; its whole ideology and programme were based on the premise of capitalism's inevitable *crisis*. The party's strategy and tactics were orientated towards battles with bosses and the state over wage *reductions*, not increases, over *deteriorations* in workers' standard of living, not improvements. Hence there is evidence of some of the beneficiaries of the 'miracle' shifting their political loyalties away from the PCI.[15] The Church and the Italian Catholic movement, and especially the Christian Democrats, had much the same sort of problem in coming to terms with the 'miracle'. On the one hand, they always claimed that a general improvement in levels of prosperity was the object of the Christian Democratic-led government. On the other hand:

> They maintained a sort of cultural 'distance' from the phenomenon, and a certain perplexity with regard to the system of production from which the relatively rapid improvement in the standard of living derived.[16]

Eventually, the Italian Catholic world, with some notable exceptions, managed to more or less reconcile its fundamental theological mistrust of bourgeois-individualistic capitalism with the massive economic and social benefits that that system was bringing to Italy in the 1950s and 1960s, and it did so by rationalising it along essentially Keynesian lines.[17]

The type of industrial economy that emerged under the leadership of the Christian Democrats in Italy after 1945 was virtually unique in western Europe. It was one strongly characterised by a relatively small private capitalistic sector and a relatively large state one, and by direct governmental intervention in the micro-management of state-run economic entities. The Catholic doctrine of 'social solidarity' was a better fit with a largely state-run economy. The doctrine also became the ideological cover for the *stato assistenziale*, the peculiarly Italian version of 'welfare capitalism', which was so very different from the 'social capitalism' that evolved in Germany and the Netherlands.[18] The distribution of all these sources of finance, credit, contracts, employment, social security and pension benefits was exploited by politicians of nearly all parties for essentially clientelistic ends. Thus Catholicism must be held responsible in no small way for the clientelism, the corruption and the influence of organised crime that has characterised Italian politics since the Second World War.

Ginsborg has laid another accusation at the door of Catholicism in relation to the role that it has played in Italian society over the decades. He complains about the 'ambiguities of the Catholic Church', arguing that while, on the one hand, it has in recent years urged the duty of individuals to participate in civil society and has set an example by its charitable and humanitarian activities, and its mobilisation against the ills that afflict it such as the Mafia, on the other hand it still subordinates wider society to the family in its general pronouncements, thus undermining the effort to develop a stronger sense of civic consciousness and responsibility in Italians.[19] Current demands for 'the defence of the family' in the face of attempts to introduce same-sex unions are simply an echo of this long-held Catholic stance. Similarly, the 'defence of the unborn child' has put the Church at odds with the liberal democratic emphasis upon individual human rights, in this case of women.

Ginsborg has also made the point that from the 1980s onwards, 'Trade unions, mass parties, churches, all faced crises of cohesion and participation.'[20] Certainly, the decline and fall of the PCI and the Christian Democrats was in part a result of these 'secularising' processes, 'secularising' understood in the sense of eroding the bases of *both* ideological sub-cultures. But in the case of the Christian Democrats they had begun to suffer the direct or indirect effects of secularisation and the impact of the Second Vatican Council in the geographical locations of their sub-culture as early as the 1960s, and for this, but also for other reasons, had gone a-whoring after false gods in the south, increasingly replacing shared beliefs and faith and family networks with largely clientelistic (and criminal) networks in order to win votes. In consequence, they suffered further electoral losses in Lombardy and the Veneto at the hands of the leagues. In the longer term, what proved fatal to the Christian Democrats was the decline of their support in the embedded Catholic sub-culture of northern and eastern Italy *and* becoming part of the clientelistic structure of the south.

The Church and politics

During the Liberal era, the Church responded to the perceived threat from the Liberal State and its ruling class through the mass mobilisation of the laity (as it did elsewhere in Europe) – using modern forms of mass organisation, and also exploiting such 'modern' means as the press and railways – and, initially, through the enforcement of their abstention from the political process as a form of protest. But in response to the emergence of a Marxist-inspired working class movement from the 1880s onwards, it accepted the logic of the formation of clerico-moderate alliances with acceptable elements of the Liberal ruling class and, eventually, the gradual re-entry of Catholics into national politics. In the post-First World War period, under the aegis of Benedict XV, it went along with the new, Wilsonian, democratic vogue and permitted the ending of political abstentionism (abolition of the *non expedit*) and the emergence of a 'Catholic' political party, the PPI, and a Catholic trade union confederation, CIL. But it was never really very comfortable giving such political freedom to the Catholic laity; Cardinal Gasparri, and many of the Italian bishops, barely tolerated the PPI and its participation in the system of democratic, parliamentary government. The threat of Bolshevism in Italy, though grossly exaggerated on all sides, provided the excuse for Pius XI to entirely dispense with the PPI and turn back to an arrangement with which he and Gasparri were much more comfortable, a direct interlocutory relationship with a new authoritarian state, Fascism. For in the Vatican, Fascism in the early to mid 1920s seemed to be like just any one of the many authoritarian regimes that flourished in inter-war Europe, and bore such a reassuring resemblance to the semi-authoritarian, monarchical regimes that had prevailed in Europe prior to the First World War. It was not obvious to most people at the time that Italian Fascism would turn out to be more than just any old authoritarian regime, and would seek to develop into a fully-fledged totalitarian dictatorship.

After the end of the Second World War, when the Fascist dictatorships had been defeated and discredited by the Holocaust and other genocides, and the 'Catholic' dictatorships of Portugal and Spain were in 'the doghouse' as far as the Western Allies were concerned, the Vatican still kept its preference for the establishment of a cosy, secure, authoritarian or semi-authoritarian regime in Italy, as has been seen in Chapter 7. Even after the victory of the Christian Democrats, and democracy, in 1948, some in the Vatican pushed for a ban on the PCI similar to that imposed on its counterpart, the KPD, in the German Federal Republic.[21] This episode, and the earlier unwillingness to accept De Gasperi and the Christian Democrats as the best political defence of the Church's interests, demonstrate that at bottom the Vatican was not comfortable with democracy or with democratic Catholic parties of virtually any hue, and this had been true all the way through the pontificates of Leo XIII, Pius X and Pius XI: only that of Benedict XV saw a grudging acceptance of the necessity of political Catholicism operated in *prima persona* by the laity, in the form of the (original) PPI. Despite Leo XIII's encyclical *Graves De Comuni Re*[22] establishing the principle that no form of government is to be preferred over another and his practical attempt to implement that policy by encouraging a *Ralliement* of French Catholics to the Third Republic, the Catholic Church has unwillingly accepted political democracy until relatively recent times. And despite John XXIII's attempt to 'liberate' Italian Catholic politicians from the chains of Vatican control, the leadership of Italy's episcopate have been equally unwilling to let Italian Catholic politicians make their own decisions and choose their own alliances. Catholic parties, however large or small, have usually been regarded as a hindrance, an impediment to what the men of the Vatican, trained in its diplomacy, regard as the ideal arrangement, that is, top level negotiations with the powers that be. The present situation, in which the Italian bishops by their magisterial pronouncements can directly influence the choice of the voters at election time and in referendums, and the politicians in Parliament, on the issues that really matter to the Church, must seem to them to be infinitely better than having to rely upon a 'Catholic' party.

The presence of the papacy

The Church's modus operandi in Italian politics is closely connected with the fact that, as in other periods of Italian history, the absolutely distinguishing characteristic of Italian Catholicism in the modern period has been the way in which it has been strongly conditioned by the presence of the papacy in the Italian peninsula. That presence has brought advantages and disadvantages. Because of the presence of the papacy in the peninsula, the Church in Italy has also been able to draw upon exceptional resources, in particular, the prestige of the papacy as an international institution and its worldwide diplomatic influence: the most obvious example of the latter would be Pius XII's 'special relationship' with Roosevelt. The papacy's international role and prestige, which were recognised by Mussolini himself in his maiden speech (see Chapter 5, p. 80) gave Italian Catholicism additional 'resources'. The international nature of what might be regarded, and was indeed regarded by Gioberti, as an essentially 'Italian' institution was crucial at certain key moments in the history of modern Italy. The papacy as an institution is by its very nature *charismatic,* by virtue of its claim to be historically the *oldest* existing Italian institution and its explicitly infallible claims after 1870, regardless of the personal charisma or otherwise of the occupants of the Chair of St Peter. Thus, in relation to the Savoyard monarchy after 1861, the papacy had a huge advantage, and it has to be said that after the death of Victor Emmanuel II in 1878 neither of the subsequent occupants of the Italian throne, Humbert I and Victor Emmanuel III, displayed much in the way of personal charisma: since Humbert II was king for only just over a month in 1946, his reign can be discounted. Similarly, the construction of a personality cult around Mussolini from the late 1920s onwards, the 'cult of the Duce', suffered from the existence of a pre-existing cult around the person of the pope: when it was brought to Mussolini's attention by a provincial prefect in 1929 that an enterprising local printer had produced a postcard to commemorate the Lateran Pacts, bringing together cameo portraits of Duce, pope and king, with that of the pope in the middle and slightly raised above the other two, the Duce immediately intervened to ban its sale.[23]

Another advantage was the number of Catholic pilgrims – hundreds of thousands, and since the middle of the last century, millions – from all over the world who have flocked to Rome since the development of railways, steamships and later air travel and constitute a 'reserve' army to reinforce the mobilisation of Italian Catholics during the various holy years: in the Holy Year of 2000, it has been estimated that between 30 million and 35 million 'pilgrims' visited Rome.[24] And Italians, especially Romans, could not ignore the *economic* benefits that the presence of the papacy thus brought to Italy (including the millions of non-Catholic tourists drawn to the Eternal City). The crowds of pilgrims were ably exploited by Leo XIII and Pius XI respectively to defend Christian/Papal Rome against attempts by both the liberals and the Fascists to create a 'third' Rome, National or Fascist as the case may be. And for Pius XII the success of Holy Year in 1950 was his answer to Stalin's scornful query at Yalta about the number of the 'pope's divisions'.

But the presence of the papacy brought definite disadvantages. As Carlo Falconi has described it, the papacy has tended to treat the Italians as a 'levitical people', that is as a nation whose essential function and *raison d'être* is to be in the service of the Church:

> Italy . . . given the presence of the Holy See in Rome, has always been regarded by the latter as its strategic and demographic hinterland, necessary in order to guarantee the physical and moral survival of its central organs. A country which, of course, has its own government in order to provide for its normal needs, as along, that is, as the government knows how to adapt its autonomy to the needs of the Vatican, which is concerned, above all, to preserve the Italians as an essentially levitical people. Was this not what Papa Ratti was aiming at with the Concordat?[25]

This 'servitude' is the price that Italian Catholicism has paid for the many benefits of the presence of the papacy. In the first place, the Italian Church has been subordinated to the wider policies of the Vatican in a way in which Catholicism in other countries has not: when an 'Italian' church finally emerged, it was firmly under the direct control of the Secretariat of State, which took all decisions regarding, in particular, the question of Catholics in politics, and the organisation and role of Catholic Action. The Vatican has also tended to treat the Italian peninsula as its hinterland or 'backyard', so to speak, putting Italian Catholics in an initially awkward position during the First World War (see Chapter 5, p. 71). During the early stages of the Cold War, while it is true that Pius XII used his massive influence to overwhelm the neutralist and even 'pacifist' elements in the Christian Democratic Party in support of

De Gasperi's desire that Italy should enter NATO, it should also be remembered that the pope hesitated for a long time precisely because he feared that Italian membership of the Western Alliance would compromise the papacy's diplomatic neutrality in the developing global struggle.[26]

The presence of the papacy has undermined the authority of the Italian state in two other very specific ways. Because of the international nature of the papacy, it has claimed a status of quite extraordinary privilege for the Italian Church, setting it up as an *equal* of the state, first by the terms of Article Seven of the Constitution (see Chapter 7, pp. 114–15) and then by the revised Concordat of 1984 (see Chapter 8, p. 157). As Italian parliamentarians have pointed out many times, this position of privilege is quite exceptional, indeed, unique among sovereign states; it calls into the question the very sovereignty of the state in modern democratic theory and practice.[27] Even if as Guido Formigoni claims 'Catholic supra-nationalism (or anti-nationalism) was not the major factor impeding the development of a cohesive national identity in Italy', it can still be argued that the presence of the papacy did for a long time constitute a serious obstacle (there were definitely others) to the consolidation of the Italian nation state after unification. The 'Roman Question' undermined the loyalty to the unified state of several million Italians well into the twentieth century. Only, perhaps, after the Second World War, under the Christian Democratic regime, did millions of Italian Catholics feel completely comfortable with their national identity, feel that they were living in a 'Catholic Italy'. Ironically, given the historically negative role played by Catholicism in the development of Italian national identity and unity, today the wheel has come full circle. Over the last decade or so, the Italian Church has become one of the staunchest defenders of the unified Italian state not only against the anti-southern policies of Umberto Bossi and the Lega but also against their secessionist aspirations for a 'Republic of Padania' in northern Italy, liberated from Roman control.

The impact of church–state relations in Italy on the development of the Catholic Church worldwide

If the presence of the papacy has very much conditioned the history of Italian Catholicism in the modern period, then, vice versa, the experience of Italian Catholicism over the last 160 years has had a powerful impact upon the development of the papacy as an institution and consequently upon the overall development of Catholicism as a worldwide religion. The experience of liberalism in Italy has clearly had an impact on the rest of the Church and on the papacy's relations with the rest of the world, as has been seen in Chapter 3: without that Italian experience, there would almost certainly not have been the Syllabus of Errors, or possibly even Papal Infallibility. These two developments contributed massively to the rise of the modern, centralised, 'Romanised' Catholic Church.[28] Ironically, the Italian experience of anti-clerical legislation and violence was far less horrific than that of France, Mexico (or other Latin American countries), Portugal or Spain, indeed, virtually every other Catholic country. A particular consequence of the papacy's Italian experience in the nineteenth century was that the Liberal Revolution, with its destruction of the temporal power of the popes and the latter's subsequent rejection of the Law of Guarantees, and with it permanent Italian government financial support, forced the papacy to become almost completely dependent upon the offerings of the faithful, i.e. Peter's Pence, which in turn intensified the 'personality cult' around the pope.[29] Again, the experience of relations with Italian Fascism, especially the reasonable success of the Lateran Pacts of 1929 in the medium term, predisposed the Vatican towards negotiating the *Reichskonkordat* with another dictatorship, the new Nazi regime in Germany, despite some misgivings on the part of both Pius XI and his secretary of state, Cardinal Pacelli.

The impact of this Italian experience on the men of the Vatican, who until the 1960s at the earliest were almost all *Italians*, can also be seen in the attempts to impose the Italian model of Catholic Action upon organisations of Catholic militants throughout the world and the Catholic Church's crusade against Communism from the late 1940s onwards. Though the assaults upon the Church in the countries of eastern Europe were, of course, crucially important, the experience of the threat of the West's largest Communist party in the pope's backyard was also a key factor. In Australia, for example, Catholic Action's obsession with the Communist threat led to a split in the Australian Labour Party. The Catholic-dominated Democratic Labour Party that thus emerged from the split would effectively keep the Australian Labour Party (ALP) from power at a federal level until the 1970s.[30] In America, too, of course, there was a Catholic crusade against Communism, especially during the early years of the Cold War. And even in America popular devotions could be given a distinctly anti-Communist flavour, thus a preacher at the Forty Hours Devotion argued that it was actually patriotic to attend the Devotion because: 'Our nation is lined up against godless enemies, men who deny Christ . . . When you generously, fearlessly and lovingly attend the devotions during these three days, you are showing the godless that you still believe in God'.[31]

This is no coincidence: under the leadership of Cardinal Spellman, archbishop of New York and close friend of Pius XII, American Catholicism, like Catholicism in Italy, was arguably most confident, and most influential, in national life precisely during the Cold War period.

What all this tells us is that if the history of modern Italy cannot be fully understood without some knowledge of the history of the papacy, then neither can the modern history of the papacy be understood without a knowledge of Italian history.

The secular alternative and the future of Catholicism in Italy

The other side of the coin of this story of the strength of 'papal' Catholicism in Italy in the modern period is the comparative weakness of all of its opponents, liberalism, Fascism and Communism and, above all, secular humanism. Those who have opposed 'clericalism', the economic, legal, political and social influence in Italian society enjoyed by the institutional church, have so frequently lost their battles with it. To repeat Ezio Mauro's claim, there is the lack of a 'laic culture, conscious and confident of itself and its values, and capable of giving substance to them in politics and legislation'.[32] But why is this so? Such a culture has a long and honourable history in Italy, arguably all the way from Dante and Machiavelli, through the thinkers of the Enlightenment and French Revolution, the supporters of Garibaldi, the anti-clerical enthusiasts of nineteenth-century Freemasonry, as well as the anti-clericals of both Futurism and Fascism, down to such parties as the PLI, the PRI in the post-1945 period and the Partito Radicale from the 1970s onwards, not to mention the even more radical anti-clericalism of the Marxist parties, PSI and PCI. Yet, this culture *is* feeble, it is weak in the face of the Church. History tells us that, when the chips are down, Italian Catholicism's critics have usually preferred to defer to the Church. The failure to pass a divorce law in Liberal Italy, Fascism's deference to the Catholic social-sexual agenda, even when Mussolini's racial proclivities were becoming more pronounced, Togliatti's 'sell-out' over Article Seven of the Constitution and the more recent rows over assisted fertility and same-sex unions are clear examples of this phenomenon. They all ultimately indicate a fear of Catholic power and the consequences of opposing it.

This weakness may be attributed to a number of factors, but especially to the presence and power of the papacy and the consequent failure of a Protestant Reformation in Italy. Thanks to the effectiveness of the papal Inquisition, sixteenth-century reformers such as Peter Martyr and Giordano Bruno were quickly despatched and the Counter-Reformation ruled supreme. Protestantism came to be seen as un-Italian, anti-national. Hence there has not been a 'non-conformist' religious alternative to Catholicism in Italy, a counterculture from which a stronger form of Italian secularism might ultimately have drawn some nourishment. It was, and remained, dependent upon the importation of ideas from abroad. One could also argue that after 1922, liberal secularism was crushed between the totalitarian ideologies of Fascism, Communism and 'papal' Catholicism, but Verucci claims that the turning point came much earlier: the period 'between the end of the nineteenth century and the early part of the twentieth saw the abandonment on the part of the conservative bourgeoisie of anti-clericalism',[33] and the development of that process has been traced in Chapter 3 of this book.

More recently, however, there have been vigorous stirrings of secularist feeling, indeed anti-clericalism, in Italy. The experience of the second Berlusconi government, from 2001 to 2006, with its general attitude of deference towards the Italian Bishops' Conference, especially on the issue of bioethics, stirred up sharp protests from elements in the centre-left coalition, especially from the residual Marxist left — the Partito dei Comunisti d'Italia and Rifondazione Communista. Since then, the graffiti — complete with death threats against Cardinal Bagnasco, president of the Italian bishops — that appeared during the battles over the legalisation of same-sex unions in early 2007 suggest that what has outraged many on the Marxist and non-Marxist left is not so much the essentially homophobic tone of many ecclesiastical utterances as the feeling that once again the Church is 'bullying' and bulldozing Italy with its own moral agenda. Whatever happens to the legislation in question, and to the Prodi government, it seems likely that secularist/anti-clerical resistance to that agenda can only increase in strength.

In the period under discussion, Italian Catholicism has clearly demonstrated the capacity to meet the challenges of modernisation and to survive, and even to flourish, in changing conditions. Indeed, in consequence, the relationship between Italian Catholicism and modernisation has not always been one of conflict, it has not always resulted in defeat or retreat, and at certain times and in certain circumstances, Italian Catholicism has responded very imaginatively and effectively to the challenges posed by the forces of change — political, economic and social — and adapted accordingly. In the course of 150 years, the Italian Church has survived both the Liberal and Fascist 'revolutions' and has subsequently seen off liberalism, Fascism and Communism. It remains to be seen how it will fare in the longer term under a 'regime' of global, consumerist capitalism, whose unrestrained individualism has been identified by both Paul VI and Paul II, rightly, as probably the most insidious of all the enemies of Catholicism.

GLOSSARY AND
ABBREVIATIONS

ACI	Azione Cattolica Italiana. The very influential, centralised organisation of Italian Catholic Action created by Pius XI.
ACLI	Associazioni Cattoliche Lavoratori Italiani. Organisation of Catholic workers founded in 1944 as a pressure group inside the unified trade union movement which was largely Communist-dominated. They played an important role in the split which led to the formation of the CISL, q.v.
ACS	Archivio Centrale dello Stato (Rome). Central State Archive.
AGIP	Agenzia Generale Italian di Petrolio. Italian General Agency for Petrol.
ALP	Australian Labour Party.
assessore	One of the members of the *giunta*, or executive committee, of a local council responsible for one of its departments.
Avanguardia Operaia	Workers' Vanguard. Extra-parliamentary group to the left of the Communists.
Balilla	Opera Nazionale Balilla. The official Fascist youth organisation between 1932 and 1937.
black aristocracy	That part of the aristocracy of Rome and the former Papal States that remained loyal to the pope and boycotted the court of the king of Italy established in Rome after 1870.
braccianti	Agricultural labourers with no stable employment. They were usually employed by the hour or sometimes by the day.

Camera del Lavoro	Local organisation of Socialist/Communist-dominated trade unions prior to the advent of Fascism.
capellani del lavoro	Work or factory chaplains.
cassa di risparmio	A local savings bank or credit union especially created to assist peasants and artisans.
catechism	A book containing a summary of essential Catholic beliefs, organised in a question/answer formula, used to teach schoolchildren.
CCD	Centro Cristiano Democratico. Christian Democratic Centre.
CCI	Consorzio delle Cooperative di Consumo. Consortium of Consumer Cooperatives.
CDU	Cristiani Democratici Uniti. Unified Christian Democrats.
CEI	Conferenza Episcopale Italiana. Italian Bishops' Conference.
CGIL	Confederazione Generale Italiana del Lavoro. Socialist/Communist-dominated trade union movement after 1944.
CGL	Confederazione Generale del Lavoro. Socialist-controlled trade union confederation prior to the advent of Fascism.
CIL	Confederazione Italiana del Lavoro. Catholic-dominated trade union movement, as opposed to CGL (q.v.) between 1919 and 1926.
CISL	Confederazione Italian dei Sindacati Liberi. Catholic-led breakaway from the CGIL in 1947.
clerico-moderate	Political alliance of conservative liberals and Catholics, first at a local electoral level and then at the national one, to oppose the Socialist Party. The term was also sometimes used about Catholics who participated in such an alliance.
clientelism	A form of vote-gathering whereby the candidate buys the support of groups of voters through tangible, material rewards, i.e. jobs, pensions, contracts, promotions etc.
CLN	Comitato di Liberazione Nazionale. The National Liberation Committee that constituted the political leadership of the Armed Resistance against the German occupying forces and the forces of the Fascist

	regime (Repubblica Sociale Italiana) restored in September 1943.
Cobas	Comitati di Base. Unofficial, grass roots trade union groups.
Coldiretti	Catholic organisation of peasant farmers ('direct cultivators') that played a key role in the politics of agriculture and consequently the Christian Democratic Party.
Confindustria	The Italian (industrial) employers' organisation.
culti ammessi	Literally 'permitted cults'. The non-Catholic religious organisations recognised and regulated by Fascist law after 1929.
curialist	A cardinal belonging to the Roman Curia (q.v.) and hence during a conclave one of the group of cardinals seeking to defend the interests of the Curia from outsiders, i.e. cardinals who are archbishops of residential sees.
Destra Storica	Historic Right. The conservative liberal grouping of politicians who, as heirs of Cavour, ruled Italy between 1861 and 1876.
DGPS	Direzione Generale della Pubblica Sicurezza. General Directory of Public Safety.
dicastery	Department of the Roman Curia.
diritti alla stola	Fees for baptism, marriage and funeral ceremonies.
DS	Democratici di Sinistra. Democrats of the Left.
ecclesiology	An idea of the way in which the (usually Catholic) Church should operate, especially in regard to the relationship between the ecclesiastical hierarchy and the laity.
EEC	European Economic Community.
ENI	Ente Nazionale Idrocarburi. National Hydrocarbon Corporation.
Estrema	Extreme Left. Grouping of democrats, radicals and even republicans to the left of the Sinistra (q.v.) in the Italian Parliament.
FASC	Federazione Associazioni Scautisti Cattolici. National Italian organisation of Catholic scouts disbanded by the Fascist regime in the late 1920s.
fasci siciliani	Organisations of artisans and peasants in Sicily who engaged in protests against economic conditions during the 1890s.

Fourteen Points	Promulgated by US President Woodrow Wilson in January 1918, as the basis for international peace and harmony.
Forty Hours Devotions	A set of devotions before the exposed Blessed Sacrament lasting for forty hours, i.e. the time that Christ is supposed to have lain in the tomb.
FUCI	Federazione Universitari Cattolici Italiani. Italian federation of Catholic university students.
GCI	Gioventù Cattolica Italiana. Italian Catholic (male) youth organisation founded in the 1860s.
GFCI	Gioventù Femminile Cattolica Italiana. Italian female Catholic youth organisation founded in the 1870s.
GIAC	Gioventù Italiana dell'Azione Cattolica; a later name of GCI.
giornalieri	Agricultural labourers usually employed on a daily basis.
glebe	A portion of land assigned to the parish priest for his cultivation or letting.
GNP	gross national product.
ICAS	Istituto Cattolico di Attività Sociali. The wing of the Catholic movement after 1914 that was responsible for such activities as peasant leagues and cooperatives and credit institutions.
imprimatur	Strictly speaking, ecclesiastical approval for the publication of a book, but often used in a wider sense to mean endorsement of ideas.
IOR	Istituto per le Opere di Religione. Institute for the Works of Religion. Otherwise known as the Vatican Bank.
IRI	Istituto per la Ricostruzione Industriale. Industrial Reconstruction Institute: state industrial holding company.
Liberal Italy (or the Liberal State)	The name given by historians to the period of Italian history between unification in 1861 and the coming to power of Fascism in 1922, on the basis that the regime was ruled by the conservative liberal class which had unified Italy.
Lotta Continua	Permanent Struggle. Extra-parliamentary group to the left of the Communists.
mezzadri	Peasants who worked the land on the basis of a contract whereby they divided their produce with the landlord in lieu of money rent.

Mgr	Monsignor.
MI	Ministero dell'Interno. Ministry of the Interior.
Movimento Laureato	Graduates' Movement. The organisation of Italian Catholic university graduates. From the ranks of it and FUCI (q.v.) came large numbers of politicians of the post-war Christian Democratic Party.
MPL	Movimento Politico dei Lavoratori. Italian Workers' Movement.
MSI	Movimento Sociale Italiano. Italian Social Movement – post-war neo-Fascist party.
NATO	North Atlantic Treaty Organization.
non expedit	Literally 'it is not expedient'. A decree of the Sacred Penitentiary of the Roman Curia (q.v.) that prohibited Italian Catholics from participating as either candidates or voters in Italian parliamentary elections.
ONARMO	Opera Nazional Assistenza Religiosa e Morale agli Operai. National Organisation for Moral and Religious Support to the Workers.
Opera dei Ritiri Operai	Organisation for Workers' Retreats.
Opera Nazionale Balilla	Balilla. The official Fascist youth organisation between 1932 and 1937.
opere pie	Pius works. Charitable activities and bodies under church supervision, usually operating at a parish level.
PCI	Partito Communista Italiano. Italian Communist Party.
PDS	Partito dei Democratici di Sinistra. Party of the Democratic Left.
PDUP	Partito Democratico dell'Unita Proletaria. The Democratic Party of Proletarian Unity.
PLI	Partito Liberale Italiano. Italian Liberal Party.
PNF	Partito Nazionale Fascista. National Fascist Party.
PPI	Partito Popolare Italiano. Italian People's Party – moderate, Catholic centre party.
PPV	personal preference voting.
prefect	Civil servant governor of a province, appointed by and directly answerable to the Ministry of the Interior in Rome. Modelled on the departmental *préfet* in the Napoleonic system of centralised control of local government.

PRI	Partito Republicano Italiano. Italian Republican Party.
PSDI	Partito Socialista Democratico Italiano. Italian Democratic Socialist Party.
PSI	Partito Socialista Italiano. Italian Socialist Party.
PSU	Partito Socialista Unitario. Unitary Socialist Party.
RAI	Radio Audizioni Italiana. Italian Radio and Television.
revolutionary syndicalists	A radical element of the Italian working class movement prior to the advent of Fascism which advocated continuous strikes, culminating in a massive general strike, to overthrow the capitalist, bourgeois order.
Roman Curia	The central government of the Roman Catholic Church based in the Vatican and other buildings scattered around Rome.
salariati	Agricultural workers with reasonably fixed employment and pay.
Sinistra	The Left. The opposition to the Destra Storica (q.v.) in the Italian Parliament. They came to power in 1876.
Tangentopoli	Journalistic expression used to describe bribery and corruption scandals and trials in Italy, 1992–96.
tithe	A tax consisting of a tenth part of the value of the annual produce of the land, usually payable to the parish priest.
UDR	Unione Democratica per la Repubblica. Democratic Union for the Republic.
Unione del Lavoro	The Catholic equivalent of the Camera del Lavoro (q.v.).

NOTES

1 Introduction

1   Daniele Menozzi, *La Chiesa cattolica e la secolarizzazione*, Turin: Einaudi, 1993, p. 3.
2   See, for example, P. Borzomati, *Chiesa e Società Meridionale: Dalla Restaurazione al secondo dopoguerra*, Roma: Edizioni Studium, 1982, and G. De Rosa, *Chiesa e Religione Popolare nel Mezzogiorno*, Roma-Bari: Laterza, 1978.
3   See, for example, H. Mcleod (ed.), *European Religion in the Age of Great Cities, 1830–1930*, London and New York: Routledge, 1995, which has essays on places from St Petersburg to Spain, but nothing on Italy; also by the same author, *Secularisation in Western Europe, 1848–1914*, Basingstoke: Macmillan, 2000, and H. McLeod and W. Ustorf (eds), *The Decline of Christendom in Western Europe, 1750–2000*, Cambridge: Cambridge University Press, 2003.
4   H. McLeod, *Religion and the People of Western Europe 1789–1970*, Oxford: Oxford University Press, 1981.
5   F. Lannon, *Privilege, Persecution and Prophecy: The Catholic Church in Spain 1875–1975*, Oxford: Oxford University Press, 1987.
6   N. Atkin and F. Tallett, *Priests, Prelates and People: A History of European Catholicism since 1750*, Oxford: Oxford University Press, 2003.
7   D. Kertzer, 'Religion and Society, 1789–1892', in John A. Davies (ed.), *Italy in the Nineteenth Century*, Oxford: Oxford University Press, 2000, and A. Kelikian, 'The Church and Catholicism', in A. Lyttelton (ed.), *Liberal and Fascist Italy*, Oxford: Oxford University Press, 2002.
8   J. Dunnage, *Twentieth Century Italy: A Social History*, London: Longman, 2002.
9   C.A. Jemolo, *Church and State in Italy, 1850–1950*, Oxford: Blackwell, 1960, and D.A. Binchy, *Church and State in Fascist Italy*, Oxford: Oxford University Press, 1970.
10 John F. Pollard, *The Vatican and Italian Fascism, 1929–1932: A Study in Conflict*, Cambridge: Cambridge University Press, 1985.
11 Richard A. Webster, *The Cross and the Fasces: Christian democracy and Fascism in Italy*, Stanford CA: Stanford University Press, 1959, and J. N. Moloney,

The Emergence of Political Catholicism in Italy: Partito Popolare Italiano, 1919–1926, London: Croom Helm, 1977.

12   See, for example, R. Leonardi and D. A. Wertman, *Italian Christian Democracy: the Politics of Dominance*, Basingstoke: Macmillan, 1989, and M. Donavan, 'Italy', in D. Hanley (ed.), *Christian Democracy in Europe: a Comparative Perspective*, London: Pinter, 1996.

2 Catholicism and the Liberal Revolution

1   For an analysis of the role of the Church under the *Ancien Régime* in Europe, see H. Jedin (ed.), *History of the Church; Vol. VI, the Church in the Age of Absolutism and Enlightenment*, London: Bournes & Oates, 1981.

2   Ibid, Introduction.

3   See D. Carpanetto and G. Ricuperati, *Italy in the Age of Reason, 1685–1789*, London: Longman, 1987, especially Chapters 9, 14, 15 and 16.

4   The best survey of these changes is to be found in S. Woolf, *A History of Italy 1700–1860: The Social Constraints of Political Change*, London: Methuen, 1979, Chapter 6.

5   Carpanetto and Ricuperati, *Italy in the Age of Reason*, p. 219.

6   Frank J. Coppa, *The Modern Papacy since 1789*, London: Longman, 1998, p. 4.

7   N. Atkin and F. Tallett, *Priests, Prelates and People: A History of European Catholicism since 1750*, Oxford: Oxford University Press, 2003, p. 21.

8   Woolf, *A History of Italy*, pp. 184–5.

9   Ibid, p. 191.

10   Ibid, p. 203.

11   Ibid.

12   F. Agostini, 'La riforma statale della Chiesa nell'Italia napoleonica', in G. De Rosa, T. Gregory and A. Vauchez (eds), *Storia Dell'Italia Religiosa, III. L'Età Contempranea*, Rome-Bari: Laterza, 1995, p. 23; see also E.E.Y. Hales, *Revolution and the Papacy, 1769–1846*, London: Eyre and Spottiswoode, 1960, pp. 104–5.

13   Atkin and Tallett, *Priests, Prelates and People*, p. 81.

14   H. Jedin (ed.), *History of the Church: Vol. VII, The Church between Revolution and Restoration*, London: Bournes & Oates, 1981, p. 125.

15   *Storia della Chiesa. Dalle origini ai giorni nostri, XXI/2, Il Pontificato di Pio IX*, di R. Aubert, 1st ed. italiana alla 2nd ed. a cura di G. Martina, S.J., Turin: Editrice S.A.I.E., 1964, p. 772.

16   Ibid.

17   Ibid, p. 769.

18   Ibid, 'Clero italiano e la sua azione pastorale', p. 789.

19   Atkin and Tallett, *Priests, Prelates and People*, p. 81.

20   Christopher F. Black, *Church, Religion and Society in Early Modern Italy*, Basingstoke: Palgrave-Macmillan, 2004, p. 86.

21   Ibid, pp. 86–8.

22   G. De Rosa, *Chiesa e Religione popolare nel Mezzogiorno*, Rome-Bari: Laterza, 1978, p. 56; see also P. Stella, 'Il clero e la cultura nell'Ottocento', in

De Rosa *et al.*, *Storia Dell'Italia Religiosa, III*, pp. 96–7, for an overview of the complexities of parish organisation in the south.

23 See G. De Rosa, 'Il Clero Ricettizio di Pisticci dalla Restaurazione all'unificazione nazionale' in *Ricerche di Storia Sociale e Religiosa*, n. 24, luglio-dicembre, 1983, pp. 115–32

24 Ibid, p. 121.

25 De Rosa, *Chiesa e Religione*, p. 56.

26 The concept of 'popular religion' is a seriously contested one: for a survey of the debate, see Michael P. Carroll, *Veiled Threats: the Logic of Popular Catholicism in Italy*, Baltimore MD and London: the Johns Hopkins University Press, 1996, pp. 5–15.

27 G. De Rosa, *La Religione Popolare*, Rome: Edizioni Paoline, 1981, p. 23.

28 Ibid, p. 26; for a discussion of religiosity in nineteenth century, see also P. Stella, 'Prassi religiosa, spiritualità e mistica nell'Ottocento', in De Rosa *et al.*, *Storia dell'Italia Religiosa, III*, pp. 115–42.

29 Atkin and Tallett, *Priests, Prelates and People*, p. 42.

30 Woolf, *A History of Italy*, p. 184.

31 Atkin and Tallett, *Priests, Prelates and People*, p. 65.

32 P. Borzomati, *Chiesa e Società Meridionale: Dalla Restaurazione al secondo dopoguerra*, Rome: Edizioni Studium, 1982, p. 16.

33 John Milton, 'On the Late Massacre in Piedmont', in *The Poetical Works of John Milton*, Edinburgh: William P. Nimmo & Co., 1884, pp. 364–5.

34 Woolf, *A History of Italy*, p. 244.

35 *Storia d'Italia, Annali 11**, Gli Ebrei in Italia*, a cura di Corrado Vivanti, II, *Dall'Emancipazione a oggi*, Turin: Einaudi, 1997, p. 1094.

36 Ibid.

37 Derek Beales and Eugenio F. Biagini, *The Risorgimento and the Unification of Italy*, London: Pearson Education, 2002, pp. 93–4.

38 Jedin, *History of the Church*, VII, pp. 127–8.

39 Ibid, p. 127.

40 Ibid, p. 128.

41 Ibid, pp. 126–7.

42 Ibid, p. 128–9.

43 Hales, *Revolution and the Papacy*, pp. 230–4.

44 Ibid, p. 234.

45 Woolf, *A History of Italy*, pp. 246–55.

46 Ibid, pp. 303–9.

47 Ibid, pp. 331–8.

48 E.E.Y. Hales, *Pio Nono: A Study in European Politics and Society in the Nineteenth Century*, London: Eyre and Spottiswoode, 1956, pp. 42–7.

49 Woolf, *A History of Italy*, pp. 250–2 and 320–1.

50 Ibid, pp. 329–30.

51 H. Hearder, *Italy in the Age of the Risorgimento, 1790-1870*, London: Longman, 1983, pp. 195–7.

52 Hales, *Pio Nono*, p. 76.

53 Woolf, *A History of Italy*, p. 372.

54   Beales and Biagini, *The Risorgimento*, pp. 254–5.
55   F. Della Peruta, 'Gli ebrei nel Risorgimento ed emancipazione', in C. Vivanti (ed.), *Storia d'Italia: Annali II, Gli ebrei in Italia*, Turin: Einaudi, 1997, pp. 1166–7.
56   Ibid.
57   Ibid, p.1167.
58   Ibid, pp. 1161–7.
59   D. Kertzer, *The Kidnapping of Edgardo Mortara*, London: Picador, 1997.
60   For the text of the Statuto (Constitution) granted by King Charles Albert to his people in 1848, see Beales and Biagini, *The Risorgimento*, pp. 254–5.
61   Woolf, *A History of Italy*, pp. 437–43.
62   Ibid, p. 438.
63   O. Chadwick, *A History of the Popes: 1830–1914*, Oxford: Clarendon Press, 1999, p. 137.
64   Ibid, pp. 139–41.
65   Ibid, pp. 140–1.
66   For some rather interesting first-hand accounts of the encounters between Garibaldi's troops and supportive local clergy, see G.C. Abba, *The Diary of One of Garibaldi's Thousand*, translated and introduced by E.R. Vincent, Oxford: Oxford University Press, 1962.
67   Chadwick, *A History,* pp. 155–60.
68   For the best account of this episode, see Hales, *Pio Nono*, pp. 221–7.
69   Chadwick, *A History*, pp. 153–4.
70   Ibid, p. 154.
71   Ibid, pp. 154–5.
72   John A. Davis, *Conflict and Control: Law and Order in Nineteenth Century Italy*, Basingstoke: Macmillan, 1988, pp. 168–70.
73   Ibid, p. 170.
74   As quoted in Hales, *Pio Nono*, p. 258.
75   C. Clark and W. Kaiser (eds), *Culture Wars: Secular-Catholic Conflict in Nineteenth Century Europe,* Cambridge: Cambridge University Press, 2003.
76   Chadwick, *A History*, pp. 176–9, and Hales, *Pio Nono*, p. 258.
77   As cited in Ernst C. Helmreich (ed.), *A Free Church in a Free State? The Catholic Church in Italy, Germany, France 1864–1914*, Lexington MA: D.C. Heath & Co., 1964, pp. 4–5.
78   Clark and Kaiser, *Culture Wars*, p. 29.
79   See John F. Pollard, *Money and the Rise of the Modern Papacy: Financing the Vatican, 1850–1950*, Cambridge: Cambridge University Press, 2005, pp. 31–2.
80   Ibid, p. 38.

3 The Catholic recovery

1   See N. Atkin and F. Tallett, *Priests, Prelates and People: A History of European Catholicism since 1750*, Oxford: Oxford University Press, 2003, Chapter 4.
2   V. Viaene, 'Catholic Mobilisation and Papal Diplomacy during the Pontificate of Pius IX (1846–1878)', in E. Lamberts, *The Black International: Internationale Noir (1870–1878)*, Brussels: Institut Belgique de Rome, 2002, pp. 135–78.

3   A.C. Jemolo, *Church and State in Italy, 1850–1950*, Oxford: Basil Blackwell, 1960.

4   D.A. Binchy, *Church and State in Fascist Italy*, Oxford: Oxford University Press, 1970, pp. 383–4.

5   Ibid, p. 384.

6   Ibid.

7   *Storia della Chiesa, XXI/2, Restaurazione e Crisi Liberale, Il Pontificato di Pio IX*, a cura di C. Nuselli, Turin: Editrice S.A.I.E., 1975, p. 764.

8   *Storia della Chiesa, XXI/2, La Chiesa nella Societa Industriale (1878–1922)*, a cura di E. Guerierro e A. Zambarbieri, Cinisello Balsamo, MI: Edizioni Paoline, 1990, p. 772, fn. 24.

9   Ibid.

10   X. Toscani, *Secolarizzazione e frontiere sacerdotali*, Bologna: Il Mulino, 1982, p. 55.

11   M. Pappenheim, '*Roma o morte*: Culture Wars in Italy', in C. Clark and W. Kaiser, *Culture Wars: Secular-Catholic Conflict in Nineteenth Century Europe*, Cambridge: Cambridge University Press, 2003, pp. 206–7.

12   For an example of this process in Rome, see Carlo Fiorentino, 'The Political and Social Transformations in the Early Years of Rome Capital of Italy', in Lamberts, *The Black International*, pp. 184–7.

13   R. Zangheri, 'Catasti e storia della proprietà terriera', in *Storia D'Italia, V. Documenti 1*, Turin: Einaudi, 1973, p. 133.

14   *Storia della Chiesa, XXI/2, La Chiesa nella Societa Industriale*, p. 807.

15   G. Rocca, 'La Vita Religiosa dal 1878–1922', in ibid, pp. 137–40.

16   *Annuario Pontificio per l'anno 1948*, Vatican City: Tipografia Poliglotta Vaticana, 1948, pp. 695–719, and Rocca, 'La Vita Religiosa', p. 141.

17   Ibid.

18   Rocca, 'La Vita Religiosa', p. 141.

19   See M. Clark, *Modern Italy, 1871–1995*, 2nd ed., London: Longman, 1996, pp. 82–3 for a description of the wonderful variety of ways in which the religious orders got round the law, often with the connivance of the authorities.

20   P. Stella, 'Prassi religiosa, spiritualità e mistica nell'Ottocento', in G. De Rosa, T. Gregory and A. Vauchez (eds), *Storia dell'Italia Religiosa. III, L'Età Contempranea*, Rome-Bari: Laterza, 1995, p. 135.

21   C. Carlen (ed.), *The Papal Encyclicals, 1740–1878*, Ann Arbor MI: Pierian Press, 1990, pp. 1–5, 81–4, 145–6, 271–6, 315–19, 355–9, 375–80 and 447–8.

22   John F. Pollard, *Money and the Rise of the Modern Papacy: Financing the Vatican, 1850–1950*, Cambridge: Cambridge University Press, 2005, pp. 58–9.

23   Christopher Clark, 'Introduction: The European culture wars', in Clark and Kaiser, *Culture Wars*, pp. 21–3.

24   *Storia della Chiesa, XXI/2, La Chiesa nella Società Industriale*, p. 772.

25   V. Viaene, 'Brilliant Failure. Wladimir Czachi, the Legacy of the Geneva Committee and the Origins of the Vatican's Press Policy from Pius IX to Leo XIII', in Lamberts, *The Black International*, pp. 231–56.

26   C. Seton-Watson, *Italy from Liberalism to Fascism*, London: Methuen, 1967, pp. 60–1.

27   A. Coletti, *Il divorzio in Italia. Storia di una battaglia civile e democratica*, Roma: Giulio Savelli Editore, 1974, p. 13.

28   M. Seymour, *Debating Divorce in Italy. Marriage and the Making of Modern Italians*, Basingstoke: Palgrave-Macmillan, 2007.

29   Ibid.

30   Coletti, *Il divorzio*, pp. 36–7.

31   C. Duggan, *Francesco Crispi: From Nation to Nationalism,* Oxford: Oxford University Press, 2002, pp. 384–7.

32   Pollard, *Money*, p. 42.

33   For an abridged text of the Law of Guarantees, see John F. Pollard, *The Vatican and Italian Fascism, 1929–1932: A Study in Conflict*, Cambridge: Cambridge University Press, 1985, pp. 195–6.

34   Ibid, p. 196.

35   Jemolo, *Church and State*, pp. 50–1.

36   Seton-Watson, *Italy*, p. 57

37   For an example of this process, see John F. Pollard, *The Unknown Pope: Benedict XV (1914–1922) and the Pursuit of Peace*, London: Cassell, 1999, p. 70, where the prefect's report on Monsignor Giacomo Della Chiesa (later Benedict XV), who had been nominated to become archbishop of Bologna, is quoted in part.

38   C. Falconi, *Cardinal Antonelli: vita e carriera del Richlieu italiano nella chiesa di Pio IX*, Milan: Rizzoli, 1983, p. 494.

39   In the face of state intransigence even Pius was occasionally forced to compromise, as in his agreement in 1866 that Nazari di Calabiana, a candidate acceptable to the government, be archbishop of Milan: see O. Chadwick, *A History of the Popes 1830–1914*, Oxford: Oxford University Press, 1998, p. 156.

40   Seton Watson, *Italy*, p. 55, fn. 2

41   For a biographical essay on Leo XIII, see P. Levillain (ed.), *The Papacy: An Encyclopedia*, London: Routledge, 2002, 3 vols, II, pp. 933–6.

42   Seton-Watson, *Italy*, pp. 221–4.

43   Ibid, p. 223.

44   C. Carlen (ed.), *The Papal Encyclicals, 1878–1903*, Ann Arbor MI: Pierian Press, 1990, p. 92.

45   Jemolo, *Church and State*, p. 81.

46   Duggan, Francesco Crispi, p. 331

47   Clark, *Modern Italy*, p. 107 and Seton-Watson, *Italy*, p. 228.

48   Duggan, *Francesco Crispi*, pp. 486–94.

49   Ibid, p. 546.

50   Clark, *Modern Italy*, p. 105.

51   Duggan, *Francesco Crispi*, pp. 378–81 for a description of the funeral and pp. 432–50 on Crispi's ideas about 'making Italians', i.e. giving them a real sense of national identity.

52   Seton-Watson, *Italy*, p. 225.

53   S. Pivato, *Movimento operaio e istruzione popolare nell'Italia liberale: Discussioni e ricerche*, Milan: F. Angeli, 1986, p. 24.

54   For an analysis of the crisis, see Clark, *Modern Italy*, pp. 101–7.

55   Ibid, p.105.

56   For biographical essays, see Levillain, *The Papacy*, II, pp. 1197–9 and C. Falconi, *The Popes in the Twentieth Century: From Pius X to John XXIII*, London: Weidenfeld & Nicolson, 1967, pp. 1–88.

57   Falconi, *The Popes in the Twentieth Century*, pp. 21–2.

58   C. Carlen (ed.), *The Papal Encyclicals, 1903–1939*, Ann Arbor MI: Pierian Press, 1990, pp. 10–28, Ad Diem Illum Laetitissimum.

59   Levillain, *The Papacy*, II, p. 1198.

60   Ibid, p. 1197.

61   M. Guasco, 'La formazione del clero', in *Storia D'Italia, Annali 9, La Chiesa e il potere politico*, Turin: Einaudi, 1986, pp. 677–83.

62   Pollard, *Money*, p. 83.

63   Pollard, *The Unknown Pope*, p. 23.

64   Seton-Watson, *Italy*, p. 289.

65   Possibly because he updated Cavour's favourite maxim as a call for 'free religions in the sovereign state'.

66   Seton-Watson, *Italy*, p. 279.

67   Pollard, *Money*, p. 99.

68   For an explanation of 'modernism' and the struggles of Pius X against it, see D. Jodock (ed.), *Catholicism Contending with Modernity: Roman Catholic Modernism and Anti-Modernism in Historical Context*, Cambridge: Cambridge University Press, 2000, especially Introduction I.

69   Ibid.

70   Chadwick, *History of the Popes*, pp. 354–9.

71   See Pollard, *The Unknown Pope*, pp. 44–5

72   Falconi, *The Popes in the Twentieth Century*, pp. 56–7 and 59–60.

73   Jodock (ed.), *Catholicism Contending with Modernity*, p. 27.

74   For the Scotton brothers, see A. Scottà (ed.), *La Conciliazione Ufficiosa: il Barone Carlo Monti 'incaricato d'affari' del governo italiano presso la Santa Sede*, 2 vols, Vatican City: Libreria Editrice Vaticana, 1997, I, pp. 174–5 and 179.

75   *L'Unità Cattolica*, like Benigni, ended up supporting the advent of Italian Fascism: see Richard A. Webster, *The Cross and the Fasces: Christian democracy and Fascism in Italy*, Stanford CA: Stanford University Press, 1959, p. 224.

76   Jodock, *Catholicism Contending with Modernity*, p. 24

77   Chadwick, *A History of the Popes*, p. 353.

78   Jodock, *Catholicism Contending with Christianity*, p. 24.

4 Italian Catholicism and the challenges of industrial development

1   For a summary of the historiographical debates around the processes and timing of industrialisation, and the related issue of working class formation

in Italy, see J.A. Davis, 'Socialism and the Working Classes in Italy before 1914', in D. Geary (ed.), *Labour and the Socialist Movements in Europe before 1914*, Oxford: Berg, 1989, pp. 203–7.

2   V. Zamagni, *The Economic History of Italy: Recovery after Decline*, Oxford: Oxford University Press, 1993, pp. 66–74.

3   Davis, 'Socialism', pp. 198–9 and 216–17.

4   P. Corti and A. Lonni, 'Da Contadini a Operiai', in A. De Clementi (ed.), *La Società inafferabile: Proto-industria, città e classi sociali in Italia liberale*, Milan: Lavoro, 1986, pp. 196 and 243.

5   Ibid, p. 243.

6   As quoted in John Pollard, 'Religion and the Formation of the Italian Working Class', in Rick Halpern and Jonathan Morris (eds), *American Exceptionalism? US Working Class Formation in an International Context*, Basingstoke: Macmillan, 1997, p. 169.

7   John F. Pollard, *Money and the Rise of the Modern Papacy: Financing the Vatican, 1850–1950*, Cambridge: Cambridge University Press, 2005, pp. 211–12.

8   Davis, 'Socialism', p. 220.

9   As quoted in C. Snider, *L'Episcopato di Cardinale Andrea Ferrari*, vol. I, Vicenza: Neri Pozza, 1981, p. 365.

10 See, for example, F. Agostini (ed.), *Le visite pastorali di Giuseppe Callegari nella Diocesi di Padova (1884–88/1893–1905)*, Rome: Edizioni di Storia e Letteratura, 1981; A. Lazzarretto, 'Parrocci ed emigrati nel Vicentino del primo Novecento', in various authors, *Studi di storia sociale e religiosa: Scritti in onore di Gabriele De Rosa*, Naples: Ferraro, 1980, pp. 1091–112; and A. Monticone, 'L'Episcopato italiano dall'Unita al Concilio Vaticano II', in M. Rosa (ed.), *Clero e societa nell'italia contemporanea*, Rome-Bari: Laterza, 1992.

11 Monticone, 'L'Episcopato italiano', p. 278.

12 D. Menozzi, 'Le Nuove parrocchie nella prima Industrializzazione Torinese (1900–1915)', in *Rivista di Storia e Letteratura Religiosa*, 9, 1973, p. 70.

13 Ibid, p. 85.

14 Ibid.

15 L. Bedeschi, *I Capellani del lavoro: Aspetti religiosi e culturali della societa lombarda negli anni della crisi modernista*, Milan: A. Mondadori, 1977, p. 211.

16 X. Toscani, *Secolarizzazione e frontiere sacerdotali*, Bologna: Il Mulino, 1982, p. 55.

17 Bedeschi, *I Capellani del lavoro*, pp. 211–37.

18 G.B. Varnier, 'Continuita e rotture (1870–1915)', in D. Puncoh (ed.), *Il cammino della Chiesa Genovese dalle origini ai nostril giorni: Atti della Societa Ligure di Storia Patria*, Nuova Serie, Vol. XXXIX (CXIII) Fasc. II, Genoa: Societa Ligure di Storia Patria, 1994, p. 448.

19 Ibid, p. 451.

20 Ibid, pp. 455–7.

21 H. McLeod, 'The Dechristianisation of the Working Class in Western Europe (1850–1950)', *Social Compass*, XXVII, 2/3 (1986), p. 27.

22 U. Lovato and A. Castellani, 'Il beato Leonardo Murialdi e il movimento operaio cristiano', in *Italia sacra: Spiritualità e azione del laicato cattolico*, Padua: Marsilio, 1969, p. 608.

23 A. De Clemente, 'Cresciuta e ristagno proto-industriale nell'Italia meridionale', in De Clementi, *La Società inafferabile*, p. 109.

24 A. Kelikian, 'Convitti operai cattolici e forza lavoro feminile', in A. Gigli Marchetti (ed.), *Donna Lombarda*, Milan: Angeli, 1992.

25 G. Battelli, 'Clero secolare e società italiana tra decennio napoleonico e primo novecento', in Rosa, *Clero e società*, pp. 106–8.

26 Agostini, *Le visite pastorali*, p. xcviii.

27 J. Dunnage, *Twentieth Century Italy: A Social History*, London: Longman, 2002, p. 14.

28 F. Traniello and G. Campanini (eds), *Dizionario Storico del Movimento Cattolico in Italia. 1860–1980*, Turin: Casa Editrice Marietti, 1981, 1/2, p. 138.

29 Ibid.

30 Ibid, p. 140.

31 Ibid.

32 Agostini, *Le visite pastorali*, p. xcv.

33 F. Snowden, *Violence and Great Estates in Southern Italy; Apulia, 1900–1922*, Cambridge: Cambridge University Press, 1986, pp. 79–110.

34 Ibid, p. 80.

35 Ibid, p. 81.

36 See F. De Felice and V. Parlato (eds), *A. Gramsci e La questione meridionale*, Rome: Editori Riuniti, 1996, p. 151.

37 G. De Rosa, 'La parrocchia in Italia in età contemporanea', in various authors, *La parrocchia in Italia nell'età contemporanea*, Naples: Edizioni Dehoniane, 1982, p. 19.

38 Ibid, p. 25.

39 As quoted in G. De Rosa, *Vescovi, popolo e magia nel Sud d'Italia*, Napoli: Guidi, 1983, p. 262.

40 As quoted in D. Menozzi, 'Le Nuove parrocchie', p.79 (for the Turin suburb of Borgo Vittorio), in various authors, *La parrocchia in Italia* and in Bedeschi, *I Cappellani del lavoro*, p. 216 (Milan).

41 A. Albertazzi, *Il cardinale Svampa e I cattolici bolognesi 1894–1907*, Brescia: La Morcelliana, 1971, p. 890; for an account of the problems facing Della Chiesa, see John F. Pollard, *The Unknown Pope: Benedict XV (1914–1922) and the Pursuit of Peace*, London: Cassell, 1999, pp. 49–51.

42 As quoted in Pollard, *The Unknown Pope*, p. 49.

43 As quoted in ibid, pp. 49–50.

44 As quoted in ibid, p. 50.

45 G. Camaiani, 'Valori religiosi e polemica anticlericale nella sinistra democratica e del primo socialismo', in *Rivista di Storia e Letteratura*, XX, 2, 1984, p. 228, and for a broader picture of the origins of anti-clericalism in Italy, G.B. Varnier, 'Continuità e rotture (1870–1915)', in D. Puncoh (ed.), *Il cammino della Chiesa Genovese dalle origini ai nostril giorni: Atti della Societa Ligure di Storia Patria*, Nuova Serie, Vol. XXXIX (CXIII) Fasc. II, Genoa: Societa Ligure di Storia Patria, 1994.

46   C. Seton-Watson, *Italy from Liberalism to Fascism*, London: Methuen, 1967, p. 67.

47   D. Howard Bell, *Sesto San Giovanni: Workers, Culture and Politics in an Italian Town, 1880–1922*, New Brunswick NJ: Rutgers University Press, 1986, pp. 43–4, where he stresses the 'importance of the pre-factory cultural traditions and their importance in the formation of the modern working class', and an 'attitude of anti-clericalism which resulted in resistance to church influences in secular life'. Bell's work is of particular value because of his use of the diary of the parish priest of Sesto and its observations on the rise of the working class movement there.

48   Davis, 'Socialism', pp. 185–6.

49   See, for example, Bell, *Sesto San Giovanni*, p. 47 and Snowden, *Violence*, p. 86.

50   S. Pivato, *Movimento operaio e istruzione popolare nell'Italia liberale: Discussioni e ricerche*, Milan: F. Angeli, 1986, p. 24.

51   Ibid, p. 26.

52   Ibid, p. 28.

53   Ibid, p. 24.

54   As quoted in A. Azzaroni, *Socialistici anticlericali*, Florence: Parenti, 1961, p. 105.

55   Camaiani, 'Valori religiosi', p. 235 and G. Giarizzo, 'Il Socialismo e la modernizzazione del mezzogiorno', in C. Cingari and S. Fedele (eds), *Il socialismo nel Mezzogiorno d'Italia, 1892–1926*, Bari: Laterza, 1992, p. 6.

56   As quoted in Bell, *Sesto San Giovanni*, p. 244.

57   As quoted in S. Merli (ed.), *Proletariato di fabbrica e capitalismo industriale: il caso italiano, 1889–1900*, vol. 2, Florence: La Nuova Italia, 1973, doc. CCLXXX, p. 645.

58   Enrico Berlinguer, Communist Party secretary 1972–86, and author of the 'historic compromise'; his wife was a devout Catholic.

59   As quoted in V. Germani Genzini, 'Il movimento contadino nel Cremonese all'inizio del'900', in P. Della, *Braccianti e contadini nella valle Padana*, Rome: Editori Riuniti, 1975, p. 119.

60   Merli, *Proletariato di fabbrica*, doc. LXXXIX, p. 860.

61   Mcleod, 'Dechristianisation', p. 62 and Bell, *Sesto San Giovanni*, p. 60.

62   Archivio Centrale dello Stato (Rome), Ministero dell'Interno, Direzione Generale della Pubblica Sicurezza (ACS, MI and DGPS), fasc. 11, 30.09.1905.

63   Ibid.

64   Merli, *Proletariato di fabbrica*, p. 849, fn. 18.

65   Bell, *Sesto San Giovanni*, p. 47 and D. Kertzer, *Comrades and Christians: Religion and the Political Struggle in Communist Italy*, Cambridge: Cambridge University Press, 1980, p. 142.

66   Bell, *Sesto San Giovanni*, p. 26.

67   Ibid, p. 56.

68   Lovato and Castellani, 'Il beato Leonardo Murialdi', p. 610.

69   G. Rosa, 'La parrocchia in Italia', p. 25.

70   As quoted in Seton-Watson, *Italy*, 223.
71   For an account of the early stages in the development of the Catholic movement in Italy see Richard A. Webster, *The Cross and the Fasces: Christian Democracy and Fascism in Italy*, Stanford CA: Stanford University Press, 1960, pp. 3–26 and J.F. Pollard, 'Italy', in T. Buchanan and M. Conway (eds), *Political Catholicism in Europe*, Oxford: Oxford University Press, 1996, pp. 69–77.
72   For an analysis of the crisis, see John A. Davis, *Conflict and Control: Law and Order in Nineteenth Century Italy*, Basingstoke and London: Macmillan, 1988, pp. 345–52.
73   Bell, *Sesto San Giovanni*, p. 68–72
74   V. Zamagni, *The Economic History of Italy 1860–1990. Recovery after Decline*, Oxford: Clarendon Press, 1993, pp. 104–5 and L. Guiotto, *La fabbrica totale: Paternalismo industriale e Città sociali in Italia*, Milan: Feltrinelli, 1979, pp. 81–2.
75   P. Misner, *Social Catholicism in Europe: From the Onset of Industrialisation to the First World War*, New York: Crossroad, 1991, pp. 285–7.
76   Ibid, p. 254 and Lovato and Castellani, 'Il beato Leonardo Murialdi', p. 571.
77   Misner, *Social Catholicism*, p. 286.
78   C. Carlen, *The Papal Encyclicals, 1878–1903*, Ann Arbor MI: Pierian Press, 1990, pp. 241–63.
79   Lovato and Castellani, 'Il beato Leonardo Murialdi', p. 60.
80   Bedeschi, *I Cappellani del Lavoro*, p. 217.
81   Ibid, p. 226.
82   Webster, *The Cross and the Fasces*, p. 13.
83   See, for example, ACS, MI and DGPS, busta 26, partito clericale, fasc. 11, Bologna and fasc. 17, Catania for evidence of these tensions.
84   See Snider, *L'Episcopato*, p. 245 and A. Caneva, *L'Azione sindacale in Italia dall'estraneita alla partecipazion*, Brescia: La Morcelliana, 1979, p. 41.
85   Daniel D. Horowitz, *Storia del Movimento Sindacale in Italia*, Bologna: Il Mulino, 1966, pp. 186–7.
86   P. Monetti in *La Civiltà Cattolica*, 65, 1914: 1, 'Sindacalismo cristiano?', pp. 385–400; 2, 'Sindacalismo cristiano?', pp. 385–99; and 3, 'Sindacalismo cristiano?' pp. 546–59.
87   Misner, *Social Catholicism*, p. 33.
88   Horowitz, *Storia del Movimento Sindacale*, p. 187.
89   P. Hebblethwaite, *John XXIII: The Pope of the Council*, London: Geoffrey Chapman, 1984, pp. 63–4.
90   I. Lizzola and E. Manzoni, 'Proletariato Bergamasco e Organizzazioni Cattoliche: Lo Sciopero di Ranica (1909)', in *Studi e Ricerche di Storia Contemporanea*, 15 (May), 1981, pp. 15–18.
91   Ibid.
92   For a study of the origins of this 'plutocracy', see M.G. Rossi, *Le origini del partito cattolico in Italia: Movimento cattolico e lotta di classe nell' Italia liberale*, Rome: Editori Riuniti, 1977, pp. 281–310.

93 Caneva, *L'Azione sindacale*, p. 127.
94 Ibid. Local studies of Catholic trade unions and peasant leagues also confirm this: see, for example, Valeria Romani Genzini, 'Il movimento contadino nel Cremonese all'inizio del'900, in F. Della Peruta (ed.), *Braccianti e contadini nella Valle Padana*, Roma: Editori Riuniti, p. 97.
95 Seton-Watson, *Italy*, pp. 301–2.
96 Bell, *Sesto San Giovanni*, p. 60.
97 The Ministry figures are quoted in Horowitz, *Storia del Movimento Sindacale*, pp. 185–9.
98 A.Fappani, *G. Migliolo e Il Movimento Contadino Italiano*, Rome: Cinque Lune, 1964, pp. 156–63.
99 Horowitz, *Storia del Movimento Sindacale*, p. 186.
100 Ibid.
101 O. Confessore, *I cattolici e'la fede nella liberta'*, Rome: Edizioni Studium, 1989.
102 Rossi, *Le origini*, Chapter 3.
103 A. Caroleo, *Le banche cattoliche*, Milan: Feltrinelli, 1976, p. 42.
104 For this important episode see Webster, *The Cross and the Fasces*, Chapter 2.
105 Carlen, *The Papal Encyclicals, 1878–1903*, pp. 479–87.
106 For the Milan and Turin programmes, see Misner, *Social Catholicism*, pp. 241–2.
107 Webster, *The Cross and the Fasces*, Chapter 2.
108 Clark, *Modern Italy*, p. 147.
109 Ibid, p. 146.
110 The first serious study of the Catholic deputies in Parliament is G. Formigoni, *I cattolici-deputati (1904–1918)*, Rome: Edizioni Studium, 1989.
111 M. Clark, *Modern Italy*, pp. 156–7.
112 Seton-Watson, *Italy*, p. 395.
113 McLeod, 'The Dechristianisation of the Working Class', p. 210.

5 Italian Catholics, the Great War and the rise of Fascism

1 For a biography of Benedict XV, see John F. Pollard, *The Unknown Pope: Benedict XV (1914–1922) and the Pursuit of Peace*, London, Cassell, 1999.
2 Ibid, Chapters 4 and 5.
3 C. Seton-Watson, *Italy from Liberalism to Fascism*, London: Methuen, 1967, pp. 413–30.
4 Ibid, pp. 430–6.
5 On the Intervention Crisis, see ibid, pp. 436–50; on Catholic attitudes to intervention, see Richard A. Webster, *The Cross and the Fasces: Christian democracy and Fascism in Italy*, Stanford CA: Stanford University Press, 1959, pp. 44–9.
6 Ibid.
7 Pollard, *The Unknown Pope*, pp. 95–8.
8 As quoted in ibid, p. 103.

9   Ibid.

10 Ibid.

11 A Monticone, *Gl'Italiani in uniforme, 1915–1918*, Bari: Laterza, 1972, Chapter V, 'I vescovi italiani e la Guerra, 1915–1918'; see also F. Malgeri, 'La Chiesa, I cattolici e la prima guerra mondiale', in G. De Rosa, T. Gregory and A. Vauchez (eds), *Storia dell'Italia Religiosa, III, L'Età Contemporanea*, Roma-Bari: Laterza, 1995, pp. 201–3.

12 Ibid, p. 181.

13 Ibid, p. 182.

14 Pollard, *The Unknown Pope*, p. 103.

15 F. Traniello, 'L'Italia cattolica nell'era Fascista', in De Rosa *et al.*, *Storia dell'Italia Religiosa III*, p. 257.

16 M. Clark, *Modern Italy, 1871–1995*, London: Longman, 1996, pp. 188–9.

17 Pollard, *The Unknown Pope*, p. 97.

18 Ibid, p. 98.

19 Ibid.

20 Ibid, p. 131.

21 Ibid.

22 *Il Popolo D'Italia*, 28 September 1917.

23 A. Monticone, *Gl'Italiani in uniforme, 1915–1918*, Bari: Laterza, 1972, pp. xlii–xliv.

24 Pollard, *The Unknown Pope*, p. 164.

25 F. Traniello, 'L'Italia cattolica nell'era Fascista', p. 257.

26 Ibid, p. 258.

27 For an account of relations between Italy and the Vatican in war time, see Pollard, *The Unknown Pope*, Chapters 4 and 5.

28 For the diary of Monti, see A. Scottà (ed.), *La Conciliazione Ufficiosa: il Barone Carlo Monti 'incaricato d'affari' del governo italiano presso la Santa Sede*, 2 vols, Vatican City: Libreria Editrice Vaticana, 1997.

29 Pollard, *The Unknown Pope*, pp. 164–6.

30 Ibid, pp. 166–70.

31 Ibid, p. 169.

32 John F. Pollard, *The Vatican and Italian Fascism, 1929–1932: A Study in Conflict*, Cambridge: Cambridge University Press, 1985, pp. 34–6.

33 Ibid, p. 36.

34 J. Pollard, 'The Pope, Labour and the Tango', in R. Swanson (ed.), *The Use and Abuse of Time in Christian History: Proceedings of the Ecclesiastical History Society*, Woodbridge: Boydell Press, 2002, p. 376.

35 The only serious study of the Partito Popolare in English is J.N. Moloney, *The Emergence of Political Catholicism in Italy: PPI, 1919–1926*, London: Croom Helm, 1977; see also Pollard, *The Unknown Pope*, pp. 170–81.

36 Pollard, *The Unknown Pope*, pp. 173–4.

37 Ibid, pp. 173–4.

38 Ibid, p. 173.

39 Moloney, *The Emergence of Political Catholicism*, pp. 66–7.

40   P. Corner, *Fascism in Ferrara, 1915–1925*, Oxford: Oxford University Press, 1975, pp. 127–8 and J. Pollard, 'Conservative Catholics and Italian Fascism: the Clerico-Fascists', in M. Blinkhorn (ed.), *Fascists and Conservatives: The Radical Right and the Establishment in Twentieth Century Europe*, London: Unwin Hyman, 1990, pp. 38–40.

41   Moloney, *The Emergence of Political Catholicism*, pp. 55–6.

42   J.M. Foot, '"White Bolsheviks"? The Catholic Left and the Socialists in Italy, 1919–1920', in *Historical Journal*, 40, 2, 1977, pp. 420–8.

43   For a fuller analysis of the role played by the Partito Popolare in the Italian Parliament between its foundation and the Fascist March on Rome in October 1922 see Moloney, *The Emergence of Political Catholicism*, Chapters 3 and 4.

44   C. Seton Watson, *Italy from Liberalism to Fascism*, London: Methuen, 1967, pp. 510–27.

45   Pollard, *The Unknown Pope*, p. 180.

46   Foot, '"White Bolsheviks"?', pp. 420–8.

47   Pollard, *The Unknown Pope*, p. 177.

48   Ibid, p. 179.

49   For overviews of the history of the rise and fall of Italian Fascism, see P. Morgan, *Fascism in Italy, 1915–1945*, 2nd ed., Basingstoke: Macmillan, 2005, and John Pollard, *The Fascist Experience in Italy*, London: Routledge, 1998.

50   As quoted in Moloney, *The Emergence of Political Catholicism*, p. 189: for examples of Fascist violence against Catholic organisations see also pp. 84–6.

51   As quoted in Pollard, *The Vatican and Italian Fascism*, p. 22.

52   For biographical sketches of Pius XI, see P. Levillain (ed.), *The Papacy: An Encyclopedia*, London: Routledge, 2002, 3 vols, II, pp. 1209–16 and C. Falconi, *The Popes in the Twentieth Century from Pius X to John XXIII*, London: Weidenfeld & Nicolson, 1967, pp. 151–233.

53   Falconi, *The Popes in the Twentieth Century*, pp. 158–60.

54   For the text of *Ubi Arcano Dei*, see C. Carlen (ed.), *The Papal Encyclicals 1903–1939*, Ann Arbor MI: Pierian Press, 1990, pp. 225–39.

55   Pollard, *The Vatican and Italian Fascism*, p. 25.

56   Ibid, pp. 24–5.

57   Pollard, 'Conservative Catholics', pp. 33–5.

58   Pollard, *The Vatican and Italian Fascism*, p. 27.

59   See the Vatican newspaper, *L'Osservatore Romano*, editorial for 1 November, 1922.

60   John F. Pollard, *Money and the Rise of the Modern Papacy: Financing the Vatican, 1850–1950*, Cambridge, 2005, pp. 115–18.

61   Pollard, 'Conservative Catholics', pp. 35–6.

62   Moloney, *The Emergence of Political Catholicism*, pp. 181–8.

63   Ibid, p. 180.

64   Pollard, *The Vatican and Italian Fascism*, p. 34.

65   As quoted in ibid, p. 34, fn. 73.

66   Pollard, 'Conservative Catholics', pp. 38–9.

67   Ibid, p. 39.

68   Ibid, pp. 35–6.
69   Pollard, *The Vatican and Italian Fascism*, pp. 36–7.
70   Ibid, p. 37.
71   A. Acquarone, *La costruzione dello stato totalitario*, Milan: A. Mondadori, 1965; for a short general account of Italian Fascism, see Pollard, *The Fascist Experience*.
72   A. Lyttelton, *The Seizure of Power: Fascism in Italy, 1919–1929*, London: Weidenfeld & Nicolson, 1987, p. 286.
73   Pollard, *The Vatican and Italian Fascism*, p. 41.
74   Ibid, pp. 38–9.
75   Ibid.
76   For an account of the negotiations, see ibid, pp. 42–7 and D.A. Binchy, *Church and State in Fascist Italy*, Oxford: Oxford University Press, 1970, Chapters V and VI.
77   For the texts of the Lateran Agreements see Pollard, *The Vatican and Italian Fascism*, Appendix II, pp. 197–215.

6 Fascism, war and resistance

1   John F. Pollard, *The Vatican and Italian Fascism, 1929–32: A Study in Conflict*, Cambridge: Cambridge University Press, 1985, p. 197.
2   Ibid, pp. 62–3 and 66–7.
3   Ibid, pp. 69–73.
4   A. C. Jemolo, *Church and State in Modern Italy*, Oxford: Oxford University Press, 1960, p. 239.
5   As quoted in Pollard, *The Vatican and Italian Fascism*, p. 71.
6   Ibid, p. 70.
7   Ibid, p. 215.
8   Pollard, *Money and the Rise of the Modern Papacy; Financing the Vatican, 1850–1950*, Cambridge: Cambridge University Press, 2005, pp. 146–9 and 171–7.
9   As quoted in Pollard, *The Vatican and Italian Fascism*, p. 72.
10   Ibid, p. 66.
11   As quoted in ibid, p. 72.
12   As quoted in ibid, pp. 130.
13   Ibid, Chapter 6, for a full account of the crisis.
14   Peter C. Kent, *The Pope and the Duce: The International Impact of the Lateran Agreements*, London and Basingstoke: Macmillan, 1981.
15   See Pollard, *The Vatican and Italian Fascism,* p. 216 for the text of the September Accord and pp. 161–6 for an analysis of their long-term significance.
16   For an assessment of the clerico-Fascist position after 1929, see John Pollard, 'Conservative Catholics and Italian Fascism: the Clerico-fascists', in M. Blinkhorn (ed.), *Fascists and Conservatives: The Radical Right and the Establishment in Twentieth-Century Europe*, London: Unwin Hyman, 1991, pp. 43–7.

17   Charles F. Delzell, *Mussolini's Enemies: The Italian Anti-Fascist Resistance*, New York: Praeger, 1974, Chapter 3.

18   As quoted in R. Wolff, 'Italy: Catholics, Clergy, and the Church – Complex Reactions to Fascism', in R. Wolff and R. Hoensch (eds), *Catholics, the State and the European Radical Right, 1919–1945*, New York: Social Science Monographs, 1987, p. 147.

19   Delzell, *Mussolini's Enemies*, pp. 148–52.

20   For an exploration of the key role played by the concept of palingenesis in contemporary explanations of Fascism, see R. Griffin, *The Nature of Fascism*, London: Routledge, 1991, pp. 32–9.

21   Pollard, *The Vatican and Italian Fascism*, Chapter 5.

22   Ibid, pp. 189–91.

23   For an analysis of the role of the Catholic University in the 1930s, see P. Ranfagni, *I Clerico Fascisti: Le riviste dell'Universita Cattolica negli anni del regime*, Florence: Cooperativa Editrice Universitaria, 1975.

24   See *Vigilanti Cura*, in C. Carlen (ed.), *The Papal Encyclicals, 1903–1939*, Ann Arbor MI: Pierian Press, 1990, pp. 515–23.

25   John Dunnage, *Twentieth Century Italy: A Social History*, London: Longman, 2002, p. 99.

26   Pollard, *The Vatican and Italian Fascism*, pp. 153–4.

27   Wolff, 'Catholics, Clergy and Church', pp. 146–7 and p. 155, fn. 51.

28   P. Scoppola, *La proposta politica di De Gasperi*, Bologna: Il Mulino, 1977, p. 46.

29   F. Traniello, 'L'Italia Cattolica nell'era Fascista', in G. De Rosa, T. Gregory and A. Vauchez (eds), *Storia dell'Italia Religiosa. III. L'Età Contemporanea*, Roma-Bari: Laterza, 1995, p. 272.

30   Ibid.

31   Pollard, *Money and the Rise of the Modern Papacy*, p. 153.

32   Traniello, 'L'Italia Cattolica', p. 271.

33   Ibid, p. 290.

34   Pollard, *The Vatican and Italian Fascism,* p. 108; for a fuller account, see G. Peyrot, 'La legislazione sulle confessioni religiose diverse dalla cattolica', in P.A. D'Avack (ed.), *La legislazione ecclesiastica*, Milan: Istituto per la scienza dell'amministrazione pubblica, 1967, pp. 521–47.

35   Pollard, *The Vatican and Italian Fascism*, pp. 110–11.

36   Huw Thomas, 'Religious Freedom, the Lateran Pacts and the Debates in the Constituent Assembly (1946–1948)', unpublished PhD thesis, University of Wales, Swansea, 2006, pp. 43–4.

37   Pollard, *The Vatican and Italian Fascism*, p. 108 and R. de Felice, *Storia degli Ebrei sotto il fascismo*, Bari: Laterza, 1961, pp. 118–20.

38   For an account of the fate of women generally under Fascism, see V. De Grazia, *How Fascism Ruled Women: Italy, 1945*, Berkeley CA: University of California Press, 1992.

39   The text of *Casti Connubi* is in C. Carlen (ed.), *The Papal Encyclicals, 1903–1939*, Ann Arbor MI: Pierian Press, 1990, pp. 390–414.

40   Mussolini was also, ironically, the Italian premier who first gave votes to women, in local elections in 1925, only to abolish local elections the following year.

41   P. Willson, *Modern Italy; Journal of the Association for the Study of Modern Italy*, vol. 1, Autumn 1996, 2, pp. 44–62.

42   Pollard, *The Vatican and Italian Fascism*, p. 107–8.

43   Ibid, p. 107.

44   See the entry on 'Ruralisation' in C.P. Blamires (ed.), *Historical Dictionary of World Fascism*, Oxford: ABC-Clio, 2006.

45   See A. Kersevan and P. Visintin (eds), *Giuseppe Nogara: luci ed ombre di un arcivescovo, 1928–1945,* Udine: I Quaderni del Picchio, 1992, pp. 56–61.

46   P. Willson, *Peasant Women and Politics in Fascist Italy: The Massaie Rurali*, London: Routledge, 2002, p. 187.

47   For the text of *Quadragesimo Anno*, see Carlen, *The Papal Encyclicals, 1903–1939*, pp. 415–43.

48   Richard A. Webster, *The Cross and the Fasces: Christian Democracy and Fascism in Italy*, Stanford CA: Stanford University Press, 1959, p. 161.

49   Pollard, *The Vatican and Italian Fascism*, p. 139.

50   V. De Grazia, *Culture of Consent: Mass Organisations of Leisure in Fascist Italy*, Cambridge: Cambridge University Press, 1982.

51   As quoted in Willson, *Peasant Women*, pp. 186–7.

52   Pollard, *The Vatican and Italian Fascism*, pp. 50–3.

53   As quoted in ibid, p. 203.

54   Ibid, chap. 4 and Kent, *The Pope and the Duce*, Chapters 6 and 7.

55   Pollard, *The Vatican and Italian Fascism*, pp. 100–3.

56   Edward R. Tannenbaum, *Fascism in Italy: Society and Culture, 1922–1945*, London: Allen Lane, 1972, pp. 230–1.

57   A. Pellicani, *Il Papa di Tutti: La Chiesa Cattolica, Il Fascismo e il Razzismo, 1929–1945*, Milan: Sugar Editore, 1964, Chapter 4.

58   D.A. Binchy, *Church and State in Fascist Italy*, Oxford: Oxford University Press, 1970, pp. 678–9.

59   Ibid.

60   As quoted in Willson, *Peasant Women*, p. 185.

61   For the text of *Mit Brennender Sorge*, see Carlen, *The Papal Encyclicals, 1903–1939*, pp. 525–35.

62   Pollard, *Money and the Rise of the Modern Papacy*, pp. 179–80.

63   P. Morgan, *Fascism in Italy: 1919–1945*, London and Basingstoke, 2nd ed., Basingstoke: Palgrave, 2004, pp. 193–205.

64   The best study of this development is to be found in E. Gentile, *The Sacralisation of Politics in Fascist Italy*, London: Harvard University Press, 1996.

65   Ibid, Chapters 4 and 5.

66   We have little information about religious practice under Fascism, but what we know about the post-Second World War period suggests that the numbers of 'practising Catholics', i.e. those attending weekly Mass, were rather higher than suggested by Tannenbaum, *Fascism in Italy*, p. 169: see Traniello, 'L'Italia cattolica', pp. 257–99.

67   The text of *Non Abbiamo Bisogno* is in Carlen, *The Papal Encyclicals, 1903–1939*, pp. 445–58.

68   E. Fattorini, *Pio XI, Hitler and Mussolini*, Turin: Einaudi, 2007 (which is one of the first fruits of the opening of the papers of Pius XI in the Vatican Archives in September 2006) demonstrates this clearly, especially in Chapters VII and VIII.

69   For the text of the encyclical and a discussion of its genesis, see G. Passelecq and B. Suchecky, *The Hidden Encyclical*, New York and London: Harcourt Brace, 1997.

70   Webster, *The Cross and the Fasces*, p. 160; see also Pellicani, *Il Papa di Tutti*, Chapter 6.

71   Aaron Gillette, *Racial Theories in Fascist Italy*, London: Routledge, 2002, p. 76.

72   Ibid, p. 76 and D.A. Binchy, *Church and State in Fascist Italy*, Oxford: Oxford University Press, 1970, pp. 623–6.

73   I am grateful to my research student, Ms Meredith Carew of St Anthony's College, Oxford, for bringing information on this issue to my attention.

74   R. De Felice, *Mussolini il Fascista: L'organizzazione dello stato totalitario. 1925–1929*, Turin: Einaudi, 1968.

75   There is a considerable literature in Italian on relations between Catholicism and Fascism at a local level in Italy: see, for example, A. Monticone (ed.), *Cattolici e Fascisti in Umbria (1922–1945)*, Bologna: Il Mulino, 1978 and P. Pecorari (ed.), *Chiesa, Azione Cattolica e fascismo nell'Italia settentrionale durante il pontificato di Pio XI (1922–1939)*, Milan: Vita e Pensiero, 1979.

76   R Moro, 'Afascismo e antifascismo nei movimenti intellectually dell'Azione Cattolica dopo il "31" ', in *Storia Contemporanea*, VI, 4, 1975, pp. 733–801.

77   P. Scoppola, 'The State and the Church in the Fascist Period in Italy, 1922–1943', unpublished paper given at Cambridgeshire College of the Arts and Technology, 4 November 1979.

78   R.J.B. Bosworth, 'Everyday Mussolinianism: Friends, Family, Locality and Violence in Fascist Italy', in *Contemporary European History*, XVI, I, 2005, pp. 29–30.

79   Pollard, *The Vatican and Italian Fascism*, pp. 120–2.

80   Ibid, pp. 127–30 and Chapter 6.

81   There is no serious, scholarly biography of Pius XII in English: John Cornwell's, *Hitler's Pope: The Hidden History of Pius XII*, London: Viking, 1999 has its limitations; useful biographical essays are to be found in P. Levillain (ed.), *The Papacy: An Encyclopedia*, London: Routledge, 2002, 3 vols., II, pp. 1191–7 and in C. Falconi, *The Popes in the Twentieth Century: From Pius X to John XXIII*, London: Weidenfeld & Nicolson, 1967, pp. 235–303.

82   J. F. Pollard, 'The Papacy in Two World Wars: Benedict XV and Pius XI Compared', in *Totalitarian Movements and Political Religions*, 2, 3, Winter 2001, p. 90.

83   Ciano, G., *Ciano's Diary, 1939–1943*, ed. with an introduction by M. Muggeridge, London and Toronto: Heineman, 1947, pp. 26, 39–40,

186 and 248–9; G. Miccoli, 'Chiesa Cattolica e Totalitarismi', in V. Ferrone (ed.), *La Chiesa Cattolica e il Totalitarismo: Atti del Convegno Torino, 25–26 ottobre 2001*, Florence: Olschki Editore, 2004, p. 26.

84   For an interesting analysis of the increasing denunciation by *L'Osservatore Romano* of 'Northern', 'Nordic' and 'Germanic' influences on Italy, which seemed to accompany the development of the Rome-Berlin Axis after 1936, see F. Sandmann, *'L'Osservatore Romano' e il nazionalsocialismo, 1929–1939*, Rome: Riuniti, 1976, especially p. 327.

85   G. Rumi, 'La Santa Sede e la Politica di Potenza', in E. Di Nolfo, R.H. Rainero and B. Vigezzi (eds), *L'Italia e la politica di Potenza, 1938–1940*, Settimo Milanese: Marzorati, 1975, p. 17; see also F. Malgeri, 'Chiesa, clero e laicato cattolico tra Guerra e Resistenza', in G. De Rosa, T. Gregory and A. Vauchez (eds), *Storia dell'Italia Religiosa. III. L'Età Contemporanea*, Rome-Bari: Laterza, 1995, pp. 301–34.

86   D. Rodogno, *Fascism's European Empire: Italian Occupation during the Second World War*, Cambridge: Cambridge University Press, 2006, pp. 154–7.

87   Ibid, p. 156.

88   F. Malgeri, 'Chiesa e laicato cattolico tra Guerra e Resistenza', in De Rosa *et al.*, *Storia dell'Italia Religiosa. III*, pp. 313–14.

89   See T. Abse, 'Italy', in J. Noakes (ed.), *The Civilian in War: The Home Front in Europe, Japan and the USA in World War II*, Exeter: Exeter University Press, 1992.

90   Ciano, *Ciano's Diary*, p. 289.

91   Delzell, *Mussolini's Enemies*, p. 283.

92   R.N.L. Absalom, *A Strange Alliance: Aspects of Escape and Survival In Italy, 1943–1945*, Florence: Leo Olschki Editore, 1991.

93   S. Zucotti, *Beneath His Very Windows: the Vatican and the Holocaust in Italy*, New Haven CT: Yale University Press, 2000; while Zucotti absolutely refuses to recognise the role of Pius XII, she demonstrates very clearly the part played by the Church in Rome in sheltering those hiding from the Germans.

94   For an analysis of the role played by Catholics in the Resistance, see Delzell, *Mussolini's Enemies*, Chapters 5 and 7.

95   Pollard, *Money and the Rise of the Modern Papacy*, p. 196.

7 The age of Catholic 'triumphalism'

1   Richard A. Webster, *The Cross and the Fasces; Christian Democracy and Fascism in Italy*, Stanford CA: Stanford University Press, 1960, p. 214.

2   F. Chabod, *L'Italia Contemporanea (1918–1948)*, Turin: Einaudi, 1960, p. 140.

3   The best account of this complicated and tormented situation is to be found in D. Ellwood, *Italy 1943–1945*, Leicester: Leicester University Press, 1995.

4   Oliver Logan, 'Pius XII: *Romanita*, Prophesy and Charisma', in *Modern Italy*, 3, 2, November 1998, pp. 237–49.

5   See J.F. Pollard, 'Il Vaticano e la politica estera italiana', in R.J.B. Bosworth and S. Roman (eds), *La politica estera italiana, 1960–1985*, Bologna: Il Mulino, 1990, pp. 225–6.

6 Ciano, G., *Ciano's Diary, 1939–1943*, edited with an introduction by Malcolm Muggeridge, London, 1947, p. 554, entry for 5 February, 1943.

7 P. Scoppola, *La proposta politica di De Gasperi*, Bologna: Il Mulino, 1979, pp. 42–3.

8 A. Spinosa, *Pio XII. l'Ultimo Papa*, Milan: A. Mondadori, 1992.

9 P. Scoppola, in AAVV, *Don Lorenzo Milani tra Chiesa, cultura e scuola: Atti del convegno*, con introd. Di Gisueppe Lazzatti, Milan: Vita e Pensiero, 1983, p. 8.

10 It has been claimed that 52 priests were killed in this area: O. Chadwick, *The Christian Church in the Cold War*, London: Penguin, 1992, p. 15.

11 P. Ginsborg, *A History of Contemporary Italy: Society and Politics, 1943–1988*, London: Penguin, 1990, p. 71.

12 Ibid, pp. 42–3.

13 G. Poggi, 'The Church in Italian Politics, 1945–1950', in S.W. Woolf (ed.), *The Rebirth of Italy, 1945–1950*, Stanford CA: Stanford University Press, 1972, p. 147.

14 R.M. Giammanco, *The Catholic-Communist Dialogue in Italy 1944 to the Present*, New York: Praeger, 1989, p. 12.

15 The lay, liberal/radical parties consisted of: the PLI (Italian Liberal Party), the rump of the amorphous groups of liberal-conservatives who had dominated Italian politics in the pre-Fascist period; the Partito D'Azione (Action Party), an elitist, intellectual group born out of the experience of anti-Fascism and the Resistance, which would eventually mutate into the more enduring PRI (Italian Republican Party); and the PSDI (Italian Social Democratic Party), which was the result of the secession of the right wing of the Italian Socialist Party in 1947.

16 A. Riccardi, 'The Vatican of Pius XII and the Roman Party', in *Concilium*, 97, 1987, p. 40.

17 P. Hebblethwaite, 'Pope Pius XII: Chaplain of the Atlantic Alliance?', in C. Duggan and C. Wagstaffe (eds), *Italy in the Cold War: Politics, Culture and Society*, Oxford: Oxford University Press, 1995, p. 75.

18 Ibid.

19 Ibid.

20 See John Pollard, 'Italy', in T. Buchanan and M. Conway (eds), *Political Catholicism in Europe, 1918–1965*, Oxford: Oxford University Press, 1996, pp. 85–6.

21 Ibid.

22 Ibid.

23 Webster, *The Cross and the Fasces*, Chapter 10 and R. Leonardi and D.A. Wertman, *Italian Christian Democracy: the Politics of Dominance*, Basingstoke: Macmillan, 1989, Chapter 2.

24 Scoppola, *La proposta politica*, Chapter 3, especially pp. 121–9.

25 As quoted in M. Clark, *Modern Italy, 1871–1995*, London: Longman, 1996, p. 215.

26 Huw Martin Thomas, 'Religious Freedom, the Lateran Pacts and the Debates in the Italian Constituent Assembly (1946–1948)', unpublished PhD thesis, University of Wales Swansea, 2005, pp. 140–205.

27 Ibid.

28 Clark, *Modern Italy*, p. 215.

29 J.F. Pollard, 'Post-war Italy: the "Papal State of the Twentieth Century"?', in E.A. Millar (ed.), *The Legacy of Fascism*, Glasgow: Glasgow University Press, 1987, p. 57.

30 Giammanco, *The Catholic-Communist Dialogue* is an excellent analysis of the dialogue from a Marxist perspective.

31 Clark, *Modern Italy,* p. 215. The Calamandrei quotation is to be found in V. Bucci, *Chiesa e Stato: Church and State Relations in Italy within the Constitutional Framework*, The Hague: Martinus Nijhof, 1969, p. 65.

32 Poggi, 'The Church', p. 147.

33 For a full account of the 'martyrdom' of the Catholic Church in central and eastern Europe, see Peter C. Kent, *The Lonely Cold War of Pius XII: The Roman Catholic Church and the Division of Europe, 1943–1950*, Montreal-Kingston: McGill-Queens University Press, 2002, Parts 3 and 4.

34 D. Keogh, 'Ireland, the Vatican and the Cold War: the Case of Italy', in *Historical Journal*, 344, 1991, pp. 932–52 and Pollard, 'Italy', p. 87.

35 Ginsborg, *Contemporary Italy*, pp. 116–18.

36 Leonardi and Wertman, *Italian Christian Democracy*, p. 166.

37 As quoted in Poggi, 'The Church', p. 143–4.

38 Scoppola, *La proposta politica*, p. 12.

39 See Bucci, *Chiesa e Stato*, pp. 17–21.

40 As quoted in ibid, p. 65.

41 See for example, Bucci, *Chiesa e Stato*, and D. Settembrini, *La Chiesa nella Politica Italiana (1944–1963)*, Milan: Rizzoli, 1973, pp. 322–30 and 489–93.

42 Ibid, pp. 482–3.

43 Ibid.

44 Bucci, *Chiesa e Stato*, Chapter III.

45 Ibid, p. 69.

46 A.C. Jemolo, *Societa civile e societa religiosa, 1955–58*, Turin: Einaudi, 1959, p. 73.

47 Settembrini, *La Chiesa*, pp. 457–82.

48 N. Kogan, *A Political History of Italy: the Post-war Period*, New York: Praeger, 1983, p. 64.

49 Ibid, pp. 60–1.

50 O. Stack, *Pasolini on Pasolini*, London: Thames & Hudson, 1969, p. 22.

51 See F. Ferraresi, *Threats to Democracy: The Radical Right in Italy after the War*, Princeton NJ: Princeton University Press, 1996, pp. 46–7.

52 Giammanco, *The Catholic-Communist Dialogue*, pp. 31–2 and 55–7.

53 S. Tarrow, *Peasant Communism in Southern Italy*, New Haven CT and London: Yale University Press, 1967, p. 39.

54 D. Kertzer, *Comrades and Christians: Religion and Political Struggle in Communist Italy*, Cambridge: Cambridge University Press, 1980, Chapter 5.

55 G. Guareschi, *The Little World of Don Camillo*, Harmondsworth: Penguin, 1969.

56 L. Faenza, *Communismo e Cattolicesimo in una Parrocchia di Campagna. Vent'anni dopo, 1959–1979*, Bologna: Capelli, 1979.

57   Giammanco, *The Catholic-Communist Dialogue*, p. 57.
58   P.A. Allum, 'Uniformity Undone: Aspects of Catholic Culture in Post-war Italy', in Z. Baranski and R. Lumley (eds), *Culture and Conflict in Post-war Italy: Essays on Mass and Popular Culture*, Basingstoke: Macmillan, 1990, pp. 82–3.
59   P. Ginsborg, 'Family, Culture and Politics', in Baranski and Lumley (eds), *Culture and Conflict*, p. 29.
60   Allum, 'Uniformity Undone', p. 82.
61   As quoted in Ginsborg, *Contemporary Italy*, p. 181.
62   Allum, 'Uniformity Undone', p. 85.
63   Ibid.
64   Ibid.
65   See J.F. Pollard, *Money and the Rise of the Modern Papacy: Financing the Vatican, 1850–1950*, Cambridge: Cambridge University Press, 2005, pp. 204–5.
66   Ibid.
67   For an account of the origins of this Catholic economic 'block' in the Fascist period, see ibid, pp. 175–7.
68   Allum, 'Uniformity Undone', p. 185.
69   Ibid and S. Gundle, 'Cultura di massa e modernizzazione: Vie Nuove e Famiglia Cristiana dall Guerra fredda alla societa di consumi', in Pier Paolo D'Attore (ed.), *Nemico per la pelle: sogno Americano e mito Sovieto nell'italia contemporanea*, Milan: F. Angeli Editore, 1991, pp. 235–65.
70   G. Galli, *La Finanza Bianca: La Chiesa, I soldi, il potere*, Milan: Mondadori, 2004, p. 98.
71   P.A. Allum, 'The Changing Face of Christian Democracy', in C. Duggan and C. Wagstaffe (eds), *Italy in the Cold War: Politics, Culture and Society*, Oxford: Berghan, 1995, pp. 121–2.
72   Ibid, pp. 125–6.
73   Kent, *The Lonely Cold War*, pp. 175–6, 164 and 228–9 respectively.
74   Logan, 'Pius XII', p. 238.
75   Ibid.
76   As quoted in Keogh, 'Ireland, the Vatican and the Cold War', p. 943.
77   Logan, 'Pius XII', pp. 242 and 244.
78   The fullest account of his role is to be found in G. Zizola, *Il microfono di Dio. Pio XII, Padre Lombardi e i cattolici italiani*, Milan: A. Mondadori, 1990.
79   Ibid, pp. 57–9.
80   A. Riccardi, 'La Chiesa cattolica in Italia nel secondo dopoguerra', in G. De Rosa, T. Gregory and A. Vauchez (eds), *Storia dell'Italia Religiosa III. L'Età Contemporanea*, Roma-Bari: Laterza, 1995, p. 346.
81   Ibid, pp. 346–7.
82   S. Luzzatto, *Padre Pio: Miracoli e politica nell'Italia del Novecento*, Turin: Einaudi, 2007, Chapter 9.
83   Riccardi, 'La Chiesa cattolica in Italia', pp. 344–5.
84   Ibid, pp. 351–2: for an examination of the state of various major Italian dioceses at the end of Pius XII's reign, see A. Riccardi (ed.), *Le Chiese di Pio XII*, Roma-Bari: Laterza, 1986.

85   Ibid.
86   C. Carlen (ed), *The Papal Encyclicals, 1939–1958*, Ann Arbor MI: Pierian Press, 1983, pp. 78–85.
87   G. Verucci, *La Chiesa nella Societa Contemporanea. Dal Primo Dopoguerra al Concilio Vaticano II*, Roma-Bari: Laterza, 1988, p. 313.
88   Ibid.
89   Ginsborg, *Contemporary Italy*, p. 182.
90   Allum, 'The Changing Face of Christian democracy', p. 125, fn. 15.
91   G. Galli, *Storia della DC*, Rome-Bari: Laterza, 1978, p. 168.
92   Allum, 'The Changing face of Christian Democracy', pp. 125–6.
93   For examples of these phenomena in Calabria and Naples respectively, see J. Walston, *The Mafia and Clientelism: Roads to Rome in Post-war Calabria*, London: Routledge, 1988, especially pp. 85–6 and 193–8, and J. Chubb, *Patronage, Power and Poverty: A Tale of Two Cities*, Cambridge: Cambridge University Press, 1982.

8 The new secularisation (1958–78)

1   The definitive biography of Pope John in English is P. Hebblethwaite, *John XXIII: Pope of the Council*, London: Geoffrey Chapman, 1984.
2   Ibid, pp. 79–90.
3   Ibid, Chapters 7–9.
4   Ibid, Chapter 10.
5   Ibid, Chapter 11.
6   Ibid, Chapter 16.
7   On Vatican *Ostpolitik*, see H-J. Stehle, *Eastern Politics of the Vatican, 1917–1979*, Athens OH: Ohio University Press, 1981 and J. Luxmoore and J. Babuich, *The Vatican and the Red Flag: The Struggle for the Soul of Eastern Europe*, London: Geoffrey Chapman, 1999.
8   The definitive biography of Paul VI in English is P. Hebblethwaite, *Paul VI: The First Modern Pope*, London: Geoffrey Chapman, 1993.
9   P. Ginsborg, *A History of Contemporary Italy: Society and Politics, 1943–1988*, London: Penguin, 1990 and D. Sassoon, *Contemporary Italy: Economy, Society and Politics since 1945*, 2nd ed., London: Longman, 1997, Chapter 2.
10   For the statistics of the 'miracle' see Sassoon, *Contemporary* Italy, pp. 28–9.
11   Ibid, pp. 29–34.
12   Ibid, pp. 31–2.
13   Ginsborg, *Contemporary Italy*, p. 220.
14   R.M. Giammanco, *The Catholic-Communist Dialogue. 1944 to the Present*, New York: Praeger, 1989, p. 21.
15   Hebblethwaite, *Paul VI*, p. 262.
16   Ginsborg, *Contemporary Italy*, p. 220.
17   Hebblethwaite, *Paul VI*, p. 266.
18   Ibid, fn. 2.
19   Hebblethwaite, *John XXIII*, p. 347.
20   Ibid.

21   Ibid, p. 334.

22   Ginsborg, *Contemporary Italy*, p. 182.

23   J. Dunnage, *Twentieth Century Italy. A Social History*, London: Longman, 2002, p. 165.

24   Ibid, p. 164.

25   The author witnessed the powerful attraction of Britain to young Italians of all classes during the periods when he lived and worked in several parts of Italy in the 1960s and 1970s; the great dream was to visit 'swinging London'.

26   G. Moliterno (ed.), *Encyclopedia of Contemporary Italian Culture*, London: Routledge, 2000, p. 593, 'Toscani, Oliviero'.

27   Dunnage, *Twentieth Century Italy*, p. 166: Benedict, twenty or thirty years before had had a particular horror for the then latest dance craze, the Tango; see J.F. Pollard, 'The Pope, Labour and the Tango', in R. Swanson (ed.), *The Use and Abuse of Time in Christian History: Proceedings of the Ecclesiastical History Society*, Woodbridge: Boydell Press, 2002, p. 381.

28   A. D'Angelo, 'Il Tirocinio del Dopoguerra: La Nunziatura D'Italia (1949–1962)', in A. Melloni and M. Guasco (eds), *Un Diplomatico Vaticano Fra Dopoguerrae Dialogo: Mons. Mario Cagna (1911–1986)*, Bologna: Il Mulino, 2003, pp. 61–2.

29   Ibid, where he also says that RAI's 'code of self-discipline' was approved by Pius XII himself.

30   Ginsborg, *Contemporary Italy*, p. 241.

31   S. Gundle, 'Cultura di Mass e modernizzazione: *Vie Nuove e Famiglia Cristiana* dalla Guerra fredda alla societa dei consumi', in P.P.D'Attore (ed.), *Nemici per la pelle: sogno Americano e mito Sovieto nell'Italia contemporanea*, Milan: Franco Angeli, 1991, pp. 235–68.

32   C. Duggan,' Italy in the Cold War Years', in C. Duggan and C. Wagstaffe (eds), *Italy in the Cold War: Politics, Culture and Society*, Oxford: Oxford University Press, 1995, p. 22.

33   D. Sassoon, *Contemporary Italy, Economy, Society and Politics since 1945*, London: Longman, 1997, p. 177.

34   John Pollard, 'Italy', in T. Buchanan and M. Conway (eds), *Political Catholicism in Europe, 1918–1965*, Oxford: Oxford University Press, 1996, pp. 91–2.

35   A. Riccardi, 'La Chiesa italiana fra Pio XII e Paolo VI', in G Lazzati (ed.) *Don Lorenzo Milani tra Chiesa, cultura e scuola: Atti del convegno*, introduction by Giuseppe Lazzati, Milan: Vita e Pensiero, 1983, p. 37.

36   As quoted in Hebblethwaite, *John XXIII*, p. 380.

37   Ginsborg, *Contemporary Italy*, Chapter 8.

38   Ibid, pp. 280–3.

39   Sassoon, *Contemporary Italy*, p. 177.

40   Hebblethwaite, *John XXIII*, p. 490.

41   Ibid.

42   Riccardi, 'La Chiesa italiana', p. 45.

43 Richard P. O'Brien, 'The Church (*Lumen Gentium*)', in Adrian Hastings (ed.), *Modern Catholicism: The Second Vatican Council and After*, London: SPCK, 1991, pp. 92 and 104; F.L. Cross and E.A. Livingstone, *The Oxford Dictionary of the Christian Church*, 3rd ed., Oxford: Oxford University Press, 1997, p. 602.

44 Aidan Kavanagh, 'Liturgy (*Sacrosanctum Concilium*)', in Adrian Hastings (ed.), *Modern Catholicism: The Second Vatican Council and After*, London: SPCK, 1991, pp. 71–3.

45 A. Melloni, 'Da Giovanni XXIII alle Chiese italiane del Vaticano II', in De Rosa, Gregory and Vauchez, *Storia dell'Italia Religiosa III*, p. 376.

46 Ibid, p. 375.

47 Ibid, p. 367. See also M. Cuminetti, *Il dissenso cattolico in Italia, 1965–1980*, Milan: Rizzoli, 1983, pp. 135–9.

48 Cuminetti, *Il dissenso cattolico*, Chapter IV.

49 As quoted in ibid, pp. 258–9.

50 C. Carlen (ed.), *The Papal Encyclicals, 1958–1981*, Ann Arbor MI: Pierian Press, 1990, p. 125.

51 Ginsborg, *Contemporary Italy*, p. 302.

52 Ibid, p. 303: for a more detailed analysis of Catholic 'revolt', see also R. Lumley, *States of Emergency: Cultures of Revolt in Italy from 1968 to 1978*, London: Verso, 1990, Chapter 6.

53 M. Clark, *Modern Italy, 1871–1995*, London: Longman, 1996, p. 371.

54 Giammanco, *The Catholic-Communist Dialogue*, p. 129.

55 Ginsborg, *Contemporary Italy*, p. 361.

56 Cuminetti, *Il dissenso cattolico*, p. 114.

57 Ibid, p. 224.

58 Ibid, pp. 269–71.

59 Riccardi, 'La Chiesa italiana', p. 42.

60 See G. Urquhart, *The Pope's Armada: Unlocking the Secrets and Mysteries of Powerful New Sects in the Church*, London: Corgi, 1996.

61 Sassoon, *Contemporary Italy*, p. 126.

62 N. Kogan, *A Political History of Italy: the Post-war Period*, New York: Praeger, 1983, p. 221.

63 Ginsborg, *Contemporary Italy*, p. 356.

64 *Catechismo Della Chiesa Cattolica; Testo integrale e commento teologico*, Vatican City: Libreria Editrice Vaticana, 1993, p. 277.

65 Ibid.

66 S.S. Aquaviva, *The Decline of the Sacred in Industrial Society*, Oxford: Oxford University Press, 1979, p. 79.

67 Robert Leonardi and Douglas A. Wertman, *Italian Christian Democracy: the Politics of Dominance*, Basingstoke: Macmillan, 1989, p. 178.

68 Clark, *Modern Italy*, p. 371.

69 Aquaviva, *The Decline of the Sacred*, p. 82.

70 See, for example, James M. O'Toole, *Habits of Devotion: Catholic Religious Practice in Twentieth Century America*, Ithaca NY and London: Cornell University Press, 2004.

71 Melloni, 'Da Giovanni XXIII alle Chiese', p. 376.

72 Ibid, p. 377.

73 L. Milani, *Esperienze pastorali*, Florence: Liberia editrice fiorentina, 1958 and G. Bevilacqua, *Equivoci: mondo moderno e Cristo*, Brescia: La Morcelliana, 1953.

74 S. Burgalassi, *Le Cristianità Nascoste*, Bologna: EDB, 1970, pp. 164–8.

75 L. Faenza, *Il Communismo e il Cattolicesimo in una Parrocchia*, Milan: EDB, 1959, p. 79.

76 Hebblethwaite, *Paul VI*, p. 264.

77 Ibid.

78 Sassoon, *Contemporary Italy*, p.177.

79 G. Galli and A. Nannei, *Il Mercato di Stato: Capitalismo assistenziale*, Milan: Sugar Editore, 1984, p. 60.

80 G. Ricossa, 'Italy, 1920–1970', in C. Cipolla (ed.), *The Fontana Economic History of Europe: Contemporary Economies*, Glasgow: Fontana, 1972, p. 287.

81 M.V.S. Posner and S.J. Woolf, *Italian Public Enterprise*, London: Duckworth, 1967, pp. 55–6 and 68–9 and Ginsborg, *Contemporary Italy*, pp. 163–5.

82 G. Galli, *La sfida perduta; biografia politica di Enrico Mattei*, Milan: Saggi Bompiani, 1972, pp. 249–50.

83 Ginsborg, *Contemporary Italy*, pp. 146–7.

84 Ibid, pp. 171–81; G. Galli, *Storia della D.C.*, Rome-Bari: Laterza, 1978, Chapters 9 and 10; P.A. Allum, *Politics and Society in Post-war Naples*, Cambridge: Cambridge University Press, 1973, pp. 172–3; and P. Farneti, 'Patterns of Changing Support for the Christian Democrats in Italy, 1946–1976', in B. Denitch (ed.), *Legitimation of Regimes*, London: Sage, 1979, p. 213.

85 Sassoon, *Contemporary Italy*, p. 120.

86 See M. Seymour, *Debating Divorce in Italy. Marriage and the Making of Modern Italians*, Basingstoke: Palgrave-Macmillan, 2007, especially Chapter 8.

87 Clark, *Modern Italy*, p. 380.

88 Seymour, *Debating Divorce*, p. 216; see the little pamphlet containing the statements of three Catholic intellectuals, Pietro Scoppola, Gian Paolo Meucci and Luigi Pedrazzi in various authors, *Cattolici e referendum. Per Una Scelta di Libertà*, Roma: Coines Edizioni, 1974.

89 See G-F. Pompei, *Un Ambasciatore in Vaticano, Diario 1969–1977*, Bologna: Il Mulino, 1998, pp. 361–4.

90 Hebblethwaite, *Paul VI*, p. 664.

91 Melloni, 'Da Giovanni XXIII alle Chiese, p. 382.

92 Ginsborg, *A History*, Chapter 10.

93 Sassoon, *Contemporary Italy*, pp. 196 and 242–3.

9 Religious pluralism in Italy

1 M. Clark, *Modern Italy, 1871–1995*, London and New York: Longman, 1996, pp. 387–90.

2   For biographies of John Paul II, see M.J. Walsh, *John Paul II*, London: Fount, 1995 and G. Weigel, *Witness to Hope: The Biography of Pope John Paul II*, London: Cliff Books, 2001.

3   For the strength of Ruini's grip on the Italian Church, see Sandro Magister, 'The Church and the End of the Catholic Party', in M. Caciagali and David I. Kertzer (eds), *Italian Politics, A Review: Vol. II, the Stalled Transition*, Oxford: Westview Press, 1996, pp. 226–7.

4   M. D. de Franciscis, *Italy and the Vatican: The 1984 Concordat between Church and State*, New York: Peter Lang, 1989, p. 7.

5   See C. Raw, *The Money Changers*, London: Harper Collins, 1992, p. 34–7.

6   For the list of their names and their reasons, see various authors, *Cattolici e Referendum: Per Una Scelta di Libertà*, Rome: Coines, 1974.

7   For an insider's account of these intrigues, see G-F. Pompei, *Un Ambasciatore in Vaticano, Diario 1969–1977*, Bologna: Il Mulino, 1998.

8   Clark, *Modern Italy*, p. 409.

9   de Franciscis, *Italy and the Vatican*, p. 201.

10   For the text of the 1984 Concordat and consequent Italian legislative measures see ibid, pp. 225–307.

11   Clark, *Modern Italy*, p. 405.

12   As quoted in de Franciscis, *Italy and the Vatican*, p. 226.

13   Ibid, p. 244.

14   Ibid, p. 186.

15   Ibid, pp. 165–6.

16   R. Cartocci, *Fra Lega e Chiesa: L'Italia in cerca di integrazione*, Bologna: Il Mulino, 1994, p. 167.

17   Ibid, p. 183.

18   de Franciscis, *Italy and the Vatican*, p. 225.

19   M.A. Manacorda and M. Vigli (eds), *Stato e Chiese. Il potere clerical in Italia dopo il 'nuovo concordato' del 1984 tra Craxi e Wojtyla*, Trezzano sul Naviglio MI: Mille Lire, 1995, p. 50.

20   Ibid, pp. 51–3.

21   Ibid, p. 53.

22   Ibid, pp. 51–4.

23   Ibid, p. 54.

24   D. Sassoon, *Contemporary Italy: Economy, Society and Politics since 1945*, London: Longman, 1997, p. 177.

25   Clark, *Modern Italy*, p. 177.

26   Ibid, p. 409.

27   Sassoon, *Contemporary Italy*, p. 177.

28   E. Hobsbawm, *The Age of Extremes: The Shorter Twentieth Century, 1914–1991*, London: Abacus, 1995, pp. 416–18.

29   Clark, *Modern Italy*, p. 412.

30   Ibid, p. 413.

31   Sassoon, *Contemporary Italy*, p. 186.

32   Ibid.

33   *Il Corriere Della Sera*, 16 August, 1994, 'Processo al funzionario Dc'.

34   Clark, *Modern Italy*, p. 252–3.
35   Ibid, p. 414.
36   Clark, *Modern Italy*, pp. 413–19.
37   Ibid, pp. 416–19.
38   See G. Andreotti, *Ad Ogni Morte di Papa. I Papi che ho conosciuto*, Milan: Rizzoli, 1982.
39   Orazio La Rocca, 'E il Vaticano non ama più I giudici di "Mani pulite"', in *La Repubblica*, 11 January, 1994.
40   Ibid.
41   P. Ginsborg, *Italy and its Discontents: Family, Civil Society and the State, 1980–2001*, London: Penguin, 2001, p. 134.
42   P. Nicotri, *Tangenti in confessionale: Come I preti rispondono a corrotti e corruttori*, Venice: Marsiglio, 1993.
43   Ibid, pp. 123–6.
44   Ibid, pp. 141–6.
45   G. Bedani, 'Church and State in Italian History. Origins of the Present Crisis', unpublished professorial lecture given at University College of Swansea, 1994, p. 23.
46   Ibid, p. 24.
47   'Church Must Promote Moral Renewal', *L'Osservatore Romano*, English Weekly Edition, 10 January 1994 and Marco Politi, 'La lettera del papa', *La Repubblica*, 7 January, 1994.
48   Sassoon, *Contemporary Italy*, pp. 244–5.
49   For an excellent account of the prolonged period of crisis, see Ginsborg, *Italy and its Discontents*, Chapter 9.
50   Magister, 'The Church and the End of the Catholic Party', p. 230.
51   Ibid, p. 231.
52   Ibid.
53   A. Riccardi, 'La vita religiosa', in P. Ginsborg (ed.), *Stato Dell'Italia: il bilancio politico, economico, sociale e culturale di un paese che cambia*, Milan: B. Mondadori, 1998, pp. 347–8.
54   R.M. Giammanco, *The Catholic-Communist Dialogue in Italy 1944 to the Present*, New York: Praeger, 1989, pp. 27–8.
55   Giuseppe Dalla Torre, 'Minoranze musulmane in Italia nel XX secolo', in De Rosa *et al.*, *Storia dell'Italia Religiosa III*, pp. 464–5.
56   http://italpolblog.blogspot.com (09.02.04).
57   Dalla Torre, 'Minoranze musulmane', p. 483.
58   'Islamici si convertono: "La loro vita e adesso in pericolo"', in *La Repubblica*, 18 September 2007.
59   Ilvio Diamanti, 'Il valore della questione cattolica', in *La Repubblica*, 16 December 2005.
60   'Pubblico and Privato', in *Corriere della Sera*, 29 April 2001.
61   Diamanti, 'Il valore della questione cattolica'.
62   Riccardi, 'La vita religiosa', p. 338.
63   See M. Iadanza (ed.), *Chiesa e Società Civile nel Mezzogiorno. La memoria, l'analisi e il progetto*, Rome: Borla, 1992, for a Catholic view of the Church's role in the south of Italy.

64   Ibid, p. 7.

65   Quoted by Patricia Clough, 'The Pope Condemns Mafia in Angry Plea', *The Independent*, May 10, 1993.

66   Riccardi, 'La vita religiosa', p. 347.

67   G. Urquhart, *The Pope's Armada: Unlocking the Secrets and Mysteries of Powerful New Sects in the Church*, London: Bantam Press, 1996; Riccardi, 'La vita religiosa' says surprising little about Catholic associationalism, old or new, but F. Garelli, *Religione e Chiesa in Italia*, Bologna: Il Mulino, 1991 dedicates Chapter VI to a thorough sociological and statistical analysis of it.

68   Urquhart, *The Pope's Armada*, p. 279.

69   G. Moliterno (ed.), *Encyclopedia*, p. 210.

70   Riccardi, 'La vita religiosa', pp. 342–3.

71   Garelli, *Religione e Chiesa*, Chapter V and Ginsborg, *Italy and its Discontents*, pp. 130–1.

72   M. Blondet, *I Nuovi Barbari: Gli Skinheads Parlano*, Milan: FDF Edizioni, 1993, pp. 133–8.

73   http://elezionistorico.interno.it/index.php

74   Antonello Caporale, 'Prodi via con 25 ministri', *La Repubblica*, 18 May, 2006, pp. 1–17.

75   For an analysis of the tension between the Lega and the Church, see R. Cartocci, *Fra Lega e Chiesa*, Bologna: Il Mulino, 1994.

76   There is no good biography of Prodi in any language: see a very sympathetic account in Carlo Valentini, *Prodi: la mia Italia; il nuovo leader parla di sè e propone la medicina per guarire il paese*, Bologna: Carmenta, 1995.

77   Diamanti, 'Il valore della questione cattolica'.

78   Ibid.

79   Ibid.

80   For an analysis of the role of the Church during the referendum, see C. Martini, 'Il referendum sulla fecondazione assista', in G. Amyot and L. Verzichelli (eds), *Politica in Italia. I fatti e le interpretazioni, 2006*, Bologna: Il Mulino, 2006.

81   Diamanti, 'Il valore della questione cattolica'.

82   As quoted in ibid.

10 Conclusion

1   See C. McKevitt, 'San Giovanni Rotondo and the Cult of Padre Pio', in J. Eade and M.J. Sallnow (eds), *Contesting the Sacred*, London: Routledge, 1991 and S. Luzzatto, *Padre Pio: miracoli e politica nell'Italia del '900*, Turin: Einaudi, 2007.

2   See the entry for Lefebvre in Roy P. Domenico and Mark Y. Hanley (eds), *Encyclopedia of Modern Christian Biography*, Westport CT: Greenwood Press, 2006, pp. 328–9.

3   See the entry on Stefano Jacini in *Dizionario Biografico degli Italiani*, vol. 61, Rome: Treccani, 2003, pp. 729–32.

4   L. Faenza, *Il Comunismo e il Cattolicesimo in una Parrocchia*, Milan: EDB, 1959, p. 181: even before the end of the war, Padre Mariano Cordovano, the Vatican's leading theological expert had warned that 'No one can be a good Catholic and a Socialist at the same time' (*L'Osservatore Romano*, 23 July 1944).

5   Faenza, *Il Comunismo*, p. 185.

6   G. Sani, 'Mass-Level Response to Party Strategy', in D.L.M. Blackmer and S.G. Tarrow (eds), *Communism in Italy and France*, Princeton NJ: Princeton University Press, 1975, p. 496.

7   See the entry for Adriano Ossicini in Domenico and Hanley (eds), *Encyclopedia of Modern Christian Biography*, pp. 421–2.

8   As of September 2007, Livia Turco, regarded by the Italian press as 'cattocommunista', was standing for the leadership of the new party against Walter Veltroni, formerly of the PCI-PDS-DS.

9   Sandro Magister, 'The Church and the End of the Catholic Party', in M. Caciagali and David I. Kertzer (eds), *Italian Politics, A Review: Vol. II, the Stalled Transition*, Oxford: Westview Press, 1996, p. 232.

10   See Tracy Koon, *Believe, Obey and Fight: the Political Socialisation of Youth in Fascist Italy, 1922–1943*, Chapel Hill NC and London: University of North Carolina Press, 1985, pp. 250–2.

11   V. De Grazia, *The Culture of Consent: The Mass Organisation of Leisure in Fascist Italy*, Cambridge: Cambridge University Press, 1982, especially Chapter 8.

12   A.J. Gregor, *Italian Fascism as Developmental Dictatorship*, Princeton NJ: Princeton University Press, 1979.

13   Richard J.B. Bosworth, '*L'Anno Santo* (Holy Year) in Fascist Italy 1933–4', draft of an unpublished article, p. 4.

14   David I. Kertzer, *Comunisti e Cattolici: la lotta religiosa in Italia comunista*, Milan: Franco Angeli, 1981, p. 19.

15   See A. Iandolo, 'The PCI and the Unforgettable 1956', MPhil thesis for Cambridge University, 2007, pp. 16 and 17, and G. Gozzini and R. Martinelli, *Storia del Partito Comunista. VII. Dall'Attentato a Togliatti all'VII Congresso*, Turin: Einaudi, 1998, pp. 418–36 and 527–30.

16   Ada Ferrari, *La Cultura Riformatrice: uomini, techniche, filosofie di fronte alol sviluppo (1945–1968)*, Roma: Edizioni Studium, 995, p. 13.

17   Ibid, p. 10.

18   See, for example, K. Van Kersbergen, *Social Capitalism: A Study of Christian Democracy and the Welfare State*, London: Routledge, 1995.

19   P. Ginsborg, *Italy and its Discontents: Family, Civil Society and the State, 1980–2001*, London: Penguin, 2001, p. 31.

20   Ibid, pp. 129–30.

21   A. Riccardi, *Il 'Partito Romano' nella secondao dopo-guerra (1945-1954)*, Brescia: Morecelliana, 1983.

22   For the text of this encyclical, see C. Carlen (ed.), *The Papal Encyclicals, 1978–1903*, Ann Arbor MI: Pierian Press, 1990, pp. 479–86.

23   Archivio Centrale dello Stato (Central State Archives, Rome), Ministero dell'Interno (Interior Ministry), DGPS (General Directory of Public Security), G1, busta (box) 94, second quarter of 1929.

24   Bosworth, '*L'Anno Santo* (Holy Year) in Fascist Italy 1933–4', p. 5.

25   C. Falconi, *The Popes in the Twentieth Century: From Pius X to John XXIII*, London: Weidenfeld & Nicolson, 1967, pp. 292–3.

26   N. Kogan, *A Political History of Italy: The Post-war Period*, New York: Praeger, 1983, p. 81.

27   Huw Thomas, 'Religious Freedom, the Lateran Pacts and the Debates in the Constituent Assembly (1946–1948)', unpublished PhD thesis, University of Wales, Swansea, 2006, p. 179.

28   John F. Pollard, *Money and the Rise of the Modern Papacy: Financing the Vatican, 1850–1950*, Cambridge: Cambridge University Press, 2005, pp. 6–7.

29   Ibid, p. 45.

30   Ross Fitzgerald, *Pope's Battalions: Santamaria, Catholicism and the Labor Split*, St Lucia, Queensland: University of Queensland Press, 2003, Chapter 5.

31   As quoted in James M. O'Toole, *Habits of Devotion: Catholic Religious Practice in Twentieth Century America*, Ithaca NY and London: Cornell University Press, 2004, p. 97.

32   As quoted in Ilvio Diamanti, 'Il valore della questione cattolica', in *La Repubblica*, 16 December, 2005.

33   See also A. Lyttelton, 'An Old Church and a New State: Italian Anti-clericalism 1876–1915', in *European Studies Review*, 13, 2, April 1983, pp. 225–48.

BIBLIOGRAPHY

Archival and periodical sources

Annuario Pontificio per l'Anno 1948, Vatican City: Tipografia Poliglotta Vaticana, 1948.

Archivio Centrale dello Stato (Rome), Ministero dell'Interno, Direzione Generale della Pubblica Sicurezza (ACS, MI, DGPS).

La Civiltà Cattolica (authoritative Jesuit fortnightly, published in Rome).

Il Corriere Della Sera (Milan).

The Independent (London).

L'Osservatore Romano (official newspaper of the papacy, published and printed in the Vatican).

La Repubblica (Rome).

Histories of Italy in the modern period

Acquarone, A., *La costruzione dello stato totalitario*, Milan: A. Mondadori, 1965.

Beales, Derek and Eugenio F. Biagini, *The Risorgimento and the Unification of Italy*, London: Pearson Education, 2002.

Carpanetto, D. and G. Ricuperati, *Italy in the Age of Reason, 1685–1789*, London: Longman, 1987.

Chabod, F., *L'Italia Contemporanea (1918–1948)*, Turin: Einaudi, 1960.

Ciano, G., *Ciano's Diary, 1939–1943*, ed. with an introduction by M. Muggeridge, London and Toronto: Heineman, 1947.

Clark, M., *Modern Italy, 1871–1995*, 2nd ed., London: Longman, 1996.

De Felice, R. *Mussolini il Fascista: L'organizzazione dello stato totalitario. 1925–1929*, Turin: Einaudi, 1968.

Duggan, C., *Force of Destiny: the History of Italy since 1796*, London: Penguin, 2007.

—— *Francesco Crispi: From Nation to Nationalism*, Oxford: Oxford University Press, 2002.

Dunnage, J. *Twentieth Century Italy: A Social History*, London: Longman, 2002.

Ellwood, D., *Italy 1943–1945*, Leicester: Leicester University Press, 1995.

Ginsborg, P., *A History of Contemporary Italy: Society and Politics, 1943–1988*, London: Penguin, 1990.

—— *Italy and its Discontents: Family, Civil Society and the State, 1980–2001*, London: Penguin, 2001.

Kogan, N., *A Political History of Italy: the Post-war Period,* New York: Praeger, 1983.

Lyttelton, A., *The Seizure of Power: Fascism in Italy, 1919–1929*, London: Weidenfeld & Nicolson, 1987.

Morgan, P., *Fascism in Italy, 1915–1945*, 2nd ed., Basingstoke: Macmillan, 2005.

Pollard, John, *The Fascist Experience in Italy*, London, 1998.

Sassoon, D., *Contemporary Italy: Economy, Society and Politics since 1945*, 2nd ed., London: Longman, 1997.

Seton-Watson, C., *Italy from Liberalism to Fascism*, London: Methuen, 1967.

Woolf, S., *A History of Italy 1700–1860: The Social Constraints of Political Change*, London: Methuen, 1979.

Zamagni, V., *The Economic History of Italy: Recovery after Decline*, Oxford: Oxford University Press, 1993.

History of the Church and the papacy

Atkin, N. and F. Tallett, *Prelates, Priests and People: A History of European Catholicism Since 1750*, Oxford: Oxford University Press, 2003.

Black, Christopher F., *Church, Religion and Society in Early Modern Italy*, Basingstoke: Palgrave-Macmillan, 2004.

Carlen, C. (ed.), *The Papal Encyclicals*, 6 vols, Ann Arbor MI: Pierian Press, 1990.

Catechismo Della Chiesa Cattolica; Testo integrale e commento teologico, Vatican City: Libreria Editrice Vaticana, 1993.

Chadwick, O., *The Christian Church in the Cold War*, London: Penguin, 1992.

—— *A History of the Popes: 1830–1914*, Oxford: Clarendon Press, 1999.

Clark, C. and W. Kaiser (eds), *Culture Wars: Secular-Catholic Conflict in Nineteenth Century Europe*, Cambridge: Cambridge University Press, 2003.

Coppa, Frank J., *The Modern Papacy since 1789*, London: Longman, 1998.

Cornwell, John, *Hitler's Pope: The Hidden History of Pius XII*, London: Viking, 1999.

Cross, F.L. and E.A. Livingstone, *The Oxford Dictionary of the Christian Church*, 3rd ed., Oxford: Oxford University Press, 1997.

Falconi, C., *Cardinal Antonelli: vita e carriera del Richlieu italiano nella chiesa di Pio IX*, Milan: Rizzoli, 1983.

—— *The Popes in the Twentieth Century: From Pius X to John XXIII*, London: Weidenfeld & Nicolson, 1967.

Fattorini, E., *Pio XI, Hitler e Mussolini*, Turin: Einaudi, 2007.

Hales, E.E.Y., *Pio Nono: A Study in European Politics and Society in the Nineteenth Century*, London: Eyre and Spottiswoode, 1956.

—— *Revolution and the Papacy, 1769–1846*, London: Eyre and Spottiswoode, 1960.

Hastings, Adrian (ed.), *Modern Catholicism: The Second Vatican Council and After*, London: SPCK, 1991.

Hebblethwaite, P., *John XXIII: Pope of the Council*, London: Geoffrey Chapman, 1984.

—— *Paul VI: The First Modern Pope*, London: Geoffrey Chapman, 1993.

Helmreich, Ernst C. (ed.), *A Free Church in a Free State? The Catholic Church in Italy, Germany, France 1864–1914*, Lexington MA: D.C. Heath & Co., 1964.

Jedin, H. (ed.), *History of the Church: Vol. VI, the Church in the Age of Absolutism and Enlightenment*, London: Bournes & Oates, 1981.

Jodock, D. (ed.), *Catholicism Contending with Modernity: Roman Catholic Modernism and Anti-Modernism in Historical Context*, Cambridge: Cambridge University Press, 2000.

Lamberts, E. *The Black International: Internationale Noir (1870–1878)*, Brussels: Institut Belgique de Rome, 2002.

Levillain, P. (ed.), *The Papacy: An Encyclopedia*, 3 vols, London: Routledge, 2002.

Luxmoore, J. and J. Babuich, *The Vatican and the Red Flag: The Struggle for the Soul of Eastern Europe*, London: Geoffrey Chapman, 1999.

Passelecq, G. and B. Suchecky, *The Hidden Encyclical*, New York and London: Harcourt Brace, 1997.

Pollard, John F., *Money and the Rise of the Modern Papacy: Financing the Vatican, 1850–1950*, Cambridge: Cambridge University Press, 2005.

—— 'The Pope, Labour and the Tango', in R. Swanson (ed.), *The Use and Abuse of Time in Christian History: Proceedings of the Ecclesiastical History Society*, Woodbridge: Boydell Press, 2002.

—— *The Unknown Pope: Benedict XV (1914–1922) and the Pursuit of Peace*, London: Cassell, 1999.

Scottà, A. (ed.), *La Conciliazione Ufficiosa: il Barone Carlo Monti 'incaricato d'affari' del governo italiano presso la Santa Sede*, 2 vols., Vatican City: Libreria Editrice Vaticana, 1997.

Stehle, H-J., *Eastern Politics of the Vatican, 1917–1979*, Athens OH: Ohio University Press, 1981.

Storia della Chiesa. Dalle origini ai giorni nostri, XXI/2, Il Pontificato di Pio IX, di R. Aubert, 1st ed. italiana alla 2nd ed. a cura di G. Martina, S.J., Turin: Editrice S.A.I.E., 1964.

Storia della Chiesa, XXI/2, La Chiesa nella Societa Industriale (1878–1922), a cura di E. Guerierro e A. Zambarbieri, Cinisello Balsamo (MI): Edizioni Paoline, 1990.

General works on the history of the Church in Italy

Agostini, F. (ed.), *Le visite pastorali di Giuseppe Callegari nella Diocesi di Padova (1884–88/1893–1905)*, Rome: Edizioni di Storia e Letteratura, 1981.

Binchy, D.A., *Church and State in Fascist Italy*, Oxford: Oxford University Press, 1970.

Borzomati, P., *Chiesa e Società Meridionale: Dalla Restaurazione al secondo dopoguerra*, Roma: Edizioni Studium, 1982.

De Rosa, G., *Chiesa e Religione Popolare nel Mezzogiorno*, Roma-Bari: Laterza, 1978.

—— *La Religione Popolare*, Rome: Edizioni Paoline, 1981.

——, T. Gregory and A. Vauchez (eds), *Storia Dell'Italia Religiosa, III. L'Età Contempranea*, Rome-Bari: Laterza, 1995.

Jemolo, C.A., *Church and State in Italy, 1850–1950*, Oxford: Blackwell, 1960.

Kelikian, A., 'The Church and Catholicism', in A. Lyttelton (ed.), *Liberal and Fascist Italy*, Oxford: Oxford University Press, 2002.

Kertzer, D., 'Religion and Society, 1789–1892', in John A. Davies (ed.), *Italy in the Nineteenth Century*, Oxford: Oxford University Press, 2000.

Monticone, A., *Gl'Italiani in uniforme, 1915–1918*, Bari: Laterza, 1972.

Pollard, John F., *The Vatican and Italian Fascism, 1929–1932: A Study in Conflict*, Cambridge: Cambridge University Press, 1985.

Scoppola, P., 'The State and the Church in the Fascist Period in Italy, 1922–1943', unpublished paper given at Cambridgeshire College of the Arts and Technology, 4 November, 1979.

Storia d'Italia, Annali 11**, Gli Ebrei in Italia, a cura di Corrado Vivanti, II, *Dall'Emancipazione a oggi*, Turin: Einaudi, 1997.

Traniello, F. and G. Campanini (eds), *Dizionario Storico del Movimento Cattolico in Italia. 1860–1980*, 4 vols, Turin: Casa Editrice Marietti, 1981.

Webster, Richard A., *The Cross and the Fasces: Christian democracy and Fascism in Italy*, Stanford CA: Stanford University Press, 1959.

Other secondary works

Abba, G.C., *The Diary of One of Garibaldi's Thousand*, translated and introduced by E.R. Vincent, Oxford: Oxford University Press, 1962.

Absalom, R.N.L., *A Strange Alliance: Aspects of Escape and Survival In Italy, 1943–1945*, Florence: Leo Olschki Editore, 1991.

Abse, T., 'Italy', in J. Noakes (ed.), *The Civilian in War: The Home Front in Europe, Japan and the USA in World War II*, Exeter: Exeter University Press, 1992.

Albertazzi, A., *Il cardinale Svampa e I cattolici bolognesi 1894–1907*, Brescia: La Morcelliana, 1971.

Allum, P.A. *Politics and Society in Post-war Naples*, Cambridge: Cambridge University Press, 1973.

—— 'Uniformity Undone: Aspects of Catholic Culture in Post-war Italy', in Z. Baranski and R. Lumley (eds), *Culture and Conflict in Post-war Italy: Essays on Mass and Popular Culture*, Basingstoke: Macmillan, 1990.

Andreotti, G., *Ad Ogni Morte di Papa. I Papi che ho conosciuto*, Milan: Rizzoli, 1980.

Aquaviva, S.S., *The Decline of the Sacred in Industrial Society*, Oxford: Oxford University Press, 1979.

Azzaroni, A., *Socialistici anticlericali*, Florence: Parenti, 1961.

Baranski, Z. and R. Lumley (eds), *Culture and Conflict in Post-war Italy: Essays on Mass and Popular Culture*, Basingstoke: Macmillan, 1990, pp. 82–3.

Battelli, G., 'Clero secolare e societa italiana tra decennio napoleonico e primo novecento', in M. Rosa (ed.), *Clero e societa nell'italia contemporanea*, Rome-Bari: Laterza, 1992.

Bedani, G., 'Church and State in Italian History: Origins of the Present Crisis', unpublished professorial lecture given at University College of Swansea, 1994.

—— *Politics and Ideology in the Italian Workers' Movement: Union Development and the Changing Role of the Communist Sub-culture in Post-War Italy*, Oxford: Berg, 1995.

Bedeschi, L., *I Capellani del lavoro: Aspetti religiosi e culturali della societa lombarda negli anni della crisi modernista*, Milan: A. Mondadori, 1977.

Bell, D. Howard, *Sesto San Giovanni: Workers, Culture and Politics in an Italian Town, 1880–1922*, New Brunswick NJ: Rutgers University Press, 1986.

Bevilacqua, G., *Equivoci: mondo moderno e Cristo*, Brescia: La Morcelliana, 1953.

Blamires, C.P. (ed.), *Historical Dictionary of World Fascism*, Oxford: ABC-Clio, 2006.

Blondet, Maurizio, *I Nuovi Barbari: Gli Skinheads Parlano*, Milan: FDF Edizioni, 1993.

Bosworth, R.J.J., 'Everday Mussolinism: Friends, Family, Locality and Violence in Fascist Italy', in *Contemporary European History*, XIV, i, 2005.

Bucci, V., *Chiesa e Stato: Church and State Relations in Italy within the Constitutional Framework*, The Hague: Martinus Nijhof, 1969.

Burgalassi, S., *Le Cristianità Nascoste*, Bologna: EDB, 1970.

Camaiani, G., 'Valori religiosi e polemica anticlericale nella sinistra democratica e del primo socialismo', in *Rivista di Storia e Letteratura*, XX, 2, 1984.

Caneva, A., *L'Azione sindacale in Italia dall'estraneita alla partecipazion*, vol. 1, Brescia: La Morcelliana, 1979.

Caroleo, A., *Le banche cattoliche*, Milan: Feltrinelli, 1976.

Carroll, Michael. P., *Veiled Threats: The Logic of Popular Catholicism in Italy*, Baltimore MD and London: Johns Hopkins University Press, 1996.

Cartocci, R., *Fra Lega e Chiesa: L'Italia in cerca di integrazione*, Bologna: Il Mulino, 1994.

Chubb, J., *Patronage, Power and Poverty: A Tale of Two Cities*, Cambridge: Cambridge University Press, 1982.

Coletti, A., *Il divorzio in Italia. Storia di una battaglia civile e democratica*, Roma: Giulio Savelli Editore, 1974.

Confessore, O., *I cattolici e'la fede nella libertà*, Rome: Edizioni Studium, 1989.

Corner, P., *Fascism in Ferrara, 1915–1925*, Oxford: Oxford University Press, 1975.

Cuminetti, M., *Il dissenso cattolico in Italia, 1965–1980*, Milan: Rizzoli, 1983.

D'Angelo, A., 'Il Tirocinio del Dopoguerra: La Nunziatura D'Italia (1949–1962)', in A. Melloni and M. Guasco (eds), *Un Diplomatico Vaticano Fra Dopoguerrae Dialogo: Mons. Mario Cagna (1911–1986)*, Bologna: Il Mulino, 2003.

Davis, John A., *Conflict and Control: Law and Order in Nineteenth Century Italy*, Basingstoke and London: Macmillan, 1988.

—— 'Socialism and the Working Classes in Italy before 1914', in D. Geary (ed.), *Labour and the Socialist Movements in Europe before 1914*, Oxford: Berg, 1989.

De Clementi, A. (ed.), *La Società inafferabile: Proto-industria, città e classi sociali in Italia liberale*, Milan: Lavoro (sic), 1986.

De Felice, F. and V. Parlato (eds), *A. Gramsci e La questione meridionale*, Rome: Editori Riuniti, 1996.

de Franciscis, M. D., *Italy and the Vatican: The 1984 Concordat between Church and State*, New York: Peter Lang, 1989.

De Grazia, V., *How Fascism Ruled Women: Italy, 1945*, Berkeley CA: University of California Press, 1992.

Delzell, Charles F., *Mussolini's Enemies: The Italian Anti-Fascist Resistance*, New York: Praeger, 1974, Chapter 3.

De Rosa, G., *Chiesa e Religione popolare nel Mezzogiorno*, Rome-Bari: Laterza, 1978.

—— 'La parrocchia in Italia in età contemporanea', in various authors, *La parrocchia in Italia nell'eta contemporanea*, Naples: Edizioni Dehoniane, 1982.

—— 'Il Clero Ricettizio di Pisticci dalla Restaurazione all'unificazione nazionale' in *Ricerche di Storia Sociale e Religiosa*, n. 24, luglio-dicembre, 1983, pp. 115–32.

Donavan, M., 'Italy', in D. Hanley (ed.), *Christian Democracy in Europe: a Comparative Perspective*, London: Pinter, 1996.

Erba, A., *'Proletariato di Chiesa' per la cristianità' La Faci tra curia romana e fascismo dale origini alla conciliazione*, 2 vols, Roma: Herder, 1990.

Faenza, L., *Il Communismo e il Cattolicesimo in una Parrocchia*, Milan: EDB, 1959.

—— *Communismo e Cattolicesimo in una Parrocchia di Campagna. Vent'anni dopo, 1959–1979*, Bologna: Capelli, 1979.

Fappani, A., *G. Migliolo e Il Movimento Contadino Italiano*, Rome: Cinque Lune, 1964.

Farneti, P., 'Patterns of Changing Support for the Christian Democrats in Italy, 1946–1976', in B. Denitch (ed.), *Legitimation of Regimes*, London: Sage, 1979.

Ferraresi, F., *Threats to Democracy: The Radical Right in Italy after the War*, Princeton NJ: Princeton University Press, 1996.

Ferrone, V. (ed.), *La Chiesa Cattolica e il Totalitarismo: Atti del Convegno Torino, 25–26 ottobre 2001*, Florence: Olschki Editore, 2004.

Foot, J.M., ' "White Bolsheviks"? The Catholic Left and the Socialists in Italy, 1919–1920', in *Historical Journal*, 40, 2, 1977.

Formigoni, G., *I cattolici-deputati (1904–1918)*, Rome: Edizioni Studium, 1989.

—— *L'Italia dei cattolici. Fede e nazione dal Risorgimento alla Repubblica*, Bologna: Il Mulino, 1998.

Furlong, P. 'Authority, Change and Conflict in Italian Catholicism', in Thomas M. Gannon, S.J. (ed.), *World Catholicism in Transition*, New York: Macmillan Publishing Company, 1988, pp. 116–32.

Galli, G., *La sfida perduta; biografia politica di Enrico Mattei*, Milan: Saggi Bompiani, 1972.

—— *Storia della DC*, Rome-Bari: Laterza, 1978.

—— *La Finanza Bianca: La Chiesa, I soldi, il potere,* Milan: Mondadori, 2004.

—— and A. Nannei, *Il Mercato di Stato: Capitalismo assistenziale*, Milan: Sugar Editore, 1984.

Garelli, F., *Religione e Chiesa in Italia*, Bologna: Il Mulino, 1991.

Gentile, E., *The Sacralisation of Politics in Fascist Italy*, London: Harvard University Press, 1996.

Germani Genzini, V., 'Il movimento contadino nel Cremonese all'inizio del'900', in F. Della Peruta, *Braccianti e contadini nella valle Padana*, Rome: Editori Riuniti, 1975.

Giammanco, R.M., *The Christian-Communist Dialogue in Italy 1944 to the Present*, New York: Praeger, 1989.

Giarizzo, G., 'Il Socialismo e la modernizzazione del mezzogiorno', in C. Cingari and S. Fedele (eds), *Il socialismo nel Mezzogiorno d'Italia, 1892–1926*, Bari: Laterza, 1992.

Gillette, Aaron, *Racial Theories in Fascist Italy*, London: Routledge, 2002.

Guareschi, G., *The Little World of Don Camillo*, Harmondsworth: Penguin, 1969.

Guiotto, L., *La fabbrica totale: Paternalismo industriale e Citta sociali in Italia*, Milan: Feltrinelli, 1979.

Gundle, S., 'Cultura di massa e modernizzazione: Vie Nuove e Famiglia Cristiana dall Guerra fredda alla societa di consumi', in Pier Paolo D'Attore (ed.), *Nemico per la pelle: sogno Americano e mito Sovieto nell'italia contemporanea*, Milan: F. Angeli Editore, 1991.

Hearder, H., *Italy in the Age of the Risorgimento, 1790-1870*, London: Longman, 1983.

Hebblethwaite, P., 'Pope Pius XII: Chaplain of the Atlantic Alliance?', in C. Duggan and C. Wagstaffe (eds), *Italy in the Cold War: Politics, Culture and Society*, Oxford: Oxford University Press, 1995.

Hobsbawm, E., *The Age of Extremes: The Shorter Twentieth Century, 1914–1991*, London: Abacus, 1995.

Horowitz, Daniel D., *Storia del Movimento Sindacale in Italia*, Bologna: Il Mulino, 1966.

Iadanza, M. (ed.), *Chiesa e Società Civile nel Mezzogiorno. La memoria, l'analisi e il progetto*, Rome: Borla, 1992.

Jemolo, A.C., *Società civile e societa religiosa, 1955–58*, Turin: Einaudi, 1959.

Kelikian, A., 'Convitti operai cattolici e forza lavoro feminile', in A. Gigli Marchetti (ed.), *Donna Lombarda*, Milan: Angeli, 1992.

Kent, Peter C., *The Pope and the Duce: The International Impact of the Lateran Agreements*, London and Basingstoke: Macmillan, 1981.

—— *The Lonely Cold War of Pius XII: The Roman Catholic Church and the Division of Europe, 1943–1950*, Montreal-Kingston: McGill-Queens University Press, 2002.

Keogh, D., 'Ireland, the Vatican and the Cold War: the Case of Italy', in *Historical Journal*, 344, 1991.

Kersevan, A. and P. Visintin (eds), *Giuseppe Nogara: luci ed ombre di un arcivescovo, 1928–1945*, Udine: I Quaderni del Picchio, 1992.

Kertzer, D., *Comrades and Christians: Religion and the Political Struggle in Communist Italy*, Cambridge: Cambridge University Press, 1980.

—— *The Kidnapping of Edgardo Mortara*, London: Picador, 1997.

Lannon, F., *Privilege, Persecution and Prophecy: The Catholic Church in Spain 1875–1975*, Oxford: Oxford University Press, 1987.

Lazzarretto, A., 'Parrocci ed emigrati nel Vicentino del primo Novecento', in various authors, *Studi di storia sociale e religiosa: Scritti in onore di Gabriele De Rosa*, Naples, Ferraro, 1980.

Lazzati, G. (ed.), *Don Lorenzo Milani tra Chiesa, cultura e scuola: Atti del convegno*, introduction by Giuseppe Lazzati, Milan: Vita e Pensiero, 1983.

Leonardi, R. and D. A. Wertman, *Italian Christian Democracy: the Politics of Dominance*, Basingstoke: Macmillan, 1989.

Lizzola, I. and E. Manzoni, 'Proletariato Bergamasco e Organizzazioni Cattoliche: Lo Sciopero di Ranica (1909)', in *Studi e Ricerche di Storia Contemporanea*, 15, May 1981.

Lumley, R., *States of Emergency: Cultures of Revolt in Italy from 1968 to 1978*, London: Verso, 1990.

Logan, Oliver, 'Pius XII: *Romanita*, Prophesy and Charisma', in *Modern Italy*, 3, 2, November 1998, pp. 237–49.

Lovato, U. and A. Castellani, 'Il beato Leonardo Murialdi e il movimento operaio cristiano', in *Italia sacra: Spiritualità e azione del laicato cattolico*, Padua: Marsilio, 1969.

Luzzatto, S., *Padre Pio: Miracoli e politica nell'Italia del Novecento*, Turin: Einaudi, 2007.

Mcleod, H, *Religion and the People of Western Europe 1789–1970*, Oxford: Oxford University Press, 1981.

—— 'The Dechristianisation of the Working Class in Western Europe (1850–1950)', in *Social Compass*, XXVII, 2/3, 1986.

—— (ed.), *European Religion in the Age of Great Cities, 1830–1930*, London and New York: Routledge, 1995.

—— *Secularisation in Western Europe, 1848–1914*, Basingstoke: Macmillan, 2000.

—— and W. Ustorf (eds), *The Decline of Christendom in Western Europe, 1750–2000*, Cambridge: Cambridge University Press, 2003.

Magister, Sandro, *La politica Vaticana e l'Italia, 1943–1978*, Rome: Editori Riuniti, 1979.

—— 'The Church and the End of the Catholic Party', in M. Caciagali and David I. Kertzer (eds), *Italian Politics, A Review: Vol. II, the Stalled Transition*, Oxford: Westview Press, 1996.

Malgeri, F., 'Chiesa, clero e laicato cattolico tra Guerra e Resistenza', in G. De Rosa, T. Gregory and A. Vauchez (eds), *Storia dell'Italia Religiosa. III. L'Età Contempranea*, Rome-Bari: Laterza, 1995.

Manacorda, M.A. and M. Vigli (eds), *Stato e Chiese. Il potere clerical in Italia dopo il 'nuovo concordato' del 1984 tra Craxi e Wojtyla*, Trezzano sul Naviglio, MI: Mille Lire, 1995.

Martini, C., 'Il referendum sulla fecondazione assista', in G. Amyot and L. Verzichelli (eds), *Politica in Italia. I fatti e le interpretazioni, 2006*, Bologna: Il Mulino, 2006.

Masala, Carlo, 'Born for Government: The Democrazia Cristiana in Italy', in M. Gehler and W. Kaiser (eds), *Christian Democracy in Europe since 1945*, vol. 2, London: Routledge, 2004.

Merli, S. (ed.), *Proletariato di fabbrica e capitalismo industriale: il caso italiano, 1889–1900*, vol. 2, Florence: La Nuova Italia, 1973.

Menozzi, D., 'Le Nuove parrocchie nella prima Industrializzazione Torinese (1900–1915)', in *Rivista di Storia e Letteratura Religiosa*, 9, 1973.

—— *La Chiesa cattolica e la secolarizzazione*, Turin: Einaudi, 1993.

Milani, L., *Esperienze pastorali*, Florence: Liberia Editrice fiorentina, 1958.

Milton, J., *The Poetical Works of John Milton*, Edinburgh: William P. Nimmo and Co., 1884.

Misner, P., *Social Catholicism in Europe: From the Onset of Industrialisation to the First World War*, New York: Crossroad, 1991.

Moliterno, G. (ed.), *Encyclopedia of Contemporary Italian Culture*, London: Routledge, 2000.

Moloney, J.N., *The Emergence of Political Catholicism in Italy: Partito Popolare Italiano*, 1919–1926, London: Croom Helm, 1977.

Monticone, A. (ed.), *Gl'Italiani in uniforme, 1915–1918*, Bari: Laterza, 1972.

—— *Cattolici e Fascisti in Umbria (1922–1945)*, Bologna: Il Mulino, 1978.

—— 'L'Episcopato italiano dall'Unita al Concilio Vaticano II', in M. Rosa (ed.), *Clero e società nell'italia contemporanea*, Rome-Bari: Laterza, 1992.

Moro, R., 'Afascismo e antifascismo nei movimenti intellettuali dell'Azione Cattolica dopo il "31"', in *Storia Contemporanea*, VI, 4, 1975.

Nicotri, P., *Tangenti in confessionale: Come I preti rispondono a corrotti e corruttori*, Venice: Marsiglio, 1993.

O'Toole, James M., *Habits of Devotion: Catholic Religious Practice in Twentieth Century America*, Ithaca NY and London: Cornell University Press, 2004.

Pecorari, P. (ed.), *Chiesa, Azione Cattolica e fascismo nell'Italia settentrionale durante il pontificato di Pio XI (1922–1939)*, Milan: Vita e Pensiero, 1979.

Pellicani, A., *Il Papa di Tutti: La Chiesa Cattolica, Il Fascismo e il Razzismo, 1929–1945*, Milan: Sugar Editore, 1964.

Peyrot, G., 'La legislazione sulle confessioni religiose diverse dalla cattolica', in P.A. D'Avack (ed.), *La legislazione ecclesiastica*, Milan: Istituto per la scienza dell'amministrazione pubblica, 1967, pp. 521–47.

Pivato, S., *Movimento operaio e istruzione popolare nell'Italia liberale: Discussioni e ricerche*, Milan: F. Angeli, 1986.

Poggi, G., 'The Church in Italian Politics, 1945–1950', in S.W. Woolf (ed.), *The Rebirth of Italy, 1945–1950*, Stanford CA: Stanford University Press, 1972.

Pollard, J.F., 'Post-war Italy: the "Papal State of the Twentieth Century"?', in E.A. Millar (ed.), *The Legacy of Fascism*, Glasgow: Glasgow University Press, 1987.

—— 'Conservative Catholics and Italian Fascism: the Clerico-Fascists', in M. Blinkhorn (ed.), *Fascists and Conservatives: The Radical Right and the Establishment in Twentieth Century Europe*, London: Unwin Hyman, 1990.

—— 'Il Vaticano e la politica estera italiana', in R.J.B. Bosworth and S. Romano (eds), *La politica estera italiana, 1960–1985*, Bologna: Il Mulino, 1990.

—— 'Italy', in T. Buchanan and M. Conway (eds), *Political Catholicism in Europe*, Oxford: Oxford University Press, 1996.

—— 'Religion and the Formation of the Italian Working Class', in Rick Halpern and Jonathan Morris (eds), *American Exceptionalism? US Working Class Formation in an International Context*, Basingstoke: Macmillan, 1997.

—— 'The Papacy in Two World Wars: Benedict XV and Pius XI Compared', in *Totalitarian Movements and Political Religions*, 2, 3, Winter 2001.

Pompei, G-F., *Un Ambasciatore in Vaticano, Diario 1969–1977*, Bologna: Il Mulino, 1998.

Posner, M.V.S. and S.J. Woolf, *Italian Public Enterprise*, London: Duckworth, 1967.

Ranfagni, P., *I Clerico Fascisti: Le riviste dell'Universita Cattolica negli anni del regime*, Florence: Cooperativa Editrice Universitaria, 1975.

Raw, C., *The Money Changers*, London: Harper Collins, 1992.

Riccardi, A., *Pio XII*, Bari: Laterza, 1985.

—— *Le Chiese di Pio XII*, Bari: Laterza, 1986.

—— 'The Vatican of Pius XII and the Roman Party', in *Concilium*, 97, 1987.

—— 'La vita religiosa', in P. Ginsborg (ed.), *Stato Dell'Italia: il bilancio politico, economico, sociale e culturale di un paese che cambia*, Milan: B. Mondadori, 1998.

Ricossa, G., 'Italy, 1920–1970', in C. Cipolla (ed.), *The Fontana Economic History of Europe: Contemporary Economies*, Glasgow: Fontana, 1972.

Rodogno, D., *Fascism's European Empire: Italian Occupation during the Second World War*, Cambridge: Cambridge University Press, 2006.

Rossi, M.G., *Le origini del partito cattolico in Italia: Movimento cattolico e lotta di classe nell' Italia liberale*, Rome: Editori Riuniti, 1977.

Rumi, G., 'La Santa Sede e la Politica di Potenza', in E. Di Nolfo, R. H. Rainero and B Vigezzi (eds), *L'Italia e la politica di Potenza, 1938–1940*, Settimo Milanese: Marzorati, 1975.

Sandmann, F., *'L'Osservatore Romano' e il nazionalsocialismo, 1929–1939*, Rome: Riuniti, 1976.

Scoppola, P., *La proposta politica di De Gasperi*, Bologna: Il Mulino, 1979.

Scottà, A. (ed.), *La Conciliazione Ufficiosa: il Barone Carlo Monti 'incaricato d'affari' del governo italiano presso la Santa Sede*, 2 vols, Vatican City: Libreria Editrice Vaticana, 1997.

Settembrini, D., *La Chiesa nella Politica Italiana (1944–1963)*, Milan: Rizzoli, 1973.

Seymour, M., *Debating Divorce in Italy. Marriage and the Making of Modern Italians*, Basingstoke: Palgrave-Macmillan, 2007.

Snider, C., *L'Episcopato di Cardinale Andrea Ferrari*, vol. I, Vicenza: Neri Pozza, 1981.

Snowden, F., *Violence and Great Estates in Southern Italy; Apulia, 1900–1922*, Cambridge: Cambridge University Press, 1986.

Spinosa, A., *Pio XII. l'Ultimo Papa*, Milan: A. Mondadori, 1992.

Stack, O., *Pasolini on Pasolini*, London: Thames & Hudson, 1969.

Tannenbaum, Edward R., *Fascism in Italy: Society and Culture, 1922–1945*, London: Allen Lane, 1972.

Tarrow, S., *Peasant Communism in Southern Italy*, New Haven CT and London: Yale University Press, 1967.

Ternavasio, M., *Padre Pio: La storia del santo con le stigmate*, Turin: Lindau, 2006.

Thomas, Huw, 'Religious Freedom, the Lateran Pacts and the Debates in the Constituent Assembly (1946–1948)', unpublished PhD thesis, University of Wales, Swansea, 2006, pp. 43–4.

Toscani, X., *Secolarizzazione e frontiere sacerdotali*, Bologna: Il Mulino, 1982.

Urquhart, G., *The Pope's Armada: Unlocking the Secrets and Mysteries of Powerful New Sects in the Church*, London: Corgi, 1996.

Valentini, Carlo, *Prodi: la mia Italia; il nuovo leader parla di sè e propone la medicina per guarire il paese*, Bologna: Carmenta, 1995.

Various authors, *Cattolici e referendum. Per Una Scelta di Libertà*, Roma: Coines Edizioni, 1974.

Varnier, G.B., 'Continuità e rotture (1870–1915)', in D. Puncoh (ed.), *Il cammino della Chiesa Genovese dalle origini ai nostril giorni: Atti della Societa Ligure di Storia Patria*, Nuova Serie, Vol. XXXIX (CXIII) Fasc. II, Genoa: Societa Ligure di Storia Patria, 1994.

Verucci, G., *L'Italia laica prima e dopo l'Unità, 1848–1876. Anticlericalismo, libero pensiero e ateismo nella storia italiana*, Roma-Bari: Laterza, 1981.

—— *La Chiesa nella Società Contemporanea; Dal Primo Dopoguerra al Concilio Vaticano II*, Roma-Bari: Laterza, 1988.

Walsh, M.J., *John Paul II*, London: Fount, 1995.

Walston, J., *The Mafia and Clientelism: Roads to Rome in Post-war Calabria*, London: Routledge, 1988.

Weigel, G., *Witness to Hope: The Biography of Pope John Paul II*, London, Cliff Books: 2001.

Willson, P., 'Fiori per il medico', in *Modern Italy; Journal of the Association for the Study of Modern Italy*, 1, autumn 1996, 2, pp. 44–62.

—— *Peasant Women and Politics in Fascist Italy: The Massaie Rurali*, London: Routledge, 2002, p. 187.

Wolff, R., 'Italy: Catholics, Clergy, and the Church – Complex Reactions to Fascism', in R. Wolff and R. Hoensch (eds), *Catholics, the State and the European Radical Right, 1919–1945*, New York: Social Science Monographs, 1987.

Zizola, G., *Il microfono di Dio. Pio XII, Padre Lombardi e i cattolici italiani*, Milan: A. Mondadori, 1990.

Zucotti, S., *Beneath His Very Windows: the Vatican and the Holocaust in Italy*, New Haven CT: Yale University Press, 2000.

Internet sites

http://elezionistorico.interno.it/index.php (09.04.06).
http://italpolblog.blogspot.com (09.02.04).

INDEX